ReSounding Poverty

ReSounding Poverty

Romani Music and Development Aid

ADRIANA N. HELBIG

Oxford University Press is a department of the University of Oxford. It furthers
the University's objective of excellence in research, scholarship, and education
by publishing worldwide. Oxford is a registered trade mark of Oxford University
Press in the UK and certain other countries.

Published in the United States of America by Oxford University Press
198 Madison Avenue, New York, NY 10016, United States of America.

© Oxford University Press 2023

All rights reserved. No part of this publication may be reproduced, stored in
a retrieval system, or transmitted, in any form or by any means, without the
prior permission in writing of Oxford University Press, or as expressly permitted
by law, by license, or under terms agreed with the appropriate reproduction
rights organization. Inquiries concerning reproduction outside the scope of the
above should be sent to the Rights Department, Oxford University Press, at the
address above.

You must not circulate this work in any other form
and you must impose this same condition on any acquirer.

CIP data is on file at the Library of Congress

ISBN 978–0–19–763177–5 (pbk.)
ISBN 978–0–19–763176–8 (hbk.)

DOI: 10.1093/oso/9780197631768.001.0001

For the silenced

Contents

List of Figures	ix
Preface	xi
Acknowledgments	xv
Awareness	1
1. Transitions	19
2. Interventions	33
3. Accountability	55
4. Mobilities	73
5. Networks	93
6. Tuning In	107
7. Sound Health	129
8. Release	153
Reflection	171
Notes	175
References	197
Index	213

Figures

0.1. Map of the Austro- Hungarian Monarchy, 1889. The research for this book was conducted along the Carpathian Mountain range near Unghvar (today's Uzhhorod, Ukraine). The author's family hails from the surrounding areas of Brody, Lemberg (today's Lviv, Ukraine), and Tarnopol (today's Ternopil, Ukraine). Artist: The Palmer/ Getty Images.   xviii

I.1. Evan Zajdel, "Amnesia in a Place of Remembrance," 24″ × 13″, 2013. The artist's hair, silk thread, mulberry paper, silk dupioni, willow wood.   4

I.2. Cover photo for the album *Band of Gypsies* by Taraf de Haïdouks (Nonesuch, 2001).   10

1.1. Frontman Eugene Hütz of Gypsy punk group Gogol Bordello performing live on the Zippo Encore Stage at Download Festival on June 14, 2013, Castle Donington, UK. Photo by Kevin Nixon/Metal Hammer Magazine/Future Publishing/Getty Images.   20

1.2. Twelve-year-old Roman Saveliev on Kyiv's Independence Square, December 2014. Photo by Andrew Kravchenko.   21

1.3. Romani activist Oktavia Adam (right), director of the Transcarpathian cultural- educational organization "Roma," leads participants in the celebration of International Romani Day, Uzhhorod, Ukraine, April 7, 2017. Photo: Yanosh Nemesh/ Shutterstock.   26

1.4. Taras Shevchenko, *Tsyhanka-Vorozhka* (Gypsy fortune-teller), 1841.   31

2.1. Aladar Adam (far right) performing with Romani Yag in Kyiv, 1992. Photo: Courtesy of Romani Yag.   49

2.2. Advertisement for the Romani Yag Romani Hotel-Restaurant Complex. Uzhhorod, Ukraine. 2008. Photo by author.   51

3.1. Carpathian Ensemble Tenth Anniversary Concert, University of Pittsburgh, 2018. © University of Pittsburgh.   65

3.2. Romani children who cannot afford to attend the kindergarten in Lunik IX, an urban Romani community near Košice, Slovakia, peer through the bars that "protect" the entrance to the school. Photo by author.   68

3.3. Young girls play with a "jump rope" made out of pantyhose tied together outside one of the condemned housing projects in Lunik IX, an urban Romani community near Košice, Slovakia, June 2012. Photo by author.   70

4.1. Romani musicians in Uzhhorod, early 1900s. Photo: Courtesy of Romani Yag.   83

X FIGURES

4.2. Aladar Adam's father Evhen Adam performing on violin at the popular Uzhhorod restaurant Skalia (Cave) in 1976. Photo: Courtesy of Romani Yag.   84

4.3. Concert for International Roma Day, Mukachevo, Transcarpathia, April 8, 2019, featuring Kandra Horvath (center), Dorina, Csík Laci, Tsino, and Friku.   86

4.4. Advertisement for the Pap Jazz Fest 2017, the 20th Jubilee International Roma Jazz Festival in Uzhhorod, Transcarpathia, featuring Villie Pap (Jr.), Eduard Pap, AMC Trio Unit, Villie Pap (Sr.), Erik Marienthal, Petro Poptarev, and the Pap Jazz Quintet. The concert is sponsored by the Carpathian Fund, the International Renaissance Foundation, the American Embassy in Ukraine.   89

5.1. Dorothea Lange's "Migrant Mother," Nipomo, California, 1936. Getty Images.   99

7.1. Django Reinhardt (1910–1953) playing his guitar backstage in New York in 1946. Photo by William Gottlieb/Redferns/Getty Images.   137

8.1. Roms in Bilky, Transcarpathia, crowd around the author's laptop in May 2016 to watch footage of family musicians from the early 2000s who have since passed. Photo by author.   163

8.2. A Romani house in Transcarpathia made of *saman* and scrap metal. Photo by Volodymyr Baleha/Shutterstock.   166

9.1. The author's viral picture announcing a week-long hunger strike to protest Russia's aggression in eastern Ukraine. The University of Pittsburgh's iconic Cathedral of Learning forms the backdrop. 2014. Photo: Nancy Murrell.   172

Preface

I first heard Romani music in 1996 while studying classical piano performance in Vienna, a city where my grandparents sought refuge during World War II while escaping from Nazi and Soviet occupations of western Ukraine. My father was eight years old when he was uprooted from his childhood home in Velyki Filvarky near Brody, spending his formative years in a displaced persons' camp near Murnau in the Bavarian Alps in the American zone in Allied-occupied Germany. Members of my father's family were taken as *Ost-Arbeiter*, the Nazi German designation for foreign slave workers gathered from occupied Central and Eastern Europe to perform forced labor in Germany during World War II. The family was reunited in Corning, New York, in 1953 and relocated to Newark, New Jersey, where my sister and I were born in the 1970s and grew up in a community of ethnic Ukrainian refugees, dissidents, and political émigrés. My mother was born in a displaced persons' camp in Erlangen, Germany, the only one of my grandmother's five children to survive the war. Her father had been active in the underground movement in Rava-Ruska near the Ukrainian-Polish border. As a war refugee, he used his skills as a partisan commander to organize the lives of ethnic Ukrainians in Erlangen's displaced persons' camp. My maternal grandmother, née Subtelna, was born in 1905 in Kejdantsi near Tarnopol (today's Ternopil, Ukraine), in Habsburg Galicia and lived with our family until she was ninety-five. She was fluent in five languages and taught us Ukrainian, Polish, and German. She received letters from her brother who had decided to turn back in Vienna and return home after the war, only to be sentenced to hard labor in the Siberian *gulag* for his role in the underground movement. The pages of these letters were marked through with black ink, the words crossed out by Soviet censors.

That the research for this book began in Vienna is not a coincidence. I had chosen to study abroad in the city that had played such a pivotal role in my family's routes. It was also the city of music and a place where I intended to launch my career as a classical pianist. The city, however, would serve as a circuitous route for my return to the home my family had left so many years before. As a music student living in the heart of the city, I was drawn to the music of street musicians who played near the conservatory. I was invited to the outer *Bezirke*, city districts, to spend time with the families of musicians, both Roms and non-Roms, who had fled violence in the Balkans. In intimate gatherings, I witnessed the role that music plays among people whose lives have been uprooted by war. I write this book with a reminiscence of those times because during that era of fluidity, social flux, and personal discovery, upon my return to the United States, I entered a graduate program in ethnomusicology in the Department of Music at Columbia University. By way of this prestigious American ivory tower, I later returned east, into the Carpathian Mountains, along the borders of Ukraine, Poland, Hungary, Slovakia, and Romania. It was there, in the center of the poorest, most violent, most economically and politically corrupt region at the time—Transcarpathia—that I began my study of the not (yet) globalized "Gypsy" music.

Since the 1990s, extensive volumes have been written about traditional and popular Romani music genres across the world, and these writings significantly deepened my understanding of the issues as a student. Subsequently, I, too, have contributed to this literature, particularly as it relates to Romani experiences on the territories of the former Austrian Empire. I have also engaged with Romani musicians in Pittsburgh, where I have lived and taught for more than a decade. Romani families who had immigrated from Austro-Hungary to Pittsburgh at the end of the nineteenth century formed an integral part of the city's industrial soundscape. The neighborhoods of Homestead and Braddock were home to a sizable Romani orchestra founded during the Great Depression through the Works Progress Administration (WPA). Musicians like George Batyi, whose family members played in this orchestra, have given presentations in my courses and participated in conferences I have organized on Romani music at the University of Pittsburgh. To further contextualize Romani music performance for students, I drew on my mother's expertise in the East European travel industry. I organized and led study abroad programs for undergraduates at the University of Pittsburgh, traveling with them to the Czech Republic, Poland, Slovakia, and Hungary. For many, these trips were the first they made abroad. This book incorporates their thoughts, feelings, and ideas regarding their visits to Romani music festivals, Romani Holocaust memorial sites, Romani museums, and urban and rural Romani communities.

I am not an ethnic Romni (fem.), but I come to this study with great respect and love for those who have historically had no voice in academia. As a scholar, I strive to include the varied perspectives of interlocutors I have worked alongside for minority rights, cultural rights, and equal representation. Furthermore, as a musician and an ethnomusicologist, I have learned over the years how to not only view music solely as a political act, as I grew up to perceive it in diaspora, but how to appreciate music as sound, emotional release, and even entertainment. A great sense of joy had come from organizing a student ensemble that popularized Romani music among undergraduates who were very much the same age as I was when I first heard this music. The writings within these pages incorporate their experiences as well. This book, then, is as much a synthesis of knowledge as it is a critical analysis and fresh revisiting of my experiences with Romani music over the years. It is a rethinking of old ideas in light of new political landscapes and economic spheres. It is a rewriting of well-known paradigms within Romani music studies and a reworking of old and new ethnographic materials. It is also an acknowledgment of my role in the process as a researcher, performer, and activist who has lived and worked alongside Roms, sharing their music within the framework of Romani rights advocacy.

As the title states, this book is a re-sounding—a re-articulation—of the upheavals and resurrections that have shaped Romani ways of being in the world. In my re-listenings, I have tried to retune my ears to the experiences that I, as a young researcher, was not equipped to understand, relate to, or adequately describe. This book, about life processes, memories, and hope, is also one of release from the burdens of witnessing the marginalization of a culture and its people. It does not purport to offer solutions to the injustices but, nevertheless, serves as a testament to advocacy. It is also a story written amid generational traumas of World War II, the experiences of Soviet collapse and the harsh realities of Ukrainian independence (1991), the changes brought forth during Ukraine's Orange Revolution (2004) that shaped my dissertation fieldwork, and Ukraine's Revolution of Dignity (2014) whose violence triggered the post-traumatic stress (PTS) that sidelined my initial attempts to write this book. The story within these pages has found its peace, embodied and passed on and experienced by those who have taken on these issues. It is also a story that spans continents, crosses borders, speaks in different languages, and engages with people of many backgrounds. I acknowledge the great responsibility I have felt over the years to give back and help, recognizing the sheer impracticality of some of the tasks I took on while rejoicing in the knowledge that I did my small part in time of great difficulty. The past looms large, and this book sorts the feelings and memories in a way that will help me to move forward.

While some people who have been a significant part of this project have passed on, others continue to work actively in their communities, performing, teaching, and working toward new tomorrows. It is to these family members, friends, colleagues, musicians, and all who have welcomed me into their lives that I dedicate this book with great gratitude.

Acknowledgments

Research for this book has been funded through generous grants from the American Council of Learned Societies (ACLS), the Fulbright Foundation, the International Research and Exchanges (IREX), the Institute of International Education (IIE), and the University of Pittsburgh's Global Studies Center, the Center for Russian, East European Studies (REES), the Humanities Center, the Provost's Office, and the Nationality Rooms and Intercultural Exchange Programs. Initial phases were supported by grants from the Shevchenko Scientific Society, the American Association for Ukrainian Studies, the Ukrainian Research Institute at Harvard University, and the Ukrainian Studies Program at Columbia University. The research for this project began in 1999 as part of my dissertation in partial fulfillment for the doctoral degree in ethnomusicology in the Department of Music at Columbia University. My dissertation came under the direction of Ana María Ochoa Gautier in its later stage with committee members Aaron Fox, Michael Beckerman, and the late Mark von Hagen. The research has continued over the last twenty years in terms of fieldwork, conference presentations, academic writings, and as collaborations with activists, scholars, musicians, and friends in Ukraine and in countries across Eastern and Central Europe and the Balkans.

First and foremost, I wish to thank Evhenia Navrotska, educator, activist, journalist, media consultant, and friend, without whom the Romani rights movement in Ukraine would not be where it is today. Evhenia has dedicated her life to helping Romani leaders in Transcarpathia fight against prejudice and discrimination in education and media. She was among the first people I met in the field and continues to be a guiding force for me and for others within the Romani rights movement in Ukraine. Aladar Adam, leader of the Romani Yag (Romani Fire) organization and editor of the *Romani Yag* newspaper, which I translated into English for its online format for many years, has also been a close friend and a pillar of support throughout the years. The late Josyp Adam and Maria Adam, who welcomed me into their home and into their family, have been a very large part of my life since the early 2000s. A heartfelt thanks goes to Svetlana Adam and Zoltán Boshanyi, and to their daughter, my beloved goddaughter, Nikoletta Adam. Together with Oktavia Adam, Serhyi Chichak, and their son Bardo, the Adam family has helped me in all aspects of my research. A new generation of Romani leaders led by Zola Kondur, Alia Yurchenko, Myroslav Horvat, Viktor Chovka, Petya Gabyn, and Denis Varody have offered inestimable help over the years. A very special thank you to Nataliya Zinevych, Senior Research Fellow, M. S. Hrushevsky Institute of Ukrainian Archaeography and Source Studies National Academy of Sciences of Ukraine, and to Michael Beníšek, Assistant Professor at the Romani Studies Section of the Department of Central European Studies at Charles University in Prague, whose research among Roms in Ukraine informs my own. I also wish to acknowledge Serhiy Ponomaryov, Roma Program Director at the International Renaissance Foundation, for his long-term commitment to Romani causes in Ukraine.

Having worked on Romani issues in many countries, I am grateful to Zuzana Jurková with whom I led the Romani music, culture, and human rights study abroad from the University of Pittsburgh to the Czech Republic, Poland, and Slovakia (2012) and to the Czech Republic and Hungary (2014). I express thanks to Lynn Hooker, Irén Kertész Wilkinson, and the late Speranta Radulescu for joining our students abroad. I am also grateful to the late Kateřina Jurečková from the CET[1] program in Prague/Washington, DC, and to the wonderful people at the University of Pittsburgh's Study Abroad Office and the Center for Russian and East European Studies for their continued support of all of my Romani-related projects, including research trips, courses, study abroad initiatives, concerts, conferences, and publications. A special thanks to Bob Hayden, Eileen O'Malley, Emilia Zankina, and the late Susan Hicks for their enthusiastic support during the years we collaborated through Pitt's REES. I am also grateful to Murray Barkema, Director of the Vienna Program, Central College (Iowa) for his inspiration and guidance. To all of my colleagues and friends in Austria, *Herzlichen Dank*.

I offer a deep bow of respect, *nyzkyii uklin*, to the broad network of ethnomusicologists in Ukraine who have supported my work over the years, especially Ira Dovhaliuk, Iryna Klymenko, Vera Madiar-Novak, and Viktor Shostak. I feel a great debt of gratitude to Romani music scholars Michael Beckerman, Ursula Hemetek, Lynn Hooker, Zuzana Jurková, Barbara Rose Lange, Svanibor Pettan, Carol Silverman, Irén Kertész Wilkinson, Petra Gelbart, Siv Brun Lie, the late Speranta Radulescu, and the late Katalin Kovalcik. Thank you to my University of Pittsburgh colleagues, especially Shalini Ayyagari, Andrew Weintraub, and Mathew Rosenblum, former

ACKNOWLEDGMENTS   xvii

Chair of the Department of Music, for their continued support of this research in terms of programming at the University of Pittsburgh. I wish to also acknowledge the feedback of scholars including Donna Buchanan, Naila Ceribašić, Lynn Hooker, Ana Hofman, Ian MacMillen, Noriko Manabe, David McDonald, Carol Muller, Inna Narodytskaya, Marcia Ostashevsky, Svanibor Pettan, Maria Sonevytsky, and others with whom I have, over the years, collaborated on projects relating to this research. Thank you also to Samantha Bassler for her assistance in preparing the index. To musicians George Batiy, Raif Huseni, Walt Mahovlich, Ethel Reim, Eva Salina, and others with whom I have worked over the years, thank you for sharing your talents with my students. And a special thank you to my former student-turned-colleague Jonathan Heins, who, upon graduation, co-directed the Carpathian Music Ensemble that I founded and directed at the University of Pittsburgh between 2008 and 2018.

I express my deepest love, respect, and gratitude to my beloved piano teacher Prof. Taissa Bohdanska at the Ukrainian Music Institute, to my high school music teacher Sr. Mary Gomolka at Mt. St. Mary Academy, to my music professors at Drew University Dr. Lydia Lydeen, Dr. Lynn Siebert, Dr. Norman Lowry, and the late Garyth Nair, and to my piano mentors Ana Bershadsky, Kazuko Jankovski, Seymour Bernstein, as well as the late Jan Gorbaty, for offering me strong foundations in classical music. The late Roma Pryma-Bohachevska, the Ukrainian-born prima ballerina and choreographer with whom I worked for many years as a piano accompanist for dance camps and workshops, helped foster my deep appreciation and understanding of folk music and dance traditions of Ukraine.

I express deep gratitude to my wide circle of friends, especially Kerri Stover, Alexa Milanytch, Areta Trytjak, Vicki Bixel, Cindy Abbott, and Roxy Korchynsky. Thank you to the Milanytch family, the Mykyta family, the Lew/Dobriansky family, and my extended family in Ukraine, Europe, and North America. I wish to offer a special thank you to Iryna Kliuchkovska, Director of the International Institute of Education, Culture and Diaspora Relations of Lviv Polytechnic National University and members of Lviv-Inturtrans, especially Vasyl and Luba Popovych, Iryna Potatuyeva, and Natalia Zaborska for supporting this project from its first iterations in the late 1990s. Natalia Zaborska, together with her late husband Bohdan and the extended Sobol family, have offered such a depth of support that no words of thanks would suffice.

And lastly, this project could not have been possible without the unwavering love and support of my late father and music lover, Omelan Helbig,

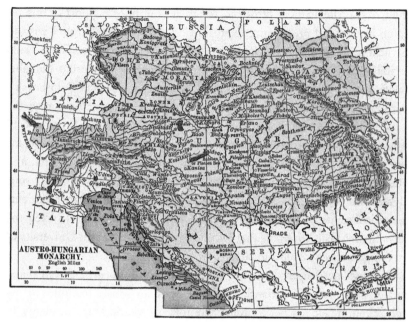

Figure 0.1 Map of the Austro-Hungarian Monarchy, 1889. The research for this book was conducted along the Carpathian Mountain range near Unghvar (today's Uzhhorod, Ukraine). The author's family hails from the surrounding areas of Brody, Lemberg (today's Lviv, Ukraine), and Tarnopol (today's Ternopil, Ukraine). Artist: The Palmer/Getty Images.

and my musically talented and ever-imaginative mother, Georgine Marijka Stadnycka Helbig. My mother, a formidable force whose insights and imagination as a travel agent specializing in Ukraine fueled my love for ethnography, continues to offer an unwavering depth of support for my career in ways that would be impossible to describe.

I write this book with great love and respect for my family's histories, joys, and traumas. To those who wish to remain unnamed, thank you for the love and support you bring into my life. Know that you remain, now and forever, close to my heart.

Awareness

There are poverties and there are poverties.

—Adrienne Rich

History is written by the rich, and so the poor get blamed for everything.

—Jeffrey Sachs

Poverty is the worst form of violence.

—Mahatma Gandhi

On a cool May afternoon in 2016, amid the blooming sakura trees gifted in 1923 to the city of Uzhhorod by the government in Vienna, a large group of attendees crowded into a nondescript classroom at the Uzhhorod National University to witness the launch of the new Romani Studies Program, a collaboration between the university, Romani activists, community leaders, and scholars that aims to familiarize students with Romani history, language, and culture through a series of courses taught over two semesters. During the event's introductions by city councilman Myroslav Horvat, a young Rom with a law degree, the projector tipped and the screen fell out of focus. A student rushed to fix it, steadying the machine with a hardcover book whose familiar binding caught my eye. Titled *Play for Me, Old Gypsy: The Role of Romani Music in the Roma Rights Movement in Ukraine* (2005), I was glad to see my doctoral dissertation continuing to be of some use. Having worked and lived among the Romani communities on the westernmost edge of Ukraine for more than twenty years, I smiled at the moment's symbolism.

The words that follow do not focus on the academic program described above, if only because such endeavors are the work of Roms whose voices are more important in such settings than mine. Instead, this book is about Roms who, like guitarist Sasha Latsko, live just a few steps away from the university but have no access to the programming inside its walls because of the poverty in which he lives. The university programming is geared for Romani students whose families, affiliated with development organizations, have established themselves as members of the bourgeoning post-Soviet middle class. The inherent class divisions within Romani communities, augmented by (in) accessibility to economic resources, play a significant role in how analyses of Romani modes-of-being are (mis)understood. By bringing us into the lived experiences of the objectified poor and the economically Othered, the words on these pages turn up the volume on the not-always-audible sound-track of Roms who, despite numerous efforts through multiple development initiatives, live in squalor and face hunger. I write this book to show that while development initiatives help *some* Roms, they cannot pull the poorest among them out of the direst situations.

Through an interdisciplinary approach drawing from the intersection of sound studies, poverty studies, and disability studies, I bring readers into the sound worlds of Roms living in the greatest degrees of poverty through stories of musical histories, tunings, performance aesthetics, and activism. I draw on my own experiences of physical and emotional traumas in the field to create space for addressing the sounds of Romani emotional and physical health as affected by the socioeconomic and personal challenges they face. My travels behind the Iron Curtain as a child in the 1980s and my witnessing of US diaspora travel experiences to independent Ukraine as a tour guide and helping reunite family members who had not seen each other since World War II have greatly informed my research. I cast such experiences as "grief tourism" due to the significant emotional toll they brought on to everyone involved. Such experiences drew me to this project through what I term "grief fieldwork," research in contexts of significant psychological and emotional hardship.

To some extent, my fieldwork echoes what Timothy Rice describes as a "new form of ethnomusicology in times (and places) of trouble" (Rice 2014, 191). In Eastern Europe, newly emerging facts about the past, especially regarding World War II history, shift present-day relationships to time and place. Broadening Rice's observation, this book accounts for shifts in memory that allow for new ethnomusicologies to emerge. Since the fall of communism, international funds have helped maintain Holocaust memorial sites like the Auschwitz concentration camp in Poland. Funds from the Polish Ministry of Culture and National Heritage, the European Union, and the Auschwitz-Birkenau Foundation as well as numerous donations from individuals as foundations have helped conserve the memorial while making it accessible to visitors. For several decades, annual visitors to Auschwitz numbered approximately 500,000. In 2019, 2.3 million people visited the Auschwitz-Birkenau Museum, contributing to a significant rise in so-called dark tourism.[1]

I traveled to Auschwitz in 2012 with students from the University of Pittsburgh to guide them through witnessing. Among the research projects resulting from this trip was Evan Zajdel's undergraduate B.Phil. thesis, which I advised, titled *Narrative Threads: Ethnographic Tourism, Romani Tourist Tales, and Fiber Art* (2013). Zajdel's nonverbal processing of these experiences resulted in five works of fiber art, including the final piece that incorporates the artist's hair. In his art piece titled "Amnesia in a Place of Remembrance," Zajdel offers a silk reinterpretation of an Auschwitz prisoner's armband (Figure I.1). The use of hair as padding in the triangle and the chenille references the Nazi practice of shaving prisoners to send the hair to German factories for use in upholstery (Zajdel 2013, 44–50). Zajdel writes, "I include my hair because my visit to Block 4 caused a complete emotional shutdown. Without this shutdown, or without my later shock in the Sauna, I could perhaps have simply buried my memories of Auschwitz and let time help me forget" (47). Zajdel argues for the credibility of artistic expression resulting from fieldwork and reminds us that emotional processing is an essential component of the research process. Echoing Zajdel, this book makes an argument for time—to learn, process, and present.

Getting Involved, Responsibly

At its core, *ReSounding Poverty* serves as an example of applied ethnomusicology. The book offers a critique of how we, as applied scholars, engage with the music and the musicians alongside whom we conduct our research. From the courses we teach to the musical performances we give, ethnomusicologists use the tools of audio and video documentation, ethnographic interviews, extended fieldwork, publications in various languages, presentations at conferences (as presenters and organizers), and classroom work to analyze, delve deeper, and exchange ideas about that which we witness and experience. In applied work, we engage with the projects framed by our interlocutors, albeit pushing such frames in new directions when appropriate. We offer our knowledge of local practice, along with our access to resources that can facilitate community-based action.

4 RESOUNDING POVERTY

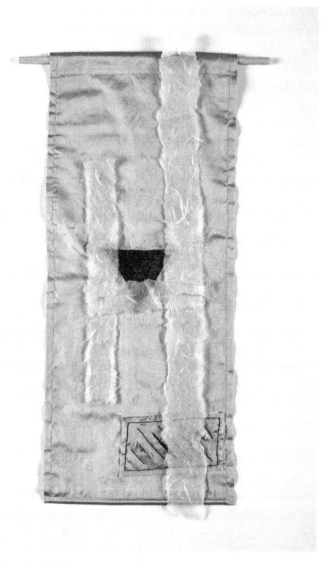

Figure I.1 Evan Zajdel, "Amnesia in a Place of Remembrance," 24″ × 13″, 2013. The artist's hair, silk thread, mulberry paper, silk dupioni, willow wood.

My applied work experience has helped me understand that, despite the alleged grassroots appearances of such actions, the success of musically informed community actions in postsocialist contexts is determined on many levels by Western economic and political forces. Western institutions play a significant role in establishing and perpetuating the global frameworks through which mediated cultural expressions are understood. Shifts within Western political and economic networks play a critical role in transforming and determining what we understand by the notion of culture and what we do in its name.

Such arguments, made in hindsight, stem from my twenty-year path as a researcher who became active in the Romani rights movement during the 1990s through affiliations with nongovernmental organizations (NGOs). These nonprofit organizations are independent of local government funding structures and are active in humanitarian agendas. At the time of my research, Western-funded nonprofit organizations were using music to advance equality discourse in Eastern Europe. My involvement in such projects stemmed from my willingness to collaborate on projects important to Romani NGO leaders, hoping that this would ultimately afford me greater access to all members of the local community. My multiple roles as researcher, musician, and unnamed behind-the-scenes policy worker determined the type of data to which I had access. Working as a minority rights advocate alongside Roms during two political upheavals in Ukraine in 2004 and 2014, I write this book sharing how exchanges between Romani musician-activists, students, and scholars were facilitated globally through development networks. At a time when academic relevance is being questioned, I draw on my experiences as a music professor and university administrator to highlight some of the complex ways that universities in the United States shape global human rights discourse.

To bring help is, by far, not the sole purpose of writing this book, but it has continued to be a guiding factor of the research. To be guided by doing good, and the pitfalls that such intervention brings, is not the same as doing good scholarship. Thus, this book is hardly a statement of advocacy, and indeed it critiques the author's involvement in such endeavors. Instead, it seeks to offer a snapshot, a feeling of what it is like, as an ethnographer and author, to have lived half a life, twenty of the forty-some years on this earth, engaging with a people who feel silenced and forgotten. Time, then, is a crucial guiding factor in this endeavor, as it has been akin to a character in a Greek tragedy that looms large, comments, disrupts, and guides. The time that has passed has also borne witness to major political upheavals that have, in their own ways, upended aspects of this research, suspending it in times of great violence and danger, and speeding it up in alternate cycles, as during the rushed preparations of court documents and testimonies[2] I prepare for Romani

6   RESOUNDING POVERTY

asylum seekers from Eastern Europe to the United States.[3] Thus, this book jumps across centuries, between the past and present, and across countries, new borders, changing laws, and new technologies. In so doing, it weaves a narrative that belongs as much to me as it does to the people whose lives I share in these pages. As I ponder the ironies of job security, grant monies, and the luxury of sabbatical time to write these words, my thoughts are always, as they have been for years, with the Romani musicians whose call for the change I echo in this book.

The Politics of Sound

While *ReSounding Poverty* is of interest to anyone wishing to know more about Romani musical traditions, it is, first and foremost, a critique of the economic structures within which Romani musics circulate. Specifically, it addresses the role of NGOs as market actors within neoliberal processes specific to the margins of Europe. It offers a micro ethnography of economic networks that function on a transnational scale and impact the daily lives of Romani musicians on the borders of the former Soviet Union and the European Union.

Lying at the heart of this book is the economic deprivation and financial poverty that frames it. In post-Soviet market economies, marred by violence and deep-rooted corruption, poverty is increasingly blamed on a lack of self-mobilization. The rhetoric of the haves and have-nots now collides with self-actualizing rhetoric from the United States, reinforced, in part, via NGOs (Round and Kosterina 2005). Everyone is responsible for their economic security. The neoliberal project, as it has taken root in formerly socialist economics, has, in following David Harvey's thinking, become a class project (Harvey 2007). NGO-salaried labor has contributed to the rise of a Romani middle class that seeks to further interests of Romani advancement in education, economics, and politics. This advancement is achieved, to an extent, through the use of cultural capital that has, through a history of Soviet manipulations, solidified dominant stereotypes of Roms as dancers and musicians. Such stereotypes reinforce rhetoric of Romani-specific skills and talents that cast Roms as emotion-generating entertainers. Such stereotypes also reinforce contemporary narratives that aim to justify the exclusion of Roms from educational and professional advancements because they are perceived to be *only* valuable to society as entertainers. Such discriminatory discourses, rooted in centuries of racist attitudes regarding Roms since their arrival from India, are inadvertently reinforced by using cultural production to draw attention to Romani rights. The circulations of such discourses operate in broader culture-driven nation-building discourses in Ukraine where post-Soviet revolutions are cast in terms of ethno-national(ist) identity formations in contexts of postcolonial violence.

Disputes over borders and territories carved from empires, kingdoms, and the Yalta Conference that determined the borders of the Ukrainian SSR by foreign leaders following the end of World War II manifested themselves in discourses rooted in the revivals of rural-based repertoires tied closely to religion, agriculture, and history (Sonevytsky 2019). Since Ukraine's independence from the Soviet Union in 1991, popular interest in pre-Soviet era musical folklore, believed to have been preserved in rural regions, has brought about a boom in amateur ensembles that travel to villages to record vocal and instrumental music and perform it on stage. Ethnomusicologists and amateur folklorists have amassed extensive collections of recordings from aging rural populations. They have documented the predominantly agrarian-related repertoire from the memories of those who lived in the region before the collectivization efforts that began in the 1930s. Collective farms changed how peasants engaged with the land, altering harvest cycles and separating them from the profoundly spiritual rituals the peasants had practiced concerning their ecosystem. This lost way of life, preserved in vocal repertoires, has found its way back through performance and is now playing a significant role in reshaping how people engage with history and the environment. In the last decade or so, such musical repertoires have been festivalized with the help of ethnomusicologists, popular musicians, and folk music groups in Ukraine and around the world, including the New York–based Ukrainian Village Voices, established in 2012 as a project that grew out of Ukrainian Women's Voices, a group established in 2008 with funds from the Center for Traditional Music and Dance.

Romani musical traditions find themselves at an intersection of three discourses. First, they have been omitted from aforementioned folk music festival events geared to foster a love for the land. Attitudes toward Romani histories of nomadism are perhaps best captured in the 1987 poem "Tsyhanska Muza" (Gypsy muse) by Ukrainian poet Lina Kostenko with its refrain, "We are a tribe / We are like peas / We roll across the world. There is no place for us." An imposed framework of Otherness and not belonging positions Roms in direct opposition to the roots-based discourse

8 RESOUNDING POVERTY

of Ukrainian folk music revivalists. Second, Romani musicians in Ukraine, many of whom were once affiliated with Moscow's Teatr Romen, established in 1931 to promote Romani identity through song and dance, are fighting for ownership regarding repertoire and performance aesthetics. Romani performance groups in Ukraine *look* and often *sound* very similar to Romani performance groups in Russia, whose extensive repertoire continues to dominate collaborations with musicians throughout the former Soviet Union and in the West, as in the case of Gogol Bordello and Via Romen.[4] Third, Roms in Ukraine are caught between aesthetics of highly stylized performances developed and cultivated for the Soviet stages and Western consumer-driven "Gypsy" aesthetics that draw non-Roms to a broad repertoire of Romani Balkan styles popularized by academics and musicians in the United States (Laušević 2006). Trying to *fit* within such frameworks has been difficult for Romani musicians in Ukraine, especially in contexts where aesthetic choices are predetermined by (predominantly) non-Rom audiences.

The (lack of) opportunity to develop new sounds or to revive older sounds results, in part, from the tragic loss of Romani lives during the Soviet-perpetrated Terror Famine of 1932–1933, *Holodomor* (literally, Death by Hunger), that killed millions of Ukrainians in central and eastern Ukraine, and the relatively undocumented and under-researched murder of thousands of Roms during the Nazi-perpetrated Holocaust, *Porajmos* (literally, the Devouring), on the territories of today's Ukraine (Kotljarchuk 2016a, 2016b). The sheer loss of human life and the exclusion from nation-building narratives has virtually silenced Romani experiences in the post-Soviet sphere. Romani performances on Ukrainian stages today are hardly an indicator of the richness of Romani repertoires and musical traditions. And yet, the complex sounds that comprise Romani intimate environs never make it to the stage because they are not what non-Rom audiences want and have been acculturated to associate with Balkan-influenced "Gypsy" music.[5]

The more involved I became in the complex webs of ethnographic and applied research, the more my research methodologies changed in response to the knowledge I gained. Nevertheless, the overall questions that guide my thinking more than twenty years since I initiated my dissertation fieldwork are, nevertheless, the same: Why are particular Romani communities so poor? What is the nature of music-making among the Romani poor? And what role do such sounds play within culture-focused development programs? Using ethnography as a lens, *ReSounding Poverty* offers at least a few answers in response.

The Romani Poor

Throughout this book I refer to the Romani poor, a category as unclear as any other. My goal, however, is to bring to attention the experiences of those who are passed over in our engagements with Romani music as it has come to be popularized on stage, in popular music, and in various traditional music scenes.[6] Perhaps readers may have already heard of the now globally famous Romani music group Taraf de Haïdouks, who hail from the rural village of Clejani, Romania. They gained international stardom through the help of the late Romanian ethnomusicologist Speranta Radulescu, Swiss ethnomusicologist Laurent Aubert, and musicians Stephane Karo and Michel Winter who became the band's managers. The group has performed in major venues worldwide and is considered one of the most important groups to have popularized Romani music among Western audiences (Figure I.2).

The global fame and financial success achieved by Taraf de Haïdouks was unfathomable to Romani musicians before the fall of socialism across Eastern Europe in 1991. Today, numerous Romani groups including Fanfare Ciocărlia, also from Romania, travel throughout Europe, the United States, and beyond on regular concert tours. Fanfare Ciocărlia has performed in Pittsburgh three times in the last decade, twice visiting my classrooms to speak with students at the University of Pittsburgh. And in that decade, I have recognized the changes in performance aesthetics, repertoire, and even rhythms and melodic ornamentations, as well as the incorporation of English alongside Romani lyrics as attempts to engage with younger audiences who come to concerts to dance and to be entertained by "Gypsies."

While the moniker "Gypsy," with its historically negative connotations, has been replaced in some (not all) musical marketing with the politically correct term "Romani" (the adjectival form of "Rom" meaning "man" in the Romani language), the music associated with Roms is increasingly succumbing to global market pressures to produce the type of world music with which non-Rom audiences can engage. Such patterns, I would argue, are present, at least within culture-focused development initiatives among Roms in Eastern Europe. Is it too far-fetched to ask whether we are, once again, in an era akin to that of the Romani restaurant musicians in Budapest who played for nineteenth-century urban elites, entertaining the masses in exchange for a subjective level of prestige allotted only to musical performers among Roms? Music scholars like Margaret Beissinger (1991, 2001, 2016), Petra Gelbart (2010), Lynn Hooker (2013), Barbara Rose Lange (2003, 2018), Alexander

Figure I.2. Cover photo for the album *Band of Gypsies* by Taraf de Haïdouks (Nonesuch, 2001).

Marković (2017), Svanibor Pettan (1996, 2001), Sonia Seeman (2019), Carol Silverman (2012), and others acknowledge the complexities working within Romani musical contexts where non-Roms engage with Romani musical repertoires but turn away from Romani realities framed by historical and systemic discrimination. Margaret Beissinger, together with coeditors Speranta Radulescu and Anna Giurchescu, illustrates how Roms play into audience perceptions of Romani corruption through appropriations of the crime-associated musical genre *manele* in Romania (Beissinger et al. 2016). Petra Gelbart draws our attention to what she terms "Gadjology," a critique of non-Roms (identified as *Gadjo* [masc.] / *Gadji* [fem.] / *Gadje* [pl.] in the Romani language) who research Roms only to use this knowledge to advance ideologies that benefit non-Roms (Gelbart 2010). Gelbart uses "Gadjology" to problematize European narratives of nationhood that write themselves into being against exoticized portrayals of Roms. Lynn Hooker delves into narratives of Hungarian music history that situate arguments of ownership as regards Romani music between the ideologies of composer Franz Liszt (1811–1886), who viewed Roms as integral performers-composers of Hungarian music, and composer Béla Bartók (1881–1945), who perceived Romani musicianship as rootless and cosmopolitan, and therefore threatening to what he deemed authentic Hungarian folk music (Hooker 2013). Barbara Rose Lange brings our attention to assimilationist processes in Hungary regarding Romani Protestantism, highlighting how Romani congregations make such music their own (Lange 2003). Alexander Marković researches Romani brass bands in Serbia. He analyzes how romanticized Orientalisms in Romani music allow non-Romani musicians to self-exoticize through Romani practices, even as the same musical elements are used to marginalize Roms as purveyors of "impure" cultural legacies in Serbian nationalist realities (Marković 2017). Svanibor Pettan extensively documents the adaptability of Romani musicians in Kosovo to non-Romani musical demands of audiences of various ethnic, religious, and linguistic groups (Pettan 1996, 2001). Sonia Seeman moves between Byzantine and Ottoman contexts to situate the historical processes by which Roms are stereotyped as and denigrated as *çingene* (Gypsies) in modern Turkey. She highlights the creative musical ways Roms have forged new musical forms to create and assert new social identities (Seeman 2019). Carol Silverman analyzes the negotiations that Romani musicians make within world music markets that advertise various Romani musical traditions from different countries under the category of "Gypsy music" (Silverman 2012).

Building on the richness of such scholarship, all of which addresses, to some extent, the nature of musical engagements among Roms and non-Roms, *ReSounding Poverty* echoes the call for advocacy for Romani-oriented discourse while drawing attention to the intimate soundscapes of the Romani poor. Drowning out academic scholarship on Romani music is the plethora of popular writing that draws musical tourists[7] to villages like Clejani[8] in search of musical authenticates within a globally mediated "Gypsy" musical phenomenon. Because such narratives have become so overpowering for musicians as well as scholars, I write this book against the very framework I helped create—the sound world of male professional musicians who have used their status within Romani communities to become the voice of Roms in politics. The historical status that male musicians carry in their communities has helped them garner enough community support as political leaders within postsocialist restructurings of Romani society. As this book narrates, after the fall of the Soviet Union, Romani musicians were among the first to capitalize on development opportunities, using their social status within Romani communities to establish culture-based organizations that served as representatives for Roms in surrounding regions.

ReSounding Poverty pushes against the crowding of increasingly affluent male voices within the growing circle of Romani elites who aim to control the narrative of (collective) Romani experiences. I acknowledge and respect many of their endeavors and describe them positively in the pages that follow. Yet as this book demonstrates, neoliberal consolidations of political and economic power are drowning out the voices of the Romani poor who have not been able to benefit from interventionist projects fully. NGOs threaten to turn resistance into a 9–5 job with a salary (Roy 2016). In the past decade, Romani musician-activists have become much more global in their outlook (Bhavnani et al. 2016; Booth et al. 2016), promoting collaborations with musicians in the West and helping to market a cosmopolitan Romani identity in Ukraine. The musical traditions of more impoverished Roms are increasingly missing from this dialogue. These are musicians who, at the time of my initial fieldwork, had been, in large numbers, forced to sell their instruments to make ends meet; in other words, they divested themselves of the very source of their income in order to survive whatever financial crises arose.[9] Their experiences constitute the core ethnographic data that inform this book.

The Audibility of Development

ReSounding Poverty analyzes the power dynamics behind public performances of music deemed "Gypsy" and deconstructs the notion of ethnic group cohesion upon which global music markets rely. Building on scholarship regarding Romani cultural agency in music, it broadens the discourse to include the role of international aid organizations in their support of cultural development initiatives that shape the rhetoric on music and musicians in Romani communities. The financial support from nonprofits in a for-profit economy that demands payment for musical labor shapes the discourse regarding the end goals for which such labor is used. How do the dynamics of aid influence identity politics among Roms in the former Soviet Union? How are such politics negotiated and reflected in musical repertoires on stage? In post-Soviet society, notions of musical skill are influenced by lingering socialist discourses regarding classical training as a marker of professional musicianship among folk and popular music artists (Helbig 2009; Lemon 2000; O'Keefe 2013). This shows that such economically and culturally mediated frameworks tend to marginalize poorer, self-taught Romani musicians as "nonprofessional" within development networks, thereby excluding them from performance opportunities, perpetuating Romani cycles of poverty in the post-Soviet era.

Through an analysis of musician experiences, *ReSounding Poverty* engages with global scholarship on development (Crewe and Harrison 1998; Edelman and Haugerud 2005; Escobar 2011; Ferguson 2015), Romani-focused development initiatives (Barany 2002; ERRC 2001, 2005, 2006, 2011, 2012; Guy 2009; McGarry 2010; Revenga et al. 2002; Ringold et al. 2005; UNDP 2002), ethnographic studies in anthropology focusing on the poor (O'Neill 2017; Spradley 2013), ethnomusicological studies on poverty (Araújo and Cambria 2013; Dirksen 2013; Fiol 2013; Harrison 2013; Harrison 2020; Moisala 2013; and Titon 2013), and applied ethnomusicology (Harrison 2013; Mackinlay et al. 2010; Pettan and Titon 2015, 2019a, 2019b, 2019c). It argues that the development aid allotted to provide economic assistance to Romani communities, when analyzed from the perspective of the performance arts, continues to marginalize the poorest among them. Through their structure and programming, NGOs choose which segments of the population are the most vulnerable and are in the greatest need of help, for instance, minorities, women, children, and the disabled. Inevitably, "Romani problems" become the responsibilities of Romani NGOs. The book asks who speaks within the Romani rights movement today. Through a closer listening to vocal inflections, physical vocalizations of health and disease, and emotional affect, *ReSounding Poverty* brings us into the back rooms of *saman*, mud and straw brick, houses not visited by media reporters and politicians, amplifying the cultural expressions of the Romani poor, silenced in the business of development.

In the second half of the book, through analyses of coughing, from tuberculosis and from smoking, I bring the lives of Romani musicians in line with global discourses on healthcare. I also bring attention to otherwise stigmatized mental health sufferings, particularly depression, anxiety, post-traumatic stress (PTS), and inter-generational trauma not only among Roms but in post-Soviet society in general. Writing against the destructive historical stereotype of *Tsyhanske schastia* (Gypsy happiness), an ironic term made popular through post-Soviet films that present Roms as resilient against

14 RESOUNDING POVERTY

poverty, this book sounds out the heretofore unacknowledged physical and psychological effects of systemic discrimination.

Book Overview

ReSounding Poverty seeks to analyze factors that influence the nature of representation for minorities in local governance in the post-Soviet era. It contributes to the literature on Roms in Eastern Europe, an area of study that lacks specific data on Roms in Ukraine, a country that has to date been coupled with scholarship on Roms in Russia (Barany 2002; Crowe 1994; Guy 2002) and Poland (Mroz 2015). The inaccuracy of merging the Russian and Ukrainian narratives stems from the fact that the nature of politics in Ukraine, with the country's numerous revolutions and violent unrest, has differed so drastically from that of Russia under President Putin's mode of rule akin to a post-Soviet dictatorship. While Putin has ordered foreign NGOs to register with the state and closely monitor their programs and interventions, in Ukraine, minority communities, identified through markers of ethnicity, gender, and sexuality, can more openly engage in civil society as promoted by international aid networks.

Using the internationally funded Romani rights movement as a model, this book questions the primacy of ethnicity as a delineating marker of identity in post-Soviet society. While it is beyond the scope of this project to engage with the historical, political, linguistic, religious, and other reasons why ethnic categories exist, ethnic identity has continued to serve as a rallying cry for social unity and division in post-Soviet Ukraine. An awareness of the harm such bounded identities create has pushed me to question whether ethnically based approaches toward the integration of minorities serve as the most effective strategies to help guarantee equal access to social goods. This book analyzes the repercussions of employing ethnicity as the main criterion for the distribution of development aid and shows that the "minorization" of specific segments of the population within international development discourse encourages various forms of internal stratification within the very minority groups that such discourse seeks to aid. In turn, such processes contribute to the further marginalization of those members with the least representative power within this discourse. In other words, this book sheds light on the ways networks of development aid function or fail to function in new market economies. In this way, it contributes to research on how neoliberal discourses of civil society shape minority politics in emerging democracies.

At its core, *ReSounding Poverty* analyzes emerging class tensions among various Romani communities as they play out in the choice of musical repertoire within the Romani rights movement in Eastern Europe. This book theorizes how music has shaped Romani identity politics since the fall of communism. It fills the gap in the literature on Romani music by focusing on the marginalized within the marginalized. Drawing attention to the unnamed poor, *ReSounding Poverty* calls out the soundscape of the impoverished. It gives voice to their everyday experiences and augments our understandings of their lives through the songs they sing and how they listen to and engage with music.

The first half of the book, comprising the Introduction and first four chapters, offers macro perspectives on how Romani music and Romani musicians engage with international programs that shape policies and attitudes regarding Roms in post-Soviet society. Through an analysis of development structures, aid programs, and on-the-ground initiatives, the data offer a broad perspective on the relationship between music and Romani rights. The second half of the book, containing a further four chapters, brings the discussion to a micro level, offering a more intimate analysis of Romani sounds. Flipping the narrative of aid, it offers a critical analysis of the everyday experiences of impoverished Roms. Moving from discussions of stage performance, film, and social media initiatives, the second half of the book brings us into the mud-floor houses of impoverished Roms. Broadening earlier discussions of music and performance aesthetics to a focus on sound and the body, the second half of the book brings us into the sonic experiences of people whose physical and mental health is shaped by the traumas and transitions of post-Soviet realities. Through an analysis of everyday struggles, it asks how the aid programs discussed in the first half of the book shape people's everyday lives.

Chapter 1—"Transitions"—offers a historical overview of Romani experiences in today's eastern and western Ukraine. It contextualizes the role of Romani musicians in the Austrian and Russian Empires and charts the trajectory of such roles from the Soviet period to the present day. It also analyzes how different state policies have contributed to distinct economic, political, and social experiences for various Romani groups. This chapter paints a historical overview of non-Rom perceptions about Roms and how Romani politicians engage with such narratives in Ukraine today through examples from literature, poetry, and art.

Chapter 2—"Interventions"—positions musicians at the forefront of the post-Soviet Romani rights movement and analyzes how musician interactions with Western-funded NGOs have shaped cultural narratives about Roms in Ukraine. The chapter examines the role of aid in postsocialist societies marred by political instability and deep-rooted corruption. Analyzing the ethnic-specific interventionist model that frames development aid for Roms, this chapter elucidates the short-term and long-term impacts of helping provide security and stability for Roms in the region. It also highlights the unintended consequences of development aid, particularly ethnic-specific aid programs in the postsocialist sphere.

Chapter 3—"Accountability"—explores the choices researchers make when the boundaries between scholarship and advocacy blur. It argues that in applied research settings, scholars highlight chosen aspects of the ethnographic encounter that benefit the people with whom we collaborate. Taking as a given the so-called observer effect, where the mere observation of a phenomenon inevitably changes that phenomenon, this chapter engages with contemporary critiques in Eastern Europe that identify NGOs as political actors that introduce modes of thought that push against the status quo. So-called agenda-setting theories, which are usually applied to media in terms of having the ability to influence the importance placed on issues in the public sphere, play a role in activist scholarship. This chapter extends this analysis to academic institutions, offering a critique of how educational programs in the United States engage with Romani music and help shape Romani rights discourses worldwide.

Chapter 4—"Mobilities"—focuses on the history of Romani musicianship in Transcarpathia, Ukraine's westernmost region that shares borders with Poland, Hungary, Slovakia, and Romania. A microethnography of music-making in Uzhhorod, Transcarpathia's administrative capital with a sizable Romani population, and home to one of Ukraine's largest Romani organization, Romani Yag (Roma Fire), the chapter charts the history of associations between Romani musicians and Romani cultural, educational, political, and human rights organizations in post-Soviet Ukraine. This chapter uses music to highlight how shifts in borders have shaped and influenced Romani music traditions. It analyzes developments in Romani music concerning local, state, and international patronage, and offers perspectives on Romani modes of self-presentation.

Chapter 5—"Networks"—offers a history of development programs for Roms in Ukraine. It analyzes their impact on local, regional, state, and international levels and evaluates the positive and often unintended consequences of such interventions. Essential to an understanding of the outcomes is that initial programming initiatives did not include Romani voices and that the patterns set in place in the early years of post-Soviet collapse set the scenes for intervention programs of the twenty-first century. This chapter focuses on programs explicitly aimed at cultural development and how culture has been used as a political tool in the context of the broader post-Soviet society. Shaped by non-Romani imaginings of Romani engagements with music, this chapter explains how and why Romani music has become so politicized and analyzes its continued importance within the Romani rights movement.

Chapter 6—"Tuning In"—asks how conditions of poverty create specific sound environments. Poverty conditions shape the way instruments sound. Historicizing discourses of tuning during the Soviet era, this chapter elucidates how prevailing post–World War II discourses influenced notions of musical skill in Ukraine regarding classical training as a marker of professional musicianship. Such economically and culturally mediated frameworks tend to marginalize poorer Romani musicians as nonprofessional (but somehow not amateur) and exclude them from performance opportunities sponsored by Romani organizations, in turn perpetuating cycles of Romani poverty in the post-Soviet era.

Chapter 7—"Sound Health"—addresses how physical health shapes impoverished sound worlds. It elucidates how disease, particularly tuberculosis, affects contemporary performance practices in Romani villages. The chapter looks critically at how coughing, a familiar soundtrack in live music performance among audiences, punctuates fieldwork recordings in communities with high tuberculosis rates. It also connects the sonic environments of coughing to that of smoking habits among Romani musicians. The relationship between the body and the state, couched within a development discourse that aligns physical health with citizenship rights, makes the biopolitical in the post-Soviet sphere audible. An analysis of musicians' health shows how performance aesthetics engage with health disparities in communities under duress.

Chapter 8—"Release"—examines expressions of emotional health among the Romani poor. It takes a critical look at the impact of living in a state of financial, emotional, and political instability and how such emotional states impact Romani psychological wellbeing. This chapter looks particularly at vocal expressions of pain and suffering. It also celebrates aural expressions of joy while pushing back at the historically rooted tropes that reduce Roms to nothing more than happy stage performers, somehow devoid of full humanity (and the attendant pain and suffering that comes with it). In discussing the processing of trauma that music allows, this chapter offers space to express raw emotion that impoverished Roms cannot afford. It also critiques the exploitation of female Romani vocality in development discourse. Breaking the silence of the visual gaze that frames development reports, this chapter analyzes the aural soundtrack that accompanies media depictions of the Romani poor.

In sum, *ReSounding Poverty: Romani Music and Development Aid* makes audible the sounds that frame a more visually focused development rhetoric. This book makes central the sounds of hungry children begging for money and singing for food, the laments of a mother worried for her children's future, the twang of an old guitar strummed by arthritic fingers, and the hoarse coughs of a musician with tuberculosis. It gives voice to economic inequalities from the perspective of the Romani poor. It honors the emotions triggered among those without access to resources that every human, rich or poor, wishes to have to live a life of relative stability.

Time passes slowly when the body is hungry. This book is written with memories of such moments. It draws on years of repeated visits to *saman* houses of Romani musicians in Transcarpathia and situates these experiences within a broader context of history, politics, and culture. Through its perspectives on aid networks, it brings us into the mud-floor homes of those whose pictures dot development reports. Grounding the ethnography within Ukraine's anti-corruption movements, including the 2004 Orange Revolution and the 2014 Revolution of Dignity, *ReSounding Poverty* offers a critical yet sensitive analysis of how, in the context of post-Soviet neoliberalism, well-meaning networks of aid allow the rich to become richer and the poor to stay the same.

1

Transitions

To experience the rise and fall of regimes, with changing rules and social orders, is unfathomable for those who have not lived through such upheavals. Despite a relatively peaceful transition to independence, Ukraine, like all post-Soviet countries, went through dire years of poverty, corruption, and political instability; it has had a much more difficult time stabilizing than have other nascent nations once part of the USSR. Ukraine, literally meaning "borderland," comprises lands that were once the Russian and the Austro-Hungarian Empires' outer reaches and have been disputed and fought over for centuries. Since gaining independence in 1991, Ukraine has experienced two revolutions, one peaceful in 2004, known as the Orange Revolution (Wilson 2005), and one violent in 2014 known as the Revolution of Dignity (Shore 2018). Since 2014, the Russian Federation has annexed the Crimean Peninsula, once a vassal state of the Ottoman Empire, and the country's eastern borders are marred by insurgent violence (Allison 2014). There has been a war in Donbas where separatists swearing allegiance to the Russian Federation have established two breakaway republics: the Donetsk People's Republic and the Luhansk People's Republic (Cavandoli 2016).[1] By 2019, more than 10,000 people had lost their lives in the conflict; and 1.8 million had been internally displaced.[2] Such ongoing upheavals contributed to a total population loss of 8 million: from 52 million in 1990, down to 44 million in 2019, due to the combined effects of outmigration and a death rate double the birth rate in 2018.[3] Moreover, the war-torn country continues to deal with the ecological and bio-political aftermath of the Chernobyl disaster, a catastrophic nuclear accident that occurred on April 26, 1986, at the No. 4 nuclear reactor in the Chernobyl Nuclear Power Plant, near the city of Pripyat, 100 kilometers from Kyiv (Brown 2019, Plokhy 2018).[4] More than 2 million people were displaced because of the accident, among them Eugene Hütz (Figure 1.1), frontman of the Gypsy-punk group Gogol Bordello of Kyiv—New York—Rio de Janeiro—whose musical style is the subject of analysis in the latter half of Chapter 6.

ReSounding Poverty. Adriana N. Helbig, Oxford University Press. © Oxford University Press 2023.
DOI: 10.1093/oso/9780197631768.003.0002

Figure 1.1 Frontman Eugene Hütz of Gypsy punk group Gogol Bordello performing live on the Zippo Encore Stage at Download Festival on June 14, 2013, Castle Donington, UK.

Photo by Kevin Nixon/Metal Hammer Magazine/Future Publishing/Getty Images.

Roms and Revolutions

International media attention has largely overlooked Romani experiences during Ukraine's tumultuous past. However, the image of Roman Saveliev, a twelve-year-old boy in homemade armor, who fought, ate, and slept alongside protestors during the 2014 Revolution of Dignity on Kyiv's Independence Square, gave rise to hope of greater Romani acceptance and integration following the war (Figure 1.2). Hailed by the international media as the "Child of the Maidan," Roman became the symbolic image of a new Ukraine, a hopeful utopia of transparency and equality; his Romani identity served as a framing narrative for media coverage.[5] A member of one of the most marginalized and discriminated-against minorities in post-Soviet Eastern Europe, the boy both captured imaginations and personified the fears of the Other through his mere presence at the center of such a pivotal political event. While international readers praised him, his *Gadje* (pl. non-Rom) neighbors in Yagotyn in the outskirts of Kyiv spoke negatively about the boy. Referring to him as a *Tsyhan*, a Gypsy, cast as *uncivilized*, they suggested that his mother, not having the economic means to support her children, did not care about the boy's whereabouts. Such statements alluded to common stereotypes about Roms as impoverished people who do not have the financial means to support their large families and therefore send their children out to beg on the

Figure 1.2 Twelve-year-old Roman Saveliev on Kyiv's Independence Square, December 2014.
Photo by Andrew Kravchenko.

streets. The neighbors also alleged that a member of the family was in prison, deploying yet another derogatory stereotype of thievery and immorality long associated with Roms. Such media reporting elucidates the disjunctures that Roms in Ukraine face: supported by international networks in efforts to self-mobilize, they are essentialized locally in terms of centuries-old stereotypes used to justify systematic modes of exclusion.

Such narratives have genuine—and often very violent—repercussions. On June 23, 2018, ultranationalists attacked an encampment of Romani laborers near Lviv in western Ukraine, killing one person and injuring several others. This attack was the sixth in a series of attacks on Roms.[6] Violence against Roms has been common in Ukraine since independence in 1991. To date, attacks have, for the most part, occurred in retaliation for problems blamed, often without justification, on Roms, who have long been scapegoats for village tensions. Often without apparent cause or conviction, Romani houses are burned and Roms violently beaten. Such events, referred to as pogroms by Romani political activists in Ukraine, are motivated by deep-rooted prejudices against Roms, despite the promise that the Revolution of Dignity held. The presence of the "Child of the Maidan" had seemed a nascent promise of Romani inclusion, rooted in newfound mutual respect and understanding.

What, then, is causing the increase in violence and discrimination against Roms in Ukraine? Anti-minority politics in neighboring Hungary, led by Viktor Orbán, echoing Vladimir Putin's ethno-nationalist policies in the Russian Federation, have fostered a platform for a growing number of nationalist groups in Ukraine (Kucharczyk and Mesežnikov 2015). The suspects in the June 2018 attack on Roms were reported to have been members of a radical group called "Sober and Angry Youth." Some members of this group have ties to the former volunteer battalion Azov, which fought in eastern Ukraine and has been implicated in numerous unlawful detention, torture, and other abuses. Since the beginning of 2018, human rights groups have documented at least two dozen violent attacks, threats, or instances of intimidation by radical groups such as C14, Right Sector, Tradytsiya i Poriadok (Tradition and Order), Karpatska Sich (self-styled after the eponymous paramilitary group formed in 1938 in the short-lived state of Carpatho-Ukraine), and others against Roms.[7] Such ongoing acts of violence have prompted some Roms to organize politically, particularly on social media. Others have attempted to leave the country. In one such case, a Romani man from Transcarpathia who had obtained a Hungarian passport based on being able to speak Hungarian, crossed the border into Hungary, and, with the help of activists, traveled to New York where he applied for political asylum.

When Transcarpathian Roms who had set up camp in the outskirts of Lviv were attacked in 2018, Kyiv-based Romani leaders reached out to international media outlets via watchdog organizations like the European Roma Rights Center (ERRC) that has, since the 1990s, been monitoring and publishing reports on Roms' living conditions, unemployment, and attitudes among non-Roms toward Roms (ERRC 2001, 2005, 2006). The ERRC, comprising a global network of activists and lawyers, and connected with a myriad of Romani rights organizations, helped bring information about the situation to an international readership. That the story went viral on English-language social media attests to how Romani activists in Ukraine now work: social media networks that crystallized during the 2014 Revolution of Dignity now help Roms bring to light stories once relegated to the shadows, dismissed, or not reported at all.

From Performers to Politicians

Numbering 350,000, Roms in Ukraine today include such culturally and linguistically diverse groups as Servy, Slovākika Roma,[8] Ungrika Roma, Vlax, and others (Barannikov 1931, 1933a; Beníšek 2013, 2017; Elšík and Beníšek 2020; Marushiakova and Popov 2004), Servy, the largest in number in the Ukrainian territories, migrated from Wallachia and Moldova and settled in eastern and southern Ukraine in the middle of the sixteenth century. The Kalederash[9] and Lovara[10] in Transcarpathia, are part of the Vlax Romani group, whose language is strongly influenced by Romanian. Slovākika (Slovak) Roma, also prominent in Transcarpathia, differ from Servy and Vlax in that they speak Central Carpathian dialects of Romani. Ungrika Roma or Rumungri[11] living in Transcarpathia often identify as Hungarian.

In 1836, in the newly acquired territories of Bessarabia (bounded by the Dniester River on the east and the Prut River on the west), Russian tsarist ministers established two new villages called Faraonivka (Pharaoh's) and Kair (Cairo), to which many Romani groups were resettled. Today, Roms in those regions are referred to by local villagers as *xvaraony* or "the Pharaoh's people," indicating the widely held false belief that Roms came from Egypt.[12] Faraonivka and Kair are unusual names for Bessarabia, but neighboring villages have equally unusual names, including Negrovo (derived from Negro); they continue to have large populations of Roms.

By the late 1800s, Russian scholars were aware that Romani history had its roots in India.[13] Soviet scholars, including linguist Aleksei Barranikov (1890–1952), founder and head of a Soviet school of specialists on Indian philology, researched Romani dialects in the territories of today's Russia and Ukraine. The knowledge he and others accrued regarding Romani-Indian connections became an integral part of Romani identity during the 1950s when the USSR began to establish stronger relationships with non-aligned countries, including India. In the arts, Teatr Romen helped popularize Romani-themed performances that drew political attention to issues relating to Romani identity and integration into Soviet society (Lemon 2000; O'Keefe 2013). Teatr Romen dramatized the Romani exodus from India in productions like *My—Tsygane* (We are Roma) and *Latcho* (Good). In the early 1980s, the company also traveled to Punjab.

On the territories of today's eastern, central, and southern Ukraine, once ruled by the Russian Empire, Roms were serfs of the crown. Those who lived on estates of Russian nobles formed choirs for the entertainment of the nobility, and many used their popularity to gain freedom. Descendants of these Romani choir performers are the musicians mentioned earlier who worked at Teatr Romen and subsequently became representatives of the Romani intellectual and political elite in post-Soviet Russia (Bobri 1961; Marushiakova and Popov 2003). These urban-based Roms made distinctions between themselves and nomadic, or *tabornye Tsygane*, camp Gypsies.

Teatr Romen's influence reverberated throughout the Soviet Union. In Transcarpathia, Romani musicians looked to Teatr Romen for aesthetic influence. Teatr Romen was a source of pride for Transcarpathian Roms and an aspirational performance stage for Romani musicians. Aladar Adam, whose journey from musician to Romani activist is documented in Chapter 4, performed at Teatr Romen when he was fifteen years old. This performance established Adam as a professional musician who would follow in the footsteps of his father Yevhen Adam, a well-known Uzhhorod-based violinist. In turn, as this book documents, Adam's respected musician status among Roms helped positioned him as a Romani rights leader in Transcarpathia following the fall of the Soviet Union.

Romani Music as Politics

The politicization of Romani culture and identity began to happen in Ukraine only after independence, a full two decades after the first World Romani Congress in London in 1971 (Acton 1974; Barany 2002; Guy 2002; Hancock 2002). Barbara Rose Lange writes that starting in the 1970s, Romani musicians in Hungary had established *folklór* (folklore) ensembles whose repertoire was based on rural family singing and dance. *Folklór* ensembles engaged with nationwide folk revival movements and offered ways for Roms to engage in multicultural political discourse (Lange 1997). Katalin Kovalcsik notes that the trend to use traditional Romani music modeled upon peasant culture as a political statement for Romani integration in Hungary began to shift in the 1980s. Discourses of mobility and hybridity coincided with the growing world music market, and many younger Romani musicians capitalized on discourses of cosmopolitanism and fusion to draw attention to Romani rights messaging. More traditional Romani music groups in Hungary like Kalyi Jag (Black Fire) incorporated elements from various Romani and non-Romani traditions from Russia, the Balkans, and Spain (Kovalcsik 2010, 63). By the late 1990s, younger Romani musicians in Hungary like the Fekete Vonat (Black Train) rap group were engaging with popular Western genres like hip-hop. Kavalcsik notes that since the fall of communism, Western genres have offered Romani musicians opportunities to reach broader audiences (Kovalcsik 2010, 65).

Established, experienced Western-based Romani political networks, working alongside development organizations that fund Romani-related endeavors, offered models for Romani communities in Ukraine to organize politically and to engage in efforts to alleviate the traumas of post-Soviet transition. They initially drew on what worked during Soviet times, namely activism through cultural expression, which Ioana Szeman identifies as a model that continues to be used by Romani activists in Romania (Szeman 2018). More than thirty years after the fall of the Soviet Union, however, the well-established networks in Ukraine are now led by a second generation of Romani activists, many of whom took over the running of Roma nongovernmental organizations established by their parents in the 1990s. They have shifted focus from the arts to law, education, and healthcare. Nevertheless, the politicized nature of music in Ukraine as a holdover from Soviet times (Hansen et al. 2019; Helbig 2006, 2014; Schmelz 2009a, 2009b; Sonevytsky 2019) forces Romani activists to engage in frameworks of cultural essentialism that, on the one hand, draw attention to Romani rights rhetoric through performance, while, on the other hand, reinforce deeply rooted cultural stereotypes that continue to impede economic advancement and social change.

Today, the Romani political movement in Ukraine is often referred to by Romani political leaders and development representatives as the "Romani Renaissance." Many Romani leaders within the Romani rights movement in Ukraine are professional artists or were employed as such in the past. Some, like previously mentioned Aladar Adam, the director of Romani Yag (Romani Fire), the largest Romani nongovernmental organization in Ukraine, and the editor of the *Romani Yag* newspaper in Uzhhorod, spent their youth working as musicians in traveling family orchestras. Other important Romani figures in Ukraine, such as Ihor Krykunov, founder of the Kyiv-based Teatr Romance, director of the Romani organization Amala, and organizer of the annual Amala Festival in Kyiv, were members of Teatr Romen. Krykunov is perhaps best known from Soviet cinema, having been typecast as a *Tsyhan* (Gypsy) in the Soviet film classic *Tsyhanka Aza* (The Gypsy Woman Aza, 1987), based on Mykhaïlo Starytskyï's novel by the same name (1888).

Figure 1.3 Romani activist Oktavia Adam (right), director of the Transcarpathian cultural-educational organization "Roma," leads participants in the celebration of International Romani Day, Uzhhorod, Ukraine, April 7, 2017.

Photo: Yanosh Nemesh/Shutterstock.

Romani cultural expression is synonymous with Romani politics in post-Soviet Ukraine. The past professions of key figures like Aladar Adam and Ihor Krykunov connect Romani cultural and political expression even more explicitly. Grant-funded projects like the *Romani Yag* newspaper and the Amala Festival reveal the complex processes that inform the conscious construction of Roms as "one people." The Romani intelligentsia in Ukraine works to unite the various linguistically and culturally diverse groups in Ukraine under the umbrella signifier "Roma." The emergent global understanding of "Roma" is that of a transnationally unified nation without a state that shares historic and linguistic roots traced back to India, from where Roms are believed to have migrated in the tenth century. This notion manifests itself, for instance, in the festival of Romani culture initiated by Ihor Krykunov in Kyiv. Particularly poignant is the festival's name, Amala, meaning "harmony" in Romani. *Amala* is also a Hindi word, derived from the Sanskrit *amal* meaning "clean, pure." As such, the title of the festival serves as a performative act. Amala emphasizes that Ukrainian Roms are culturally pure (i.e., authentic, not polluted) and can find similarities between their own cultural expressions and the multiple music and dance traditions of Roms worldwide. Such political and cultural connections are reinforced through the participation of Romani theater groups from Macedonia and Germany in the Amala Festival together with performance groups from Slovakia, Russia, and elsewhere. The international participants in the Amala Festival perform an understanding of "Roma" as a transnational diaspora and reinforce a newly defined place for Ukrainian Roms within the worldwide Romani community.

Romani intellectuals draw on the stereotypical association of *Tsyhany* (Gypsies) with movement to forge new understandings of Roms in Ukraine as members of a transnational Romani diaspora. The road and movement along that road are important unifying tropes in this construction.[14] Similarly, the exodus from India represents the collective emotional and physical hardships all Romani groups have endured throughout their history.[15] Together with common tropes like movement, migration, and diaspora utilized within the Romani rights movement, India invokes discourses of not only belonging, but of exclusion, thus making Romani integration into non-Romani society an even more daunting prospect than it already is in Ukraine today.[16]

In the 1970s and 1980s, when most of Transcarpathia's urban Romani population was employed under communism and could afford such entertainment, the main movie house in Uzhhorod played weekly Indian movies

28 RESOUNDING POVERTY

for a large number of Roms frequenting the establishment.[17] Many recall how the theater would be packed with Roms. Many Romani performers in Ukraine incorporate Indian dance movements and vocal embellishments into public performances. For Svetlana Adam in Uzhhorod, singing *po-indiĭsky* (in the Indian way) implies incorporating microtonal fluctuations into her vocal technique. Another singer from Uzhhorod preparing for a festival in Kyiv stated that she would perform in an Indian sari if she had one. Likewise, during a wedding among Roms in Lviv, if a male dancer exhibits much more exciting and intricate footwork than others, people will remark that he dances *po-indiĭsky*.[18]

In Search of Happy Gypsies

After the fall of the Soviet Union, livelihoods that had depended on a historically cultivated status of Roms as entertainers slipped away as restaurants that employed Romani musicians closed, unable to afford luxuries like *zhyvyi zvuk*, live sound, performances. Economic insecurities also led to fewer wedding celebrations altogether, and fewer still lavish ones, once a guaranteed income source for Romani musicians. State-funded cultural initiatives like Teatr Romen, established to increase Romani visibility and to foster relationships between Roms and the Soviet state, struggled to keep alive the *spektakli*, elaborate performances, that once graced its stage.

As mentioned previously, aesthetics from Teatr Romen had shaped public identities for Roms throughout the Soviet Union (Lemon 2000; O'Keeffe 2013), including cities within the former Ukrainian SSR like Kyiv, Kharkiv, Odesa, Lviv, and Uzhhorod. Images of Romani women in colorful outfits dancing to music performed by Romani men on *semi-strunnaya*, seven-stringed guitars, were both ubiquitous and largely positive. They performed many songs popularized by Soviet-era Romani-themed films, including blockbusters like *Tabor ukhodit v nebo* by Emile Loteanu (The camp ascends to the heavens, Mosfilm 1975), based on *Makar Chudra*, a novel by Maxim Gorky about the strong-willed Rada (Svetlana Toma) and Loiko Zobar (Grigore Grigoriu) the horse thief. The most-attended movie in the Soviet Union in 1976, *Tabor ukhodit v nebo* was viewed by close to 70 million people. It invented a fantasized version of nineteenth-century Transcarpathia, where the story is set. For non-Roms, the film incorporates, and thereby validates, all possible romanticized and exoticized imaginings of Romani life: magic, nomadic and carefree living, unbridled passion, music, and dance. Rada is a lover, a dancer, and a singer, who charms both Romani and non-Romani men with her beauty and strength. She does not succumb to her Romani lover, who is jealous of the attention Rada receives from a Hungarian nobleman. At one point in the Russian-language film, Rada asks, "*Chto vy za liudy, chto vam nuzhno—nichevo krim dorogy* (What kind of people are you, what do you need—nothing except the road)?" The film features a handful of Romani singers and dancers from the environs of Uzhhorod, Transcarpathia. It thus serves as the single most crucial example of acknowledgment of local Romani identity. Songs from the film appear in the repertoires of local Romani groups, and the aesthetics of Romani dancers are mimicked from the film.

That Moscow-based directors produced the film attests to the complex web of ethnic identity formations in the former Soviet Union. Legitimizing the periphery via the center, the hand of Teatr Romen's performers is evident in how Transcarpathia is exoticized. The film embodies the stereotypes that assimilated Roms living in a metropolis have about nomadic Roms, and, in turn, imposes these on all Roms in the former Ukrainian USSR. For instance, the film shows no integrated Romani or urban Romani dwellers who, according to documents, resided and performed in Transcarpathian towns. Instead, all Roms are depicted as nomadic and exhibit specific traits. Rada has the power to woo sexually and to use her "evil eye" to control the actions of men and animals. She is able to stop a runaway horse and carriage by standing in the street and gazing forcefully in the animal's direction. She can also seduce a Hungarian nobleman while driving her Romani lover, Loiko Zobar, mad to the point where he commits a crime of passion and kills her. This essentializing of alleged Romani "traits"—of temperament, emotion, unbridled sexuality, and passion—is referred to collectively in Soviet rhetoric as *Tsyhanschyna*, Gypsiness.

Alexander Barannikov, in his 1931 study "Ukrainian Gypsies," notes that the "freedom" associated with *Tsyhany* loses its romanticized allure when considering professional musician status as an entrapment. Roms had few options for employment, and the choice to become a musician or dancer was not a choice at all (Barannikov 1931, 12–13). The Soviet-era essence of *Tsyhanschyna* idealizes Roms as happy-go-lucky musicians who sing and dance away their cares. This stereotype is common in the West and perpetuated in films that feature Roms as musicians and dancers (Malvinni 2004). Romani activist George Eli has analyzed the essence of such caricatures

30 RESOUNDING POVERTY

in his critical documentary *Searching for the 4th Nail* (Eli Films/Little Dust Productions, 2009). Deciphering images from American films that have exoticized Roms as fortune-tellers, entertainers, and thieves, Eli critiques the stripping of humanity from these character archetypes through which contemporary Romani identities are molded in the imaginings of non-Roms.

In Ukraine, stereotypes of Roms are most evident through the trope of the fortune-teller as a palm reader. The palm reader differs from images of the fortune-teller peering into a glass orb, an image that, according to Eli, first appeared in American films. Neither does the fortune-teller use tarot or playing cards. Instead, the physical touch of the palm brings the fortune-teller into proximity with *Gadje*, non-Roms. Whatever their form, however, such fortune-telling exchanges connect the promise of *shchastia*, happiness, with Roms. An inherent fear and anxiety riddles interactions with Roms because of this. The belief that Roms hold the power to reveal happiness imbues Roms, especially Romani women, with great power. To that extent, this interaction is also fraught with fears of the negative, especially if the fortune-teller's message reveals a tragic fate.

Ukrainian poet and artist Taras Shevchenko (1814–1861) focuses on the economic exchange that guides the search for hope and happiness in his 1841 watercolor *Tsyhanka-Vorozhka* (Gypsy fortune-teller) (Figure 1.4). In this painting, a young Ukrainian peasant woman shows the palm of her hand to a Romani woman with a child on her back, as if to ask the *Tsyhanka* to foretell the future. Shevchenko depicts the economic difference between the women by not representing the two figures as equals. The Romani woman stands outside of the property, separated from the young peasant woman by a low wall. The Ukrainian woman turns her face away from the fortune-teller; her upright stance contrasts with the hunched figure of the *Tsyhanka-Vorozhka*, who leans down to read the palm of the peasant woman. The Ukrainian woman is clearly at home, as indicated by her bare feet and bunched apron, both of which suggest that she might have been working in the house or garden and that the visit from the *Tsyhanka-Vorozhka* is unexpected.

In contrast, Shevchenko depicts the *Tsyhanka* with a walking stick, the symbol of a nomad and an outsider who has no permanent home; she is, quite literally, on the outside looking in on the more privileged life of the Ukrainian woman. Fortune-telling offers the *Tsyhanka-Vorozhka* an emotionally charged cultural power and a symbolic voice. She is imbued with powers derived from local superstitions and fears of the Other. She can shape

Figure 1.4 Taras Shevchenko, *Tsyhanka-Vorozhka* (Gypsy fortune-teller), 1841.

realities; she can curse the receiver or offer hope in exchange for financial compensation.

As theorized by Sarah Ahmed, happiness, or the promise of it, is connected to objects and processes that ritualize the reproduction of being. Ahmed argues that to feel better is to get better, correlating the human condition with the state of emotion (Ahmed 2010, 8). Ahmed argues that "happiness imbues certain persons or ways of personhood valuable" (Ahmed 2010, 11). What are the implications of imposing the rhetoric of happiness onto an individual or a group of people? The trope of happiness is placed upon marginalized groups for many reasons and carries a host of negative consequences.

Perhaps the most damaging is that presumed happiness infantilizes people and takes away from them the agency of complex emotions.

European histories of court jesters positioned those with disabilities as entertainers. As entertainers for noble classes, Romani musicians were meant to lift up the spirits and bring energy to social gatherings. Romani suffering, allowable in the context of staged performance, was intended for the entertainment of those who consumed and observed. While non-Romani readers may have sympathized with the characters, the performers were, after all, actors on stage who moved in and out of emotions for the sake of audience reaction.

Financial rewards gleaned from the performance of *Tsyhanshchyna* began to dwindle after the fall of the Soviet Union as audiences who had once supported such performances in large numbers found themselves unable to afford the luxury of entertainment. Confusion about Moscow-led repertoires arose within Romani communities in the furthest reaches of the former Soviet Union like Transcarpathia—Ukraine's westernmost *oblast*, administrative region—home to the majority of Ukraine's Roms. Living only a few kilometers from the suddenly accessible Polish, Slovak, Hungarian, and Romanian borders, questions emerged regarding their aesthetic relationships with Ruska Roma communities in Russia, the long-assimilated urban Roms who had shaped the traditions of the Soviet Romani stage. Many Ruska Roma families trace their lineage to ancestors who once performed in Romani choirs for Russian nobility. The traditions popularized by these performers inherently differed from those of nomadic Roms and those of Roms living in the territories of Ukraine, now faced with anxieties brought forth by the consequent reorienting of self within a turbulent postcolonial space. The chapters that follow position this narrative of reorienting and, to an extent, Romani reorientalizing, within the context of Western-funded development initiatives in postsocialist Ukraine.

2

Interventions

Since Ukraine's independence in 1991, nongovernmental organizations (NGOs) have worked to fill the gaps in social welfare left behind by the collapse of the Soviet state, a situation augmented by the economic stagnation of the 1990s. Promoting human rights, gender, and ethnic equality, and civil liberties, NGOs are generally perceived in the public sphere as fighting on behalf of those who do not have the power to speak for themselves. NGOs have also been instrumental in introducing new ways of thinking and modes of being via programs that have shaped the public and private spheres, but their influence and success are debated by scholars, politicians, and economists (Kostka 2018). Their very presence has played a contested role in the post-Soviet transition. Since 2012, a law signed into power by Vladimir Putin requires all nonprofit organizations that receive foreign donations and engage in so-called political activity to register and declare themselves as foreign agents. The "foreign agents law" stands among a series of restrictive measures introduced by the Russian government in response to the anti-Kremlin protest movement that arose between parliamentary and presidential elections in the winter of 2011–2012. Among the most affected are human rights organizations. In the eyes of Russian leaders, NGOs are instruments used by the West to pave the way for a transition of power. Such discourse is rooted in Russia's experiences with its former satellite state, Ukraine, where the pro-Russian government lost power to a pro-Western leader during the 2004 Orange Revolution. NGOs have continued to work relatively unimpeded in Ukraine, and develop programs that foster the new rhetoric of civil rights discourse framing the 2014 Revolution of Dignity. That Ukraine is presently at war with Russia is no small matter, and one must take into account the responsibilities and actions attributed to NGOs in Ukraine. Programs focusing on equal rights, gender equality, free speech, open media, and educational exchange have helped foster new ways of thinking, and those new ways of thinking insist on a Ukraine that remains outside the grasp of the Kremlin.

NGOs play an important, albeit often unacknowledged, role in how post-Soviet society is shaped. They categorize people according to gender,

ReSounding Poverty. Adriana N. Helbig, Oxford University Press. © Oxford University Press 2023.
DOI: 10.1093/oso/9780197631768.003.0003

34 RESOUNDING POVERTY

race, class, and ethnicity in development discourse and foster relationships with particular population segments through their programming. Such approaches have a direct impact on Romani communities, as the analysis of the workings of Transcarpathia's largest Romani NGO Romani Yag in the latter half of this chapter demonstrates. The varying understandings regarding the role of NGOs in mediating human rights, public representation, and access to resources can serve as a case study for a broader analysis of the dialogics of development: cultural, political, and economic engagements with Western aid, and their attendant discourses have meaning in aid recipients' public and private lives. The term "dialogics" is associated predominantly with Mikhail Bakhtin, who argued that people experience and represent the world through numerous overlapping and often conflicting meanings within a shared language (Bakhtin 1982). Research confirms that a multiplicity of interacting intentions is at play among donors, individual recipients of aid, and the broader populations for whom aid is intended (Escobar 2011). Since texts predominantly take on meaning for people about their current concerns, dialogics indexes the ways meanings are constructed out of competing modes of language usage. In donor/recipient discourse, different groups of actors have diverging understandings of policy documents, grant applications, and what the financial aid should seek to accomplish.

The rise of the NGO sector in post-Soviet Ukraine has been reinforced by corruption in government, on the one hand, combined with an attained level of society's democratization and its practical implementation through a network of Western aid organizations on the other.[1] NGOs emphasize social organization beyond the influence of the state and argue that the public sphere should be autonomous and independent of government control to ensure democratic reform and progress. Such discourse was necessary, for instance, in light of the Ukrainian government's anti-democratic tendencies under former President Leonid Kuchma (1994–2004), whose anti-democratic tactics led to the eruption of the 2004 Orange Revolution. Marred by corruption, the curtailing of free speech, and an abhorrent lack of improvement in the lives of Ukraine's citizens, the ineffectiveness of Ukraine's government at the time was perhaps most succinctly captured in a popular Ukrainian saying: "*My ne zalezhni vid vlady, a vlada nezalezhna vid nas* [We are not dependent on the regime, and the regime is independent from us]." NGOs were widely perceived as one of the only ways to bring about reforms.

NGOs in Ukraine have focused their work on specific segments of the population. Women's rights NGOs have received the most attention in the scholarly literature on NGOs in Ukraine (Phillips 2005a, 2005b, 2008; Hrycak 2007; Pishchikova 2010).[2] Romani NGOs, active in Ukraine since the early 1990s, have been relatively absent from scholarly analysis, with a few exceptions (Gabrielson 2006; Helbig 2005). The high levels of Romani unemployment, illiteracy, and health insecurities in post-Soviet society are still predominantly viewed as the "problem" of Roma NGOs, instead of being a situation that needs to be addressed by the state. The presence of foreign aid has allowed the Ukrainian government to wash its hands of responsibility concerning various challenges that minority communities face.

The role of NGOs in the post-Soviet sphere has many parallels with NGOs that take on the welfare functions of the "shrinking state" in light of neoliberal processes throughout the world (Alvarez et al. 1998). The neoliberal projects aim to eliminate poverty in developing countries through free markets and free trade.[3] Couched in the rhetoric of the protection of human rights, the role of the state is minimized to serve the interests of private property owners and entrepreneurs. Institutional reforms, cuts in welfare expenditures, and privatization equate citizenship with individual integration into the market.

Anthropologists have begun to assess the darker side of this "rights talk," analyzing the cultural, economic, and political consequences of such interventions among segments of the population targeted as needing assistance from Western donors (Alvarez et al. 1998; Escobar 1995). Ideally, in a competition for resources, everyone is assumed to be an equal player and to have access to the same information. In reality, elite class power is strengthened, the organized power of the labor force is usurped, and the poor become poorer. The state no longer comprises both political entities and civil society. Rather, it positions civil society in opposition to governmental rule; this new reality charges civil society with the sole responsibility for social betterment (Escobar 1995, 78). Deep corruption augments such neoliberal agendas in the post-Soviet sphere (Wedel 2001).[4] Since 2017, amendments to a Ukrainian law on income and asset transparency now require employees of certain NGOs and investigative journalists who focus on corruption to post detailed income declarations publicly in electronic form. Critics claim the amendment is discriminatory for singling out some NGOs and being unclear in identifying them, leaving room for selective quashing of those most critical of the government.

"The Soros Gypsies"

By 1997, George Soros, the founder and chair of the Open Society Foundations, had begun to focus efforts on helping impoverished Roms in Western and Central Europe, prioritizing Romani communities in the former Soviet bloc. Romani organizations applying for funds from the Open Society Foundations did so through the framework of what they once knew best: performance. Projects with the goal of saving Romani cultural traditions, often with a specific focus on language, became the norm and were funded. While it might seem strange in terms of timing that, at the height of the economic struggle, Roms once again began to put on large-scale music and dance events, festivals, and theater productions, the performances fostered and developed the embryonic connections between Roms in Ukraine and across the European Union.

The Soros Foundation is the main philanthropic source through which representatives of Ukrainian Romani NGOs gain access to resources to implement economic development and education projects in Romani settlements. This aid is allocated according to ethnic criteria. How do internationally sponsored development projects influence conceptualizations of ethnic identity and determine meanings imbued in categories such as "national minority"? How do discourses of ethnicity, contextualized within local, national, and transnational relations of power, shape local understandings of "equality" within ethnically segregated communities in Ukraine? How do different segments of the Romani population engage with the idea of civil society as it is propagated via and in relation to international networks of financial aid?

Internationally funded NGOs play an essential role in shaping ethnic minority movements. However, a closer examination of the repercussions of employing ethnicity as the main criterion for the distribution of aid reveals that the minoritization of specific segments of the population within international development discourse encourages various forms of internal stratification within minority groups and, more broadly, encourages and confirms a certain stratification between different ethnic groups (Yúdice 2003). In turn, such processes contribute to the further marginalization of those members with the least representative power within this discourse, namely an ethnically marked underclass. Do ethnically based approaches toward the integration of minorities serve as the most effective strategy when seeking to guarantee equal access to social goods? In emphasizing the "unique" characteristics of different cultural groups, philanthropic donor programs reinforce the notion of national minorities as homogeneous communities that have markedly different needs than does the majority population. The emphasis on ethnicity as a key to entitlement for goods and services has contributed to numerous separate "cultural" struggles of individual minorities such as Crimean Tatars, Roms, and others in Ukraine. While successful on one level in procuring much-needed national and international political recognition and foreign financial support for education and culture projects, these movements do not function as collective actions along class, gender, or social lines. They are ethnically differentiated and inadvertently mirror and encourage political processes that determine individuals' social standing based on ethnicity. In other words, ethnically based development initiatives reinforce a power framework that contributes to other forms of the very marginalization they seek to alleviate.

Despite almost three decades of international financial aid, Romani settlements in Ukraine continue to reflect high (and, in some cases, increasing) levels of unemployment, poverty, malnutrition, and disease. Today's network of Romani NGOs has been responsible for implementing this aid to diminish the negative impacts of overwhelming social issues.[5] Nevertheless, research shows that NGOs do not always help the people who are in greatest need. The Ukrainian government does not recognize the autocratic nature of Western-funded NGOs within Romani communities and often mistakes Romani NGO leaders for *barony*, elected elders who historically maintained order within Romani communities. In contrast to *barony*, Romani NGO leaders are not elected by Romani communities but rather rise through the ranks with the aid of grants provided by Westerners.[6] In many Romani settlements in Transcarpathia, for instance, access to Western financial aid has allowed Romani NGOs such as Romani Yag to usurp the traditional authority of the community elder, *birov* or *baron*. *Birovs* in Perechyn, Velyka Dobron, Svaliava, Velyki Kamiati, and many other Transcarpathian towns and villages now double as representatives of Romani Yag, which emerged in the 1990s as a supra-Romani organization in Transcarpathia that has representative power on the national level in Ukraine. To a degree, the present system of intervention has kept poorer Roms impoverished and has denied them agency in terms of political and socioeconomic community-based development (Trehan and Sigona 2009). Simultaneously, it has allowed for a small percent of educated, affluent Roms to reap the benefits of philanthropic aid. In other words, within Romani communities, an elite circle of grant recipients has

38   RESOUNDING POVERTY

managed to gain control of development-based financial aid and representational power. In contrast, the majority of impoverished Roms, for whom, in theory, the grants are intended, continue to live in marginalized shantytowns on the edges of towns and villages. This phenomenon mirrors a general trend among political elites in post-Soviet Ukraine, where a small number of politically and economically powerful people have manipulated numerous state and social mechanisms to benefit personal interests.

To better understand how Romani NGO leaders garner local power, it is fruitful to analyze historical divisions among Roms that have been exaggerated through the donor network. As Ladányi and Szelényi explain, such divisions are social cleavages that form within ethnically marked groups whose exclusion from mainstream society is extreme (Ladányi and Szelényi 2006, 11). From the late nineteenth century until the fall of the Soviet Union, the most influential Roms in the Transcarpathian region included musician families who performed for non-Romani restaurant patrons. In the mid-1990s, when donor organizations began to offer cultural development grants, Romani musicians in Transcarpathia capitalized on the availability of funding and founded organizations to benefit from this financing. Romani musicians, generally more accepted in non-Romani society, were better equipped to engage with donors because they had already had greater access to education and work experience than others in their community.[7]

Representatives from minority groups in Transcarpathia often express anger that donors allegedly give larger amounts to Romani organizations than to similar organizations run by and for other ethnic groups in Transcarpathia. International funds that favor minorities are often perceived as unfair by the majority and further aggravate tense relations between various ethnic groups in Ukraine, including Hungarians, Romanians, Slovaks, and others. Such sentiments are evidenced in the sarcastic statement shared with me by an official in the National Minorities Council in Uzhhorod: "*Tsyhany tse naïbilsh pochesna natsmenshyna na Zakarpatti* [The Gypsies are the most lauded national minority in Transcarpathia]."[8]

George Soros has published numerous articles on the paradoxes and unintended consequences of the Soros Foundation's philanthropic activities in the region. He admits that financial aid often turns "recipients of charity into objects of charity" and that intervention often meets the objectives of donors rather than the needs of recipients (Soros 1994, 81). Nevertheless, Soros attempts to justify and clarify his philanthropic activities by stating that the policy of his Eastern and Central European foundations is "to collaborate, to pull resources and talent from different places, and to allow people from the region to determine their areas of focus and decide on methods of implementation" (Soros 1994, 85). Though Soros-funded projects appear to operate within what Jürgen Habermas terms an "ideal speech situation" where actors are all assumed to be oriented at reaching a mutually beneficial understanding, actors with more power and financial backing will always reap more significant benefits from the exchange (Habermas 1984). International donors make decisions without predicting the effects of particular policies on groups for whom they are intended.

The Unintended Consequences of Donor Aid

How do aid situations play out for Roms in post-Soviet society? Romani NGOs in Ukraine receive grants for administrative purposes, and the staff of NGOs such as Romani Yag (Uzhhorod) and the Association of Roma in Transcarpathia (Uzhhorod) regularly attend training programs in Uzhhorod and Kyiv. Romani NGOs such as Ame Roma [We Roma] (Zolotonosha), Romen [Roma] (Kharkiv), Terni Zor [Youth Power] (Brovary), Romano Foro [Romani City] (Cherkassy), Amaro Deves [Our Today] (Kremenchuk), Romano Kkham [Romani Sun] (Zhytomyr), and Bakhtale Terne [Lucky Youth] (Pereiaslav-Khmelnytsk), to name just a few, utilize International Renaissance Foundation grants to run educational and vocational programs and Romani culture clubs. Some Romani NGOs such as Kale Yakkha [Black Eyes] (Novomoskovsk) work with Romani women's groups and use grant money to provide ob/gyn services. Funds are also used to fight the spread of tuberculosis, which has reached epidemic proportions because of impoverished and unhealthy living conditions. Other Romani NGOs such as Romano Drom [Romani Road] (Vynohradiv) apply for support from the International Renaissance Foundation to run Romani school programs in Transcarpathian villages that provide instruction for Romani children in the Romani language and traditions. Romani Yag, among other endeavors, utilizes International Renaissance Foundation aid to sponsor Romani students at various universities in Kyiv, Lviv, Uzhhorod, Odesa, and Kharkiv, particularly in the Faculty of Law. In return for their education, Romani Yag asks these future lawyers to participate in the national Romani rights organization Chachipe [Truth] (headed by Romani Yag's director Aladar Adam) that provides counsel to Roms who cannot afford legal protection.

40   RESOUNDING POVERTY

Donor aid has made Romani citizens increasingly dependent on a growing network of Romani NGOs for representative agency. Because Romani NGOs are the most visible community-based structures, they function as gatekeepers between the state and the people. A director of a Romani NGO is referred to as *romskií lider*, a term that borrows the English word "leader" (an example of so-called project speak where a development-related word is incorporated into everyday community discourse). The NGO and its Romani leader offer social and judicial protection for Roms who live in settlements that fall under the purview of grant projects supported by one or another Romani NGO. A curious socioeconomic phenomenon has emerged: during the Soviet era, Roms worked independently of their community and had much more freedom to follow individual paths separate from the community, but the economic crisis in Ukraine today, coupled with increasing anti-Rom discrimination, makes them highly dependent on the Romani NGO in their search for work and during run-ins with the police.

To some degree, democratic freedoms have yielded fewer freedoms for poorer Roms. As was the case in many of Transcarpathia's *Tsyhanski tabory*, Gypsy camps, during the 2004, 2010, 2014, and 2019 presidential elections, Romani NGO leaders exerted great influence over how members of their respective *tabir*, camp, cast their votes.[9] NGOs present data that appeal to Western donors but use allotted financial resources for people of Romani ethnicity who might not be in relative need of aid, such as family members of particular Romani NGO leaders. This structure further marginalizes the poorest segment of the Romani population. Romani NGOs, functioning within an internal set of sociocultural hierarchies and politics, recognize that as long as there are "poor Roms," they will continue to receive donor aid.

The Business of Development

The desire to help has long-term effects that paint a poor image of the impoverished. Issues, not people, are addressed through institutions; foreign aid is a business. Without the poor, the development/poverty industry becomes obsolete. Michael Matheson Miller succinctly presents these arguments in his documentary *Poverty, Inc.* (2014). Miller's documentary opens with a critique of the 1984 song "Do They Know It's Christmas Time" written in reaction to television reports of the 1983–1985 famine in Ethiopia. The song was recorded by Band Aid, a group comprising the most prominent British and Irish musical acts at the time who sang the refrain "Feed the world, let them know it's Christmas time." It was re-recorded in 1989 as well as in 2004 by Band Aid 20, including Bono from U2 and Paul McCartney, and in 2014 by Band Aid 30, the proceeds from which went to generate funds for the United Nations to address the 2014 Ebola crisis (Stürmer et al. 2016).

Miller's documentary drives home the point that we do not need celebrities doing pop songs or campaigns, what Tanja Müller describes as "celebrity humanitarianism" (Müller 2013). Rather, we need to get rid of the poverty industry and paternalism and stop excluding the poor through partnerships to help them achieve their dreams. Miller critiques efforts by businesses like Toms that, for every pair of shoes purchased, donate a pair to a person in need. He argues that the shoe donations might put a local shoe-maker out of business. Further studies of the so-called Toms Model argue that the one-to-one model focuses more on getting consumer dollars than making a tangible impact. The Toms Model also perpetuates the global vision of the world's poor as passive receivers of aid. This damaging perspective is promoted by hand-out charities and philanthropic organizations, giving products to struggling populations without genuinely assessing the lasting effect on the community. In turn, two potentially adverse outcomes arise: the impact is either unsustainable, lasting only as long as the product does, or worse, the model promotes aid-dependency. According to Russell Reed, "aid-dependency is the phenomenon wherein populations receiving external assistance become reliant on this support, and in the most severe instances, it can stunt a community's ability to survive sustainably and without constant donation."[10] Therefore, should aid stop coming for any reason, such as an organizational pivot or a lack of funding overseas, the community may not be able to continue sustainably (Easterly and Pfutze 2008).

In some ways, cultural development grants follow the so-called Toms Model. Pushing against this structure is Nomi Dave, an ethnomusicologist and a former human rights practitioner in West Africa, who suggests conceptualizing music within the so-called capabilities network. Dave argues that using a flexible language of capabilities allows space for getting to know what people want and allowing them to pursue such goals within a development frame. This capabilities approach does not replace but instead works in conjunction with human rights discourse and aid mechanisms (Dave 2015, 13). Writing against assumptions of music's universality, Dave draws on the capabilities approach to show that music-based development initiatives often fail because of erroneous understandings of how kinds of music work in various locales (Dave 2015).

Among Roms, professional musicianship offers social status. To understand better how music functions within Romani communities, it is essential to recognize the degree of *value* that Roma place on music as a profession. The changing nature of this profession within postsocialist market economies offers significant insights into how discourses of status are now emerging as discourses of class. Distinctions once made between nomadic and settled Roma are now being drawn among Roma between the rich and the poor.

The growing interest in Romani musical traditions has contributed to a rise in the number of Romani musicians achieving international acclaim (Cartwright 2005).[11] This rise has become particularly notable since the 1990s when recordings of Romani musicians became accessible abroad and travel restrictions from formerly socialist countries allowed for Romani musicians to travel to the West. Concerts for Western audiences have drawn on historical tropes of the "Other" in the marketing of Eastern Europe and the Balkans, playing to audience expectations of Romani musicians as natural musicians who offer virtuosic, engaging entertainment.

Marketing tactics often collide with realities, especially when Romani musicians from different countries share the stage. As Carol Silverman notes, during the1999 Caravan tour, members of the Romani village ensemble Taraf de Haïdouks arrived in New York City with just a few pieces of tattered clothing and no instrument cases. Bulgarian Romani saxophonist Yuri Yunakov offered to personally take Taraf members shopping at his expense because he felt that the everyday village clothes they wore on stage would undermine the professional status of Roms as international musicians (Silverman 2007, 347). These tensions point to class differences among Roms that are not, to date, clearly articulated in Romani scholarship. If Romani elites who gained their status through their associations with aid organizations that aim to help Roms in need are the primary spokespersons for Roms of all class backgrounds, who then are the Romani poor? How do inter-group politics of poverty and marginalization play out in development discourse and cultural production?

The model that emerges among Roms in Ukraine is that of the upper-class musician as a politician. The professional status of the male musician earns him sociocultural cachet upon which he draws to advance political agendas through development networks. Having emerged in the early years of development programs, this model continues to shape discourses through initiatives led by family members of musicians who garner the same level of community respect, even if they are not professional musicians themselves. In other words, male musicians, acknowledged for their elite status in Romani society, extend class status to family members and members of the next generation.

Aid and the Limits of Ethnicity

Ethnically based grants assume a level of homogeneity among minority groups in need of financial assistance. The structure of the development network bases itself on the premise that individuals, namely Romani NGO affiliates, can represent the needs and views of the whole of the ethnic communities in which they work, putting aside their individual self-interests. Such attitudes result in simplistic approaches by NGOs, donors, and local governments in addressing people's needs. Further difficulties arise because Romani NGOs compete against each other for a limited amount of financial resources within ethnically defined funding categories. As a result, factions have arisen in Romani communities depending on which NGO individuals benefit from and consequently support. Aid money has contributed to a rising tension within Romani communities and with the general non-Romani citizenry on a local and national level.

Researchers have increasingly begun a critical assessment of local engagements with globalizing notions of civil society that have been introduced via NGOs, UNESCO, the European Union (EU), and various state-to-state programs. Scholars have argued that cultural rights function as an interchangeable concept with minority rights within cultural development practices, in which ethnicity figures as a central framework for political and social equality (Yúdice 2003). In Eastern Europe, policy initiatives and projects funded by government agencies and NGOs address minority rights issues through a lens of ethnic homogeneity that, in most cases, completely overlooks those emerging discourses of class in post-Soviet contexts that work together to influence relative cultural agency and powers of representation within a community and within society at large. Policymakers regard pluralism and the celebration of difference in the public sphere as emblematic of progressive democracy. Theoretically, each of the many cultures that make up the nation is to be treated with dignity, have access to equal representation, and be allowed to express a measure of self-identity publicly.

The embrace of ethnic difference by international institutions, networks, and governments undermines the capacity to enforce equality and create spaces for the ethnic diversity that intervention policies and programs intended to support.

Western concepts of cultural pluralism are configured as compartmentalized wholes, and, as such, cultural development programs promote ethnic relations in terms of separate diversities. Cultural borders between groups are blurred and malleable. To be truly democratic (as Western donors believe themselves to be) would be to recognize and respect such a landscape of inter-ethnic exchanges. It does not suffice to gain equal opportunity to participate in discourses that aim to eradicate the prejudices that limit marginalized groups from fully attaining their rights in a democracy. However, as Habermas recognizes, in order for an "ideal speech situation" to take place, communication must occur in a public sphere that is free of institutional coercion (Habermas 1984). Yet while such parameters may allow Habermas to assume equality between actors, equality is not built into relationships between Western givers and non-Western recipients of aid in development discourse. Though participants in UNESCO projects, for instance, appear to operate within a Habermasian "ideal speech situation," in the end, those actors with the most significant coercive power and financial backing are likely to get more of what they want in negotiations.

Many decisions are accepted without considering the effects of particular policies on groups for whom they are intended. Overlooking and silencing the actors affected by policy decisions is unjust and perpetuates structures of domination (Linklater 1998, 109). Such frameworks were institutionalized and taken for granted at the height of Western imperial restructuring in the wake of communism's collapse in the 1990s. It is time to reassess the basis of internationally sponsored approaches that have gone too far in the direction of cultural and ethnic uniqueness and position ethnic particularity as the sole cultural space for the production of minority identities in the post-Soviet era. Through their focus on homogeneous groups targeted for aid, Western models of development reinforce Soviet ethnic-bound identities that were intentionally constructed through Soviet nationality policies to divide and conquer peoples in a colonial project rooted in ethnic difference. Discourses on music, specifically traditional music, mirrored such rhetoric and solidified ideas regarding genres as bounded cultural expressions belonging to one ethnic group. Such group-specific modes of thinking have reinforced the myriad ways cultural expressions have been interpreted as extensions of homogeneous group identities.

While watchdog organizations like the European Roma Rights Center in Budapest are helping curb anti-Roma rhetoric in global media, non-Roms still privately express views of Roms as biologically lazy, thieving, and gifted only in music and dance. In countless interviews and conversations, non-Roms have stated that they believe these traits are part of *Tsyhanska krov*, Gypsy blood, and that Roms live in squalor out of choice rather than necessity. The moral framework within which Romani poverty is discussed shapes public opinion of Roms as undeserving of help because they either choose to live in squalor or are biologically preconditioned to do so. They are infantilized, their choices assumed to be predicated based on an inherent lack of morals. This dangerous rhetoric racializes the Romani poor. Non-Romani media crews and photographers often arrive in Romani communities unannounced to document living conditions in impoverished settlements (many of them with no running water, heat, or electricity), with little explanation of their presence or purpose in filming. Locals featured in such segments have expressed anger at being treated as if they are zoo animals, on display to look at but with not to interact with respectfully. Romani NGOs attempt to intervene and alter such stereotypes among the population by publishing a Romani newspaper and books and by issuing media releases for Ukrainian television. These efforts, however, have done little to change the sentiment of the public in general or the Ukrainian government in particular. This is because the "Gypsy problem" is considered the internal problem of Roms and not one of non-Romani majorities.

Social scientists have critiqued multicultural discourses and practices that function as "modes of containment and control" (Bhabha 1990, 208) within a broader project of national cohesion, a process Elizabeth Povinelli and other scholars engaged in indigenous scholarship have referred to "ethnographic entrapment" (Povinelli 2002). Such critiques are relevant in Ukraine because the emphasis on ethnic difference within the development community works in opposition to development policies that claim to support an inclusiveness agenda. In other words, the political ethnicization of the population in Ukraine, augmented through the eyes of private Western foundations with neoliberal ideological agendas, reinforces lingering socialist ethnic hierarchies in the post-Soviet context rather than offering new opportunities for sociopolitical and economic involvement. While minority social movements help to construct public spaces in which conflicts gain visibility, any gain in minority rights hinges upon the actions of existent institutions in public society and those of the state.

Well-connected organizations such as the Open Society Institute in Budapest and International Renaissance Foundation in Kyiv have stepped in where the state had allegedly failed or unable to provide in the past. Thus, Romani NGOs sponsored by the International Renaissance Foundation provide services that are, in fact, the responsibility of the Ukrainian government. These include protecting human rights, access to unbiased media, support for Romani cultural endeavors, and access to education, social security, and other benefits. However, there is a great danger that the presence of ethnically based NGOs and the government's reliance on them will continue to make it possible for the state to avoid what should be *its* responsibility to members of minority groups that are in greatest need of assistance. The situation is exacerbated because people who give and receive aid rarely contest the ethnocentric norms that pervade the Western-dominated development network.

Official statements issued by the Ukrainian government concerning Roms, in particular, reveal a great lack of awareness of and sense of obligation to address the problems at hand. According to a 2001 report provided by the government of Ukraine to the United Nations Committee on the Elimination of Racial Discrimination, racial discrimination in all its forms was declared to be eliminated in Ukraine, and the equality of every person before the law articulated as secured, without distinction based on race, skin color, or national or ethnic origin (ERRC 2001).[12] The United Nations Committee on the Elimination of Racial Discrimination rebuked this report and pointed to information regarding the continuing discriminatory treatment of Roma and violence against them and their property. Particular concerns were raised regarding reports of police brutality against the Romani population, including torture, arbitrary arrests, and illegal detention. It recommended that the Ukrainian government take immediate and effective steps to stop these abuses.[13] Rather than take responsibility, the government has, to date, blamed Roms themselves for the substandard conditions in which many live, as well as for their "inability" to advance economically, socially, and politically.

The Ukrainian government points to Romani behaviors and alleged violations of the law as justifications for their marginalization. At a meeting of the Commission on Security and Cooperation in Europe in Washington, DC, in 2018 where Romani leaders and activists met to discuss the most recent attacks on Roms, Oksana Shulyar, deputy chief of mission at the Embassy of Ukraine to the United States, acknowledged the grave humanitarian situation affecting Roms and explained how the Ukrainian government continuously tries to assist one of its nation's most vulnerable groups. She stated, "Ukraine is strongly committed to principles of tolerance and nondiscrimination of all ethnic groups, including the Romani community. Alongside the Ministry of Internal Affairs of Ukraine, law enforcement, and national security, grassroots organizations and local governments are working to create a safer community for Roma."[14] The underlying rhetoric of victim-blaming, however, is hard to root out. Moreover, such political soundbites run counter to what Romani leaders like Volodymyra Kravchenko, director of Terni Zor ("Youth Power"), a Romani organization in Brovary (Kyiv *oblast*) observe. According to Kravchenko, "The government never helped, and will not help. The difference is that now they can just take credit for it. The government thinks, 'why should we help them if they are helped by foreigners?'"[15] Local government officials address Romani-related issues solely through NGO representatives. They have made little effort to develop direct relationships with Romani citizens who live in the numerous Romani settlements, referred to as *Tsyhanski tabory*, Gypsy camps. While the term *tabir* (pl. *tabory*) implies a temporary stopover, many *Tsyhanski tabory*, especially in Transcarpathia, are more than a hundred years old. Many city councils do not consider these settlements to be part of their jurisdictions, and therefore they leave most responsibility for the welfare of these citizens to Romani NGOs. In other words, while international foundations offer financial aid for Romani projects with good intentions, this aid effectively cuts the Romani population off from other social services from the state.[16]

Young Romani activists, the second generation to engage with nongovernmental networks, have turned to social media to draw attention to local problems. Educated with the help of development programs and Western grants, they are fluent in foreign languages, including English. Many now travel often to the West, including Brussels and Washington, DC, to train people on human rights issues. They speak out against police brutality, discrimination, unemployment, and lack of access to healthcare. They fight against corruption in the economic and political sectors, rally local Roms to vote, and organize education and sports programs for young urban Roma. They are, however, few in number, and their efforts, while valiant, are overwhelmed by government ineffectiveness and stagnation in providing support and security. Thus, in critiquing development interventions, this book, de facto, critiques the lack of action on the part of Ukraine's government to assist with integrating Roms into the fabric of post-Soviet society. Roms find themselves in a situation that forces upon them a dependency on aid and allows the Ukrainian government to wash their hands of responsibilities for the country's most discriminated against minority.

The Romani Yag Organization: From Music to Romani Rights

In Transcarpathia's villages in the late 1990s, I began to hear stories of a "Romani president," a person who people said had access to money from the West and who was giving out food and medicine in Uzhhorod. It did not take long to find Aladar Adam, director of the NGO Romani Yag (Roma Fire), an organization that began as a music group. Having made his musical career in Moscow and Rostok, Adam returned to Transcarpathia when the Soviet Union collapsed. He organized his unemployed acquaintances and family members who were musicians into a performing troupe (Figure 2.1). With Romani Yag, Aladar Adam hoped to continue earning a living through performance in Uzhhorod. Such opportunities were few and far between in a country whose infrastructure was collapsing under hyperinflation rates as high as 2000 percent. By the mid-1990s, Adam found himself in a strategic position to benefit from the International Renaissance Foundation's funding opportunities that emphasized minority cultural development in Ukraine.

Through generous support from the Open Society Institute and International Renaissance Foundation, Romani Yag grew from a music ensemble to one of the most influential Romani organizations in Transcarpathia. Romani Yag continues to publish a Romani-themed newspaper in Romani and Ukrainian (with an Internet version in English). It sponsors human rights conferences, issues publications on Romani culture and language, and plays an instrumental role in the fight against anti-Romani discrimination in Ukraine. Throughout the years, Romani Yag has also run a Romani kindergarten, a sewing school for Romani women, a Romani beauty school, and a Romani museum in Uzhhorod. Today, the former offices of Romani Yag serve as a restaurant and hotel that are frequented by development aid workers who regularly visit the Romani settlements in the area. Because Adam speaks Hungarian, the native language of George Soros, he has additional advantages over Romani leaders from other parts of the country

Figure 2.1 Aladar Adam (far right) performing with Romani Yag in Kyiv, 1992.
Photo: Courtesy of Romani Yag.

that allow him to draw on cultural ties with donors in Hungary. Adam frequently travels to Budapest to meet with Romani politicians and, through their networks, broadens his options for the number of grants Romani Yag applies for and receives.

As mentioned earlier, in many Romani settlements, financial resources from development agencies have allowed Romani NGOs to overshadow or usurp the authority of the male community elder, the *birov*. Romani communities have traditionally elected the position of *birov*, or *baron*.[17] The title may be passed on to a male descendent, but the appointment must be approved by consensus. In Rakhiv, Transcarpathia, the *birov*'s widow, Anna Rostash, was elected to take on the responsibilities of settlement leadership. Mrs. Rostash also served as the representative of Rakhiv's Romani Yag office. Romani Yag has offices in Perechyn, Velyka Dobron, Svaliava, and Velyki, whose *birovs* serve as representatives to Romani Yag, which has emerged as a supra-Roma organization in Transcarpathia. Romani Yag often sponsors Romani rights training conferences in Uzhhorod to which the organization invites Romani NGO directors and staff from other regions of Ukraine.

50 RESOUNDING POVERTY

Romani Yag representatives also participate in numerous international conferences and work closely with organizations like the European Roma Rights Center in Budapest and Romani NGOs in Russia.

Western Tourists, New Audiences

In Uzhhorod, the greatest irony is that the Romani Yag NGO now runs a hotel and restaurant from the compound that once served as the organization's original office. This Romani Yag musical ensemble-turned-NGO-turned-hotel-and-restaurant is on the same street as the poorest of the three Romani settlements in Uzhhorod, gated from the surrounding impoverished Romani settlement. One of the largest Romani NGOs in Ukraine, Romani Yag hosts numerous international visitors, dignitaries, and politicians who travel to surrounding Romani settlements to conduct interviews with local Roma and to document cases of police brutality, to distribute humanitarian aid, and to track the lack of educational opportunities, unemployment, and health epidemics. The steady influx of development-related traffic inspired Aladar Adam, as Romani Yag's director, to bring tourists to the area for an authentic Romani experience. The NGO's offices were moved to another location, but the Romani Yag name, already established and recognizable as associated with Roms, was put on a hotel and Romani-themed restaurant that serves dinners around an outdoor fire on tables nestled in wagon-shaped booths (Figure 2.2). Dignitaries, researchers, and curious visitors are treated to evening entertainment with Romani music and dance, as well as traditional foods like *goulash* or *bogrash*, meat stew cooked in cauldrons in a tourist-friendly setting. A high metal fence walls off neighboring impoverished Romani neighborhoods, reinforcing a message that tourists, development aid workers, and visiting dignitaries and scholars are "protected" from the very people whom they have come to see, research, and "help."

Music brings the promise of "niche tourism," or tourism defined by a specific focus. Niche tourism beholds the illusion of unparalleled hands-on experience, satisfying entertainment, and unmatched emotional connection. A steady increase in accessibility of Romani music through the Internet, as well as through publications of travelogues by musicians and journalists and ethnographic writings by scholars, brings curious non-Roms into Romani settlements. Moreover, Romani organizations that heavily promote certain internationally

INTERVENTIONS   51

Figure 2.2 Advertisement for the Romani Yag Romani Hotel-Restaurant Complex. Uzhhorod, Ukraine, 2008.
Photo by author.

funded cultural, educational, and political projects in Romani settlements have brought Romani imagery into public discourse in the West, setting up a situation of general interest and curiosity among certain segments of the non-Romani public. In particular, development projects, as they relate to Roms, have played a significant role in positioning tourism as a capitalist resource for Roms within settlements that in no small part focus on musical entertainment.

There are many sides to the current trend. Musical tourism offers a much-needed source of income for the settlements, albeit benefiting only a select few. Visits to impoverished settlements, however, tend to evoke several controversial ideas as relating to "slum tourism" (Frenzel et al. 2012), "poverty tourism" (Frenzel 2016), "ghetto tourism" (Miller et al. 2010), "ethical tourism" (Weeden 2014), and "voluntourism" (Young 2019).[18] While it is understood that not all Roms are poor, it is the combination of dire poverty and music that give Romani settlements that extra marketing punch. Furthermore, it is increasingly positioned as the best viable option to bring much-needed cash flow into the settlements.

In eastern Slovakia, where the poverty situation in Romani settlements is on par with or worse than in the Ukraine, a mayor has recently proposed using government funds to organize poverty tourism by foreigners into Romani settlements.[19] Such tourism comes perilously close to mirroring some development aid activities, in which donors enter Romani settlements to "observe" the poverty and to assess people dying from malnutrition, lack of medical aid, and lack of essential life resources, but create instances of "poverty museums" through such consistent interactions. Such projects seek to capitalize on the poverty and popularize the allure of squalor that they attempt to obliterate.

The rise of Romani and musical niche tourism has, regrettably, been overlooked thus far in scholarly analysis *of* tourism. However, it is ripe for ethnomusicological analysis because it raises essential questions regarding agency, identity, and representative power that pose the frameworks for ethnomusicological research of Romani music.[20] Tourism forces us to take the economics of identity more seriously and place money more at the center of our analysis. Ros Derrett argues that "special interest tourists demonstrate a desire for authenticity and real experiences that offer them active identification with host communities in a non-exploitative manner" (Derrett et al. 2001, 3). Niches like music produce institutional interest activities and foster individual desires to experience music beyond the mass-marketed media product. They believe in the emotive power of music to foster personal and emotional experiences that allow them to create personal fascinations with what they have imagined by listening to the music independently. The fascination with a place as the source of the musical product, even if it comes via a packaged experience, fosters consumption rituals that demand face-to-face onsite interaction.

When tourism is instituted in a new location, it introduces a new framework of experiences that relies on specific representational strategies to draw people to travel to that particular destination. When a new location is identified, usually one person "discovers" it and lays the groundwork for institutionalizing a framed experience for that place (Kirschenblatt-Gimblett 1998). To become successful as a travel destination, it must hold promise to offer things that are not available elsewhere. The place itself becomes an object, impregnated with a particular belief and promise of activities and experiences.

Once a site becomes a tourism destination, an institutionalizing process takes place, addressing the physical needs of visitors, including food and lodging. Those within the place provide that which the visitors seek, and the process of consumption becomes cyclical. If the tourists want certain types of souvenirs (whether they are an actuality in that locale or not), the hosts offer them because it is in their interest to make money by selling their wares. A similar process happens regarding music. If a group of people arrives at a specific place, expecting a particular experience, inadvertent efforts are made to accommodate the visitors. The primary motivating factor for this type of accommodation is money.

Certain trappings have become evident in Romani villages and settlements as the increase in Romani world music consumption leads to the development of Romani musical tourism. Development grants from the European Union are sponsoring an increasing number of endeavors. Visitors are invited for the day to a select village to experience a ritual or celebration and everyday village life. The living museum model has become a valuable source of income for Romani communities, but at what cost? Musical tourism stresses its ability to offer a visitor interested in Romani culture something genuine and authentic. The marketing narrative also builds on the foreign tourist's implied wanderlust as an embodied desire for the Romani indulgence in a natural bohemian lifestyle. In this way, movement and the trope of nomadism are used to draw parallels between Roms and tourists, normalizing the behavior of tourists as natural concerning their willingness to experience hands-on events among Romani communities. In turn, Roms are exploited even more, their search-for-work migration being turned into a cultural product that can be consumed at leisure and will be—by those who can afford it.

3

Accountability

Ethnomusicologists face the complexity of representing, through ethnographic texts, people who are capable and want to represent themselves. This is evident in contexts in which interlocutors work through collective means to gain group recognition on either a local or transnational scale and believe that the ethnographer's direct or indirect involvement will help them attain their goals. Representatives from social movements express their stake in the outcome of the resulting research when they create images and publish information that directly influences the research question at hand. They aim to control the discourse regarding sensitive materials to which, in many cases, the researcher is also privy. Interlocutors anticipate that the researcher's findings will be positive and that the researcher will utilize his or her ethnographic writing as an advertisement for the interlocutors' cause. They expect the researcher to work toward the interlocutors' goals and not to diverge into other agendas.

There has been little room for such reflexivity in ethnomusicological research conducted by scholars in the former Soviet Union, where traditional music has historically been censored and controlled by the government for political means. Musical traditions once tied to a place were diffused through repertoires that were reformatted, mass-distributed, and appropriated for staged performances that broke rather than reinforced relationships to local identities. To counter such diffusions, ethnomusicologists in Ukraine today, working to revive a discipline forbidden under the Soviets in 1946, attempt to map out musical elements as they appear across the territories of Ukraine. Scholars analyze musical form, melodic structures, rhythmic patterns, and various elements to decipher patterns of diffusion to ascertain the expansive regions within which musical elements inform each other. Such distributions are mapped against the present borders of post-Soviet Ukraine. This model of ethnomusicological research reinforces the priorities of the society where ethnomusicologists (representing the ethnic majority) live and teach.

This chapter brings into dialogue divergent scholarly methodologies that frame minority-based research practices rooted in different ideologies

ReSounding Poverty. Adriana N. Helbig, Oxford University Press. © Oxford University Press 2023.
DOI: 10.1093/oso/9780197631768.003.0004

56 RESOUNDING POVERTY

while offering a space for synthesis, reflection, and understanding. It draws on experiences in fieldwork, teaching, and performance to analyze how musical performance allows applied research to be reframed and reinterpreted in disparate contexts. It highlights the complexities that frame the pendulum between ideas and action as regards music and human rights. Most important, it analyzes the role that neoliberal market processes play in shaping the musical traditions that ethnomusicologists research. The post-Soviet development of a multiparty political system, the rise of ethnic consciousness, and the overarching influence of Western-funded NGOs beg for a critically nuanced analysis that critiques such research realities. In an attempt to unpack such complexities, this chapter specifically critiques applied methodologies in development contexts. It offers a broader picture regarding the role of US-based universities within NGO networks steeped in academic rhetoric and relationships. Drawing on music-focused study-abroad programs, university music performance ensembles, and museum exhibits, this chapter analyzes the complex consequences of applied work. It also offers long-term perspectives on culture-based NGO initiatives, particularly as regards tourism in impoverished contexts. Analyzing the marketing of musical culture deemed "Romani" (or "Gypsy") NGOs, this chapter offers insights into the ethics and aesthetics of sounds, movements, and images that are produced by an emerging NGO-affiliated Romani middle class on behalf of all Roms. In other words, this chapter takes as its points of departure the fissures where minority group advocacy and individual aspiration collide.

Throughout this chapter, I give space to how I have involved myself and my students in Romani music-focused initiatives. Between 2008 and 2018, I organized and led a university-based ensemble that performed Romani music in public and academic venues and played an integral role in disseminating Romani music in local and global contexts. I organized a study-abroad program through the University of Pittsburgh in collaboration with my colleague Zuzana Jurková at Charles University in Prague, focusing on Romani music, culture, and human rights. The month-long summer program brought American and Czech students together on a tour of Romani-themed experiences in the Czech Republic, Poland, and Slovakia (2012), and in the Czech Republic and Hungary (2014). The study-abroad experience revealed that Romani NGOs play an integral part in educational initiatives, including but not limited to study-abroad programs. Working in an educational capacity with NGOs that use culture to engage with Romani rights has reinforced an integral argument that guides my teaching and research: that people working in the field of music have specific responsibilities to undo damaging stereotypes that have been imposed upon Roms through cultural policies that reinforce images of Roms as (merely) dancers and musicians. The all-too-common development model of using the arts to draw attention to political agendas pervades all aspects of Romani rights discourse.[1] However, the use of Romani music within such initiatives folds onto itself in former Soviet contexts where the stereotype of Roms as dancers and musicians pervades all aspects of Romani-related discourse in politics, economics, employment, and education.

What's at Stake

Recent scholarship conducted by US-based scholars reveals an increasing interaction among ethnomusicologists and international NGOs. NGOs are willing partners in educational endeavors, welcoming researchers and students to engage with and frequently volunteer with ongoing projects. NGOs serve as a point of destination for fieldworkers, students, and activists and function as a center through which information is disseminated. A primary destination for scholars in the field, NGOs are a vortex around which ethnographic information spins. Ethnographers reinforce the legitimacies of such organizations through engagements with them in the field.[2] On the one hand, such organizations are often the primary source of much-needed information and networks. On the other hand, such organizations have their own agendas of power. In our interactions with NGOs, applied ethnomusicologists align with certain groups over others, many times without our awareness or knowledge.

Literature in anthropology and, increasingly in ethnomusicology, documents the ever-increasing NGO sponsorship of music, dance, theater, and the arts to draw attention to broader underrepresentation and inequality issues. As Erica Haskell explains in her work on NGO music sponsorship in Bosnia and Herzegovina following the Balkan Wars, the arts are funded within parameters set by the interests of international aid, foreign embassies, and Western-funded NGOs (Haskell et al. 2008; Haskell 2015, 2017). The theme of NGO-sponsored art-making as soft power is echoed by Chérie Rivers Ndaliko, who documents how art has been mobilized by external humanitarian and charitable organizations in the war-torn Democratic Republic of the Congo. Ndaliko positions this uneasy relationship of using art to portray experience against a backdrop of war as a new form of imperial domination (Ndaliko 2016).[3] In turn, Jim Sykes de-emphasizes Western colonial narratives in his research among NGOs in postwar Sri Lanka. Analyzing how music has been used as a form of reconciliation, he shows how the emphasis on shared musical histories among populations pitted against each other through narratives of difference along ethnic lines has helped promote healing (Sykes 2018). Such ethnographies contribute to the growing literature on development in zones of conflict and war and identify the complex frameworks within which music and the arts are used as instruments of peace. They beg us to ask the following questions: Are the arts merely a form of international soft power? What agency do local musicians have in NGO networks that utilize the arts as vehicles of propaganda and reconciliation in contexts of violence and political unrest? How do musical networks set into play by NGOs interpolate with non-NGO musical activities? How do ethnographers, engaged in research projects that relate to NGO activities, set parameters for involvement?

While it may not be possible to answer these questions in full, we can begin by acknowledging that applied ethnomusicologists who work in development contexts, work with musicians who use their artistic performances to draw attention to various sociocultural, economic, and political issues (Harrison 2013; Pettan and Titon 2015). Furthermore, applied ethnomusicologists work with organizations that support and promote music and the arts as a platform for rights advocacy.[4] Applied ethnomusicologists often choose topics of study in accordance to their beliefs. We commit our professional lives to specific causes because they have meaning for us. The issues we engage with gain further meaning for us because of our involvement.[5] Through our investment of time, skill, and resources, we influence the outcomes. However, few among us acknowledge the choices we make in consciously shaping the movements we study.[6]

The changing world demands a theoretical shift regarding the scholar's positioning in the field. Contemporary modes of engagement now position both the ethnographer and the interlocutor as coauthors and co-participants of a globally mediated discourse regarding cultural politics and the political uses of culture. One may argue that the ethnographer's role is to recognize and deconstruct this globally mediated discourse in collaboration with our interlocutors. In supporting the causes of our interlocutors, we are encouraged to use the power of the institutions we affiliate with to move forward agendas of equality and rights. Yet, in doing so, we put ourselves in danger of losing our objective stance, of throwing weight behind one side of the story over another.

Such questions are crucial when considering Romani studies where scholars take responsibility for helping disseminate information that fills the tremendous gap left in global narratives that have systemically silenced Romani experiences. The narratives in this chapter echo the calls from Carol Silverman for a "reflexive turn" in Romani Studies (Silverman 2018). Silverman, well known for her research on Balkan Romani music, wears numerous hats as a scholar, activist, and performer. She has also been instrumental in facilitating networks for people worldwide to travel, meet each other, share ideas, and make and disseminate music together. Silverman points our attention to recent questions in Romani studies (and ethnomusicology) that ask, ultimately, "who generates knowledge and for what purpose?"

On Rights and Freedoms

Academic freedom, a central value in Western higher education, allows individuals to pursue knowledge free from censorship and constraint. Academic freedom presupposes that the *truth* being sought corresponds to ideas agreed upon through a peer-review process. The research model is based on a search for a good that will work for the betterment of the human condition. Nevertheless, our classroom discussions function as partial truths, what Michael Beckerman refers to as "stories," the pieces of information that we hear and learn in different places and times that we piece together as we delve into learning topics (Beckerman 2015, 293). Such stories constitute a central part of ethnographic research, mainly where we learn about musical idioms in contexts where practitioner voices are not present. When we take on the monumental task of engaging in musical traditions in educational settings, we agree to uphold the human rights of the people whose music we learn. To teach, then, is to learn responsibly and to take accountability for the information we share.[7]

Such principles have guided my work at the University of Pittsburgh. However, the Western Pennsylvanian context in which I have worked to align my applied research according to the cultural and human rights values I believe in, has proven itself quite difficult. In a city of immigrants whose dominant labor force hailed from Eastern Europe at the turn of the last century,

Roms have continuously been written out of the city's historical narratives (Piskor 2012; Spur 1959). Pittsburgh, the Steel City, drew large numbers of poor rural populations from the crumbling Austro-Hungarian Empire at the turn of the twentieth century from the very Carpathian Mountain region where I conducted my research. Lured by promises of financial gains within the coal and steel industries, these laborers were met with the stark realities of harsh working conditions, brutally long hours, mental and physical hardships in an industrially polluted region, and exploitative labor measures among robber barons like Andrew Carnegie that led to the Homestead Strike of 1892.[8] The hardships endured comprise a large part of the city lore, and locals are quick to share stories of the city's hard-work ethic and labor pride.

With the collapse of the steel industry in the 1980s and a mass exodus of unemployed workers, the city restructured itself as a medical and technology giant in the 2000s, using culture to draw educated populations to a relatively abandoned city. Alongside opera and classical music came the marketing of the city's ethnic roots, positioning Pittsburgh as a melting pot for the so-called American Dream. In areas like the South Side, where steelworkers once lived in the shocking proximity to the very steel mills that once polluted the Monongahela River and environs, certain buildings (not yet sold to investors) still reflect the history of Polish, Serbian, Croatian, Bulgarian, Macedonian, Hungarian, Slovak, Ruthenian, and Ukrainian communities. The city still boasts many Slavic folk music and dance ensembles, Slavic ethnic-themed food festivals, and Slavic heritage events.

The most iconic of the city's Slavic institutions has been the Tamburitzans, a folk dance group founded in 1937 and affiliated with Duquesne University for many decades. The Tamburitzans comprised students from Eastern Europe and the United States who performed Slavic music and dance choreographies on extensive tours through US cities in exchange for scholarships to the university.[9] Drawing their name from the *tamburitsa*, a diminutive of *tambura*, a family of string instruments from the Balkans and Near East akin to the mandolin, the "Tammies" have recorded numerous albums and have performed at a variety of folk-oriented festivals, including those sponsored by the Nationality Rooms, thirty-one classrooms inside the University of Pittsburgh's iconic Cathedral of Learning funded by and depicting the ethnic communities that constituted Pittsburgh's labor force (Kolar 1986; MacMillen 2019; March 2013).[10] That two of the city's universities would pay homage to Slavic narratives through essentialized portrayals of bounded cultures reflects how discourses of ethnicity have circulated in the city.

When laborers arrived in Pittsburgh, they organized around ethnically divided religious institutions. Many ethnic Slavic churches with golden domes still punctuate the once smoggy city's landscape. Laborers lived in tight family units, contributing to areas of the city like "Polish Hill" being populated by people who identified with the area's dominant ethnicity. Such groupings introduced a Slavic-oriented de facto nationalism into an American landscape further framed by US race relations. Romani immigrant laborers found themselves doubly marginalized—as ethnic (non-Slavic) Others and as dark-skinned racial Others. Hailing from the same regions as other Slavic immigrants, they were not welcome in the milieu of the American melting pot by fellow immigrants and were pushed to the margins in Pittsburgh's environs, settling in the areas of Braddock and Homestead further up the Monongahela River.

Pittsburgh Roms

I was unaware of Pittsburgh's Romani history until I began to perform Romani and Balkan music repertoires with friends and students around town. At one of the many Slavic-themed events, I met Romani musicians with Pittsburgh roots who shared the stories of Romani immigration to the region. I spent hundreds of hours poring through archival information relating to Roms in Pittsburgh, in part because the Romani repertoires I heard in Pittsburgh were similar to those I had heard in my travels throughout the Carpathian Basin (Ukraine, Poland, Hungary, and Slovakia). Having researched the regions from where Romani laborers immigrated to Pittsburgh, I found a particular similarity between the funeral processions for musicians described in the *Pittsburgh Courier* (1940)[11] and those that I had witnessed in Uzhhorod, Transcarpathia, more than a half-century later.[12]

Though the music performed in Pittsburgh was not described in the (many) newspaper articles that featured Romani funerals, it was interesting to note that the format of processing through the streets with instruments had been retained in the diaspora. In Transcarpathia, the highly ritualized traditional funeral processions for male Romani musicians serve as a way through which Roms lay claim to public space. Streets must be blocked off to allow for the funeral procession to pass through the town center to the cemetery. The funeral procession is led by a young man carrying a cross, followed by musicians playing violins. The coffin is carried as far as three miles from

62 RESOUNDING POVERTY

the home of the deceased to the cemetery and is followed by as many as 200 Roms in procession (the *Pittsburgh Courier* mentions a procession of sixty men with violins during a funeral procession in 1940).

In Uzhhorod, if the deceased male musician does not live in the Romani settlement or lives further from the cemetery than is possible to carry him, the body is transported by car to the town center, and the deceased is then carried in procession the rest of the way. One of the most striking characteristics of the procession is that one particular melody is played throughout. The melody is not a traditional Romani song; rather, Romani violinists in Uzhhorod play a melody they call the "Hungarian March" and attribute to the Hungarian composer Franz Liszt (1811–1886). This melody is very important in providing an aural space for the Roms procession. The style of playing is slow and somber and the effect is one of weeping violins. The melody is in minor mode and is repeated until the procession reaches the cemetery. According to some musicians, the melody attributed to Liszt has been the only one played in the procession for decades. This melody is recognized by non-Romani passersby in Uzhhorod, who associate the sound of these weeping violins solely with this Romani event. It is not known why the melody was chosen a long time ago, but we can surmise that it's name "Hungarian March" has much to do with Uzhhorod's Hungarian past.

The "Hungarian March" invokes the long history of Romani restaurant musicians in pre–World War I Hungarian Uzhhorod and redefines a non-Romani melody by a Western composer as "local" and as representative of the Romani community in Uzhhorod. Agency belongs to those who process through non-Romani spaces. Through music, Roms, many of whom are of Hungarian Romani descent, recall the prestige of Romani musicians in times past and reaffirm their historical relationship to Uzhhorod and to the surrounding geographical and cultural locale.

The Romani funeral procession serves as a poignant example of how Roms in Uzhhorod ground their lived experience in the physical world. Movement signifies a crucial aspect of this grounding. Roms do not bury their dead near the Romani settlement, but rather walk through town to the cemetery in Uzhhorod proper. Non-Roms must wait until the procession passes before continuing with their daily business. However, as one Romani man described it, "it is only in death that non-Roms treat us with respect."[13] The procession demands respect from onlookers for the Romani deceased and concurrently affirms the strength of the Romani community that participates in this ritual of collective mourning. The accompanying music roots the procession in the consciousness of those who see and hear it. A group of male musicians accompanies the deceased, followed by community elders and Romani women. No processions are held for female vocalists and instrumentalists (of which there are few). Passersby can hear the music well before the procession approaches because the sound is carried downstream by the Uzh River from the Romani settlement situated on the outskirts of Uzhhorod. By the time the procession reaches the footbridge to cross into Uzhhorod proper, news of the funeral has spread throughout the central *bazaar*, marketplace. Townspeople line the streets and wait with curiosity and in deferential respect for the procession to pass.

In Uzhhorod, much like Pittsburgh, the funeral procession and the music challenge the social and cultural canons that associate Roms with an "out-of-sight, out-of-mind" mentality among non-Roms. They expand discursive space by inscribing Romani presence into a usually non-Romani domain. The funeral processions for male Romani musicians reveal a powerful way in which Roms achieve an aural and visual stake in predominantly non-Romani spaces. The funeral memorializes ancestors and reinforces a sense of connection to land, history, community, and the attendant sense of belonging that those connections lend.

New World, Old Story

Non-Romani Slavic laborers brought anti-Romani discrimination to the New World, robbing Roms of the opportunity to live free of discrimination in the United States. They circulated stereotypes of Roms as thieves and ineffective laborers, making it difficult for Roms to be hired in the steel mills. At the same time, they also promoted the stereotype of Roms as naturally gifted musicians, allowing Roms to gain employment as restaurant entertainers for Pittsburgh's elites. During the 1930s, at the height of the Depression, when the US government was creating opportunities for out-of-work Americans, including musicians, the Braddock Works Progress Administration (WPA) orchestra employed thirty-two Roms. Steve Piskor notes that the orchestra's success was cut short when new regulations were passed that required all musicians of the orchestra to read music. Since most Romani musicians play by rote and learn by ear, the majority were cut from the WPA project (Piskor 2012, 55).

64   RESOUNDING POVERTY

Such narratives of exclusion formed the backdrop for the position into which I was hired at the University of Pittsburgh. Having researched in the same region of Eastern Europe from where the majority of immigrants hailed, I was faced with everyday challenges of teaching courses and leading a world music ensemble that offered jarringly different information that my students (and their parents, priests, and community leaders) were familiar with or wished to hear. The majority of Pittsburgh immigrants had arrived before World War I. The borders, languages, attitudes toward religion, and all that constituted the very ethnically based identities the immigrants had built, were rooted in diaspora histories of more than 100 years ago. I had to familiarize myself with nineteenth-century immigrant narratives and study maps of the Habsburg Empire like the one printed at the beginning of this book. Stories of World War II, the Holocaust, communism, the fall of communism, the Balkan wars, postsocialist corruption, and post-Soviet revolution pushed back against the stuck-in-time imaginings of Eastern Europe that heritage students brought with them into my classroom. At the same time, as a heritage professor myself, I used my teaching to help better understand my family narratives and the histories as they were taught to me by Ukrainian-identifying political émigrés and cultural elites who had fled Soviet and Nazi persecutions during World War II. These experiences reinforced my interest in *how* such narratives are constructed.

Musical performances offered contexts for negotiating such complexities. The Carpathian Ensemble that I established and directed between 2008 and 2018 offered ways through which students and I could explore the networks we lived in. With a mix of electric guitars and traditional instruments ranging from the *cimbalom*, hammered dulcimer, to the *doumbek*, goblet drum, we performed a popular repertoire of Romani music and traditional folk tunes from the Carpathian region and the Balkans (Figure 3.1).

The improvisatory and fusion approach of the Carpathian Ensemble differed in ideology and style from the Tamburitzans, whose performance style is akin to the stylized folk traditions popularized in the 1930s by the Moiseyev Dance Company in Moscow (Shay 2006). The Tamburitzans retain a to-date popular aesthetic within diaspora communities comprising colorful costumes, impressive footwork, and impeccably coordinated choreographies. Such aesthetics, popularized in Moscow in the 1930s, have remained popular through state-sponsored ensembles. Once a staple in socialist nation-building endeavors, they retain their popularity in diaspora communities in the United States. These choreographies highlight aesthetic

Figure 3.1 Carpathian Ensemble Tenth Anniversary Concert, University of Pittsburgh, 2018. © University of Pittsburgh.

elements with which Roms synchronously engage and against which they fight in complex ways.

In the end, both university ensembles were caught in a complex narrative of Romani musical representation.[14] While Duquesne University's Tamburitzans engaged with a staged folklore representation of Romani identity as popularized by socialist governments, the University of Pittsburgh's Carpathian Ensemble engaged with the student-driven "band of Gypsies" narrative that had become popular on college campuses through the aesthetics introduced by performance groups engaging with "Gypsy" music.[15]

Ethnographic Learning and Study Abroad

To push back against the imagined, I introduced "Romani (Gypsy) Music" in 2011, a course I now teach at the University of Pittsburgh every other year. Students from the Carpathian Ensemble and others taking the course for general education requirements developed individual research projects throughout the semester. One group formed the Pittsburgh Romani-Gypsy

Coalition, an activist group that draws attention to minority rights on campus. Members of the Coalition help me organize Romani-themed events on campus. In 2012, I co-organized with Zuzana Jurková, an ethnomusicologist from Charles University in Prague, a study-abroad program in Central and Eastern Europe titled "Romani Music, Culture, and Human Rights." The study-abroad program included students from the University of Pittsburgh and Charles University. In May and June 2014, students traveled to the Czech Republic and Hungary, visiting rural and urban Romani musicians and activists. Jurková's long-term involvement with the Khamoro Music Festival and her connections with the Slovo 21 NGO that organizes the festival allowed our students to learn about the inner workings of a week-long Romani music festival that features Romani musicians from different countries who perform various traditional and popular Romani music genres for Romani and non-Romani audiences on stages throughout Prague every May.[16] The study-abroad course, featured in the official booklet for the Prague's annual Khamoro Music Festival, made me recognize the role of the US educational institution as an economic and political force.

The study-abroad program, connecting two universities, facilitated exchanges among numerous musicians across many borders. Students were able to work with Gusztáv Varga, of Kalyi Yag (Black Fire) fame. Founded in 1978, Kalyi Yag helped popularize the musical folk traditions of the Vlax in Hungary, a vocal group that incorporated everyday utensils like a water jug and spoons alongside guitar accompaniments that revived the music of nomadic Roms. Kalyi Yag had its roots in the Tánchaz (dance-house) movement that popularized amateur Hungarian folk dancing in the 1970s. Kalyi Yag's popularization of traditional Romani music amidst this revival earned them the reputation as one of Hungary's most famous performing Romani groups.[17] Today, Varga runs the Kalyi Yag school, envisioned originally as a music and dance school for young Roms. It now serves as a training ground for Romani youths who wish to enter the service industry in Budapest hotels and restaurants. Though the tradition of Romani restaurant musicians in Budapest remains strong, young Roms are building on musical networks to gain social mobility. Such examples point to activist-scholarship as a series of concentric circles that build upon and loop through personal connections, institutional networks, and the ubiquitous nature of music.

Among the study-abroad experiences with undergraduates, none was more eye-opening than a visit to a Romani kindergarten in Lunik IX, an impoverished Romani housing complex outside of Košice, Slovakia, in June

2012. The kindergarten is used to welcoming international visitors due to its award-winning emphasis on art (our visit was preceded by a visit from Amnesty International the week before). We had arrived at mid-morning to be with the children before they had their lunch and took naps. Our bus dropped us off where the Košice city bus stops to bring workers home to Lunik IX. We chose to take only three cameras and decided ahead of time who would be in charge of photography and who in charge of video recording.

We walked up a hill past the socialist-era housing that has become the iconic image of Lunik IX on the Internet. These complexes were built in the 1970s with plumbing and electricity for Roma who were pushed out of housing in other parts of Košice. Since the 1970s, the buildings have fallen into disrepair. Two buildings have been condemned, and a third will be pulled down soon. Those who were once living in the buildings that were torn down have been forced to find shelter elsewhere, whether with family in other communities, or abroad. Some say that all the buildings in Lunik IX will be torn down eventually, and it will cease to exist as a community. Only those who pay their rent regularly are offered housing in other parts of the city. The 5,000–7,000 Roms who live in Lunik IX reside in terrible conditions, often without electricity and water because they cannot afford the utilities. There is a city official who stays at Lunik IX during the day to turn on utilities for those who pay, if only for one day at a time. There is no hot water in the apartments, and cold water is available for those who pay, but for only two hours every day.

The kindergarten entrance that led onto a grassy field next to the apartment buildings was protected by a cage-like structure with bars through which we entered (Figure 3.2). The city official had opened the outside door of the cage and had unlocked the kindergarten door from the outside. A woman met us at the door and proceeded to unlock a third door that led us into the kindergarten, where we were met by smiling children. The kindergarten is quite an impressive complex, with three floors and numerous hallways and doors, each unlocked as we passed through. The windows were covered with grates and mesh, and a long hallway that at one time had windows was protected by steel paneling donated by Pittsburgh-based US Steel (!), which has a plant in Košice. Košice, a center of steel production, has strong connections with Pittsburgh, the Steel City, for this very reason. The panels shut out all light, but the hallway was decorated with the students' most beautiful and creative artwork. The hallway's artwork was divided into four seasons featuring

Figure 3.2 Romani children who cannot afford to attend the kindergarten in Lunik IX, an urban Romani community near Košice, Slovakia, peer through the bars that "protect" the entrance to the school. Photo by author.

pieces in a variety of media. When we asked what we could bring to the kindergarten as a token of our visit, they asked for art supplies. We brought markers, colored pencils, crayons, and various other drawing materials that we had purchased in Krakow in preparation for the visit. The children sang for us, and in turn, we brought our instruments to play and sing for them.

As we walked through the numerous classrooms, it was clear that the kindergarten teachers care very deeply for the children and work very hard to procure materials for the school. Though the state funds the school, there is an additional tuition of ten euros a month to attend to help pay for supplies. The students receive breakfast and lunch and pay 0.23 cents (euro) for a light snack and dinner per day. This amount is, however, too expensive for some families. Those who cannot afford to send their children to the kindergarten send them to other schools, while other parents, mothers, in particular, pay for tuition through a work-exchange program with the school, helping with tasks such as maintenance, cleaning, and other jobs. The school employs two Romani cooks and had a Romani teacher, but the pay is only 450 euros a month after one has worked there for twenty-five years. Not many can afford to work there at entry-level pay if they can find a better-paying job elsewhere.

Most teachers, including the principal, are non-Romani women who choose to work there because they love the work and the children. They write grants to IBM to get computers into the classroom and other companies and organizations to help cover costs.

The students were very familiar with computers, and in one of the older classrooms, a six-year-old boy ran to the computer to start a karaoke MP3 of a song that the students danced and sang for us. The songs we heard were in Romani and Slovak, with teachers creating new songs by adding Romani words to Slovak folk melodies. Language is a critical issue in the school because some parents feel strongly that the school should only teach Slovak so that students who only speak Romani at home can better prepare to enter the Slovak-language grammar school down the hill from the settlement.

Though we were at the settlement in the middle of the day, many children were playing outside and were not in school. These were the children who could not afford tuition. My students had brought a soccer ball and we began a game. Slowly, more people began to come toward the grassy field, primarily young people who spoke to us out of curiosity. Little boys posed in front of cameras with hip-hop gestures and movements. Girls invited us to play jump rope with an improvised toy made out of tied-together pantyhose. Some older boys spoke English, and young mothers waiting to pick up their children from the kindergarten talked to us about the school (Figure 3.3).

We played and talked with the people for an hour, and then the police began to drive by. Any large gathering of Roms often evokes suspicion, and we realized we would have to disperse so as not to create any trouble for the community. The presence of the police seemed very familiar to the children, who played a game called *Polizai*, policeman. The *polizai* also figured prominently in some of the students' artwork. We were shuffled back through the steel cage, back through the labyrinth of doors and escorted by the teachers through the kindergarten classrooms, and let out the back entrance.

Police presence introduced a stark reality and a realness for the students on the study-abroad program. It motivated many to act upon their return home where, in the context of various privileges, many had never experienced forceful and potentially violent run-ins with law enforcement officials. Students became politically active, volunteering in various human rights organizations and speaking about their experiences witnessing in Lunik IX, Slovakia, and in the Auschwitz concentration camp in Poland where 21,000 Roms perished among 1.1 million victims that included 1 million Jews, 70,000–75,000 ethnic Poles, 15,000 Soviet prisoners of war, and

70   RESOUNDING POVERTY

Figure 3.3 Young girls play with a "jump rope" made out of pantyhose tied together outside one of the condemned housing projects in Lunik IX, an urban Romani community near Košice, Slovakia, June 2012. Photo by author.

10,000–15,000 others.[18] Though few students had personal connections to this history and region, the rhetoric of "being there," with reference to their physical senses, of seeing, hearing, touching, and feeling, struck home the hardest, as eclipsed by Evan Zajdel's artwork in the Introduction. It took many students months to recover and to process their feelings and many experienced serious emotional traumas.[19] However, guiding them through their process reinforced the importance of university experiences in broader networks of exchange.

As I have argued throughout this chapter, universities play a central role in human rights discourse on many levels. Offering opportunities for ethnographic learning, including but not limited to study-abroad programs, universities foster critical exchanges of ideas and strengthen networks. They also play an essential role in development infrastructure by engaging with NGOs and the agendas they propose. While our study-abroad program used existing networks to facilitate exchange, we shared the knowledge we learned upon our return to the university via conference papers and published articles that were, in turn, shared with Romani NGOs. This last point circles back to the examples of applied ethnomusicology with which I began this chapter, through which I highlighted the emphasis on relevance and positive impact that frame the discourse on applied research.

Through engagements with NGOs, universities engage with financial networks and local projects that promise to change the realities of constituents. Such networks are much broader than the nongovernment sector and must be viewed in terms of global philanthropic exchanges that move people, services, and goods into spaces deemed to be in need. They also reconstitute and refurbish physical spaces that become community sites and repositories of information and knowledge that seek to benefit those who seek assistance. The realities, however, do not always match the proposed outcomes in grant proposals. Such stories punctuate the remainder of this book. They aim less to critique the networks in place in this region and serve more to offer a broader understanding regarding the reasons for the failings of the best intentions.

4

Mobilities

Layered modernities frame Transcarpathia's disparate senses of being. The region boasts no skyscrapers, but villages, still accessed via bumpy dirt roads, now offer free WiFi, accessible from smartphones. Even five years ago, one would have been hard-pressed to find such technology here. Today, luxury cars belonging to *oligarchs*, corrupt businessmen, speed past the horse-pulled buggies of Romani metal collectors along the M06 highway connecting Kyiv to Chop, the border crossing into Hungary, which joined the European Union in 2004. Once a patched network of potholes, the highway was reconstructed for the 2012 European Soccer Championships with funds from the European Bank for Reconstruction and Development. During Soviet times, Transcarpathia was closed off to foreign tourists because it housed a build-up of Soviet armed forces that were moved there to secure the borders at the height of the Cold War. It was from Transcarpathia that the Soviet Union staged invasions of Hungary (1956) and Czechoslovakia (1968). Today, it is a modern thoroughfare for trucks with European license plates that transport goods from the European Union across Ukraine to Russia.

Transcarpathia's linguistic mix of Russian, Hungarian, Romani, Slovak, Romanian, Ukrainian, Ruthenian, and German languages create a dialect the Transcarpathians call their own (Dickinson 1999). Expressions like *Faino!*, from the English word *fine*, reflect the region's historical connections to the coal mines of Pennsylvania that welcomed workers before the collapse of Austro-Hungarian rule in 1918. The churches built by these workers are an integral part of the landscape of central and western Pennsylvania towns. So many had moved to Pittsburgh to work in the steel mills that the city had an Austrian consulate. Moreover, it was in Pittsburgh that Tomáš Masaryk, the first president of Czechoslovakia, of which Transcarpathia was a part during the Interwar Period, signed the 1918 Pittsburgh Agreement between Czech and Slovak expatriates to establish a sovereign state.

ReSounding Poverty. Adriana N. Helbig, Oxford University Press. © Oxford University Press 2023.
DOI: 10.1093/oso/9780197631768.003.0005

Transcarpathia, a Brief History

Transcarpathia, belonging to the Kingdom of Hungary before World War I, was incorporated as an autonomous region into the First and Second Czechoslovak Republics between the wars. Annexed by the Kingdom of Hungary again during World War II, it became part of the Soviet Union in 1946. Transcarpathia's separatist ideologies hold strong in post-Soviet Ukraine. In the nationwide referendum of December 1, 1991, the vast majority of the electorate voted for the "Independence of Ukraine" (90.13%), and annexation of Transcarpathia to Ukraine with the status of a "Special Self-Governing Territory" (78%). Though autonomy was not granted, Kyiv's reach beyond the Carpathians has continued to be weak. In 2018, it came to light that the Hungarian consulate had been issuing Hungarian passports to local citizens in Transcarpathia, advising them not to reveal to Ukrainian authorities that they were receiving Hungarian citizenship. Historical claims to this region are strong, and people have persistent feelings regarding with whom they align. Such allegiances are reflected in no small part in the languages people speak, in the religions they practice, and in the family stories they tell.

Linguist Michael Beníšek identifies Romani dialects in Transcarpathia as "Uzh Romani," emphasizing the geographical character of the dialect as relating to Uzh County (in the official Hungarian nomenclature *Ung vármegye*), whose territory is now divided between Slovakia and Ukraine. Beníšek divides the Slovak dialect of Uzh Romani as "Western Uzh Romani" and the heterogeneous Romani dialect spoken on the western part of Transcarpathia Ukraine as "Eastern Uzh Romani." He notes that the entire Uzh Romani dialect cluster is part of a broader continuum of Romani dialects that are classified as Central Romani. The dialect spoken in this region is often referred to interchangeably as Transcarpathian dialect of North Central Romani (Beníšek 2017, 1–4; Matras 2002, 9).

Romani communities throughout Transcarpathia speak a variety of dialects that vary according to geographical location. In urban contexts like Uzhhorod, the specific dialect varies based on family clusters and historical lineage determining contemporary settlement patterns. Due to the variety of dialects in the region, I relied on the help of local Romani speakers in settings where Romani was spoken. However, the majority of my fieldwork was conducted in Russian and local dialects of Ukrainian/Rusyn. As Beníšek notes, only a small number of Transcarpathian Roms speak any Romani dialect. According to the 2001 census, only 20.5 percent of local Roms list Romani as their mother tongue, compared to 44.69 percent in the whole

MOBILITIES 75

of Ukraine. Most Roms in Transcarpathia, especially those living in the southern and southwestern lowland adjacent to the border with Hungary, speak Hungarian as their first language. Roms living in northern and northwestern valleys of the Carpathian Mountains consider Ukrainian/Rusyn as their mother tongue (Beníšek 2017, 7).

Roms in Transcarpathia refer to themselves as *Tsyhany* or Roms. Beníšek notes that they might refer to themselves as *Slovákika* or *Slovaťika Roma* (Slovak Roms), *Ungrika Roma* or *Vengerska Rroma* (Hungarian Roms), or may identify themselves based on their geographical location, such as *Ungvārakere Rroma* (Roms of Uzhhorod), and *Radvankakere Roma* (Roms of Radvanka) (Beníšek 2017, 15). Roms from the traditional Uzhhorod Romani settlement in Shakhta are commonly referred to as *Močárika Roma* after the name of the settlement Močāra (also, Mocharky) irrespective of whether they are still living there, while the term *Šaxtakere Roma* (Roms of Shakhta) is normally used in the meaning of Roms who currently live in the Shakhta region in Uzhhorod. Within Uzhhorod, where several Romani settlements exist nowadays, Roms may be identified after the names of these particular settlements, for example, *Teľmanakere Roma* (Roma of Telmana Street), and *Xārakere Roma*, literally "Roma of the Pit," referring to Roms living in a settlement called *xār* "pit" (Beníšek 2017, 15).

Uzhhorod, Transcarpathia's administrative center, has a cosmopolitan feel. Many of the public spaces and private dwellings have been modernized in an aesthetic restructuring that locals refer to as "Euro-remont," literally, renovations in a European style. Such renovations imply modern technology, electricity, and round-the-clock access to water, something that was not possible in the USSR where limited supplies of city water allowed water flows in the morning and evening hours only. Pastel building colors, especially dull pink, yellow, green, reminiscent of Austro-Hungarian color patterns, are evocative of the color palette in Wes Anderson's film *The Grand Budapest Hotel* (2014), set in the fictional Republic of Zubrowka. Brightly colored banners hang across the bridge over the River Uzh that divides the older and newer parts of town to advertise concerts by *innozemni*, foreign, musicians, many of whom moved from the region to New York after the Soviet collapse in 1991, but return now to perform.

Life in Uzhhorod revolves around the *bazaar* in the town center, couched among two- and three-story buildings from the Hungarian era with decorative facades. Surrounded by vineyards and cobblestone streets, old Uzhhorod, with its pale yellow and pink walls, stands in great contrast to the austerely bland cement structures built by the Soviets in the newer part of town. There, the concrete Center for Culture and Children, known by its acronym PADIUN, run by Romani jazz musician Villie Pap Sr., looms in its Socialist Realist style. A large synagogue, completed in 1904 on the banks of the Uzh, repurposed in the Soviet era as a concert hall, serves as a haunting reminder of the region's war histories and traumas. At the eve of World War I, Uzhhorod was home to 5,305 Jews in a population of 16,919. In 1941, the Jewish population was 9,576.[1] Only a few hundred survived the five deportations to Auschwitz in 1944.

The fourteenth-century castle, the former residence of Ferenc II Rákóczi, leader of the Hungarian uprising against the Habsburgs in the years 1703–1711, serves as a reminder of the region's Hungarian rule. The very name of the town, Uzhhorod, Ungvár, also spelled Ongvár, Hungvár, and Unguyvar, is a name derived from *Ung*, the Hungarian name for the Uzh river, and *vár*, meaning castle, fort. Uzhhorod, the city's twentieth-century name in Ukrainian and Ruthenian, is derived from the Uzh River that divides the older and newer parts, and *horod*, meaning city.

Transcarpathia, or Zakarpattia (the Ukrainian version of the region's name), also referred to as Subcarpathia (the Hungarian version of the region's name), and known in many languages as Carpathian Ruthenia, plays an essential role in the histories of Hungary, Czechoslovakia, the Soviet Union, and independent Ukraine. A common joke from these parts gives a clearer perspective on this phenomenon: "'I was born in the Austro-Hungarian empire, went to school in Czechoslovakia, served in the Hungarian army, got married in the Soviet Union, and retired in Ukraine.' 'Oh, you must have moved often in your lifetime!' 'No, I never left Uzhhorod.'"

The lore of the Carpathian mountains in former Habsburg imaginaries is evident in the rise of the region's *zelenyi turyzm*, green tourism. The emphasis on nature, hiking, and rafting in the region's mountain rivers offer an image of a mountainous region that is remote but accessible. While the region's name embodies peripheral geopolitical perspectives, locals also point to a marker near the mountain town of Rakhiv along the Tysa River, placed there by Habsburg surveyors in 1887, that reads "Geographical Center of Europe."[2]

Ethnographic Documentations of Poverty and Prejudice

Lauded on stage as musicians and dancers but despised as neighbors, Roms have been subjected to centuries of policies that attempted to integrate Roms through forced assimilation. In the Habsburg Monarchy, which ruled western Ukrainian lands before World War I, Empress Maria Theresa (r. 1740–1780) signed into effect four decrees aimed at assimilation; the decrees rescinded the rights of Roms to own horses and wagons (1754), renamed Roms "New Citizens" and recruited Romani boys for military service (1761), ordered Roms to register with authorities (1767), and prohibited marriage between Roms (1773). Her successor, Josef II, outlawed traditional Romani clothing and the Romani language (Fraser 1992, 157–59).

Such decrees had effectively led to the crippling of Romani economies and pushed them out of dominant economies through racist rhetoric that drummed up fear of interactions among non-Roms with Roms. Ivan Franko (1856–1916) a socialist writer of Ukrainian descent, captured these realities in Carpathian territories that had passed to Hungarian rule at the time of his writing. Franko incorporated ethnographic materials into his literary output. An author, scholar, journalist, and political activist, he chronicled nineteenth-century society. Historian Yaroslav Hrytsak notes that Franko's literary works on peasant themes were designated above all for the civic and politically minded Ruthenian-Ukrainian intelligentsia (Hrytsak 2018, 243). Franko used his craft to fight for universal human rights and to fight against injustices toward the marginalized.

Written in Nahuievychi, July 1882, and rewritten 1887, Franko's short story *Tsyhany* (The Gypsies) (1882) is set in Lastivky, a poor mountain village near Upper Stryi where, as Franko describes, the river turns beyond Turka and Synevidskovy and winds between the mountains. Franko tells the story of a *gendarme*, a Hungarian policeman, who comes across a nomadic Romani family living in a cave in the woods near the village on a harsh winter day. Franko depicts the scene where the *gendarme* finds the Roms as such:

He [the *gendarme*] stopped at the very entrance to the cave, examined his sword and rifle, and then pushed the log to clear the entrance. The smoke hit his face and blinded him. He had to kneel to see anything. When the smoke diminished, the *gendarme* saw a carved cave. The gray stone walls and ceiling were arched. Moisture dripped from the walls. In the middle of the cave was a dug-out hole. The fire, covered with the half-rotten log, was burning, emitting the thick smoke. Several people were sitting around the fire, barely covered by dirty rags. The *gendarme* could not identify their faces yet; he only saw a couple of dark, scared eyes staring at him.

—"Who are you here?" he demanded angrily.

—"Gypsies, dear sir," answered a rough but tame voice.

78 RESOUNDING POVERTY

—"And what are you doing here?"

—"Living in poverty, dear sir!"

The *gendarme* barely stepped into the cave and began to look around the room at the people. Blacksmith's instruments were in the corner: a sack, an anvil, and hammers on a small cart; a small heap of dry branches for the fire in another. In the middle of the cave near the fire there was a *bed* for the family, a heap of rotten straw, dry leaves and moss. There was a rough piece of horse leather at the head, used as a blanket for the eldest.

—"And how many of you are here?—the *gendarme* asked angrily again, turning to the fire.

—"Five, dear sir, five,"—the Gypsy answered and stood, shivering with cold. The rest also stood. There was an elderly Gypsy woman, a young lad, and two little completely naked children. They all were dark with cold and swollen from hunger.

—"What do you do for a living, you, beggars?"—the *gendarme* continued.

—"We manage with the help of the Dear Lord. Just recently, our mare died, so we had some meat till today."

—"How long have you been staying here?"

—"For two weeks, dear sir."

He did not know why, but the calm and timid answers of the old Gypsy vexed the *gendarme* immensely. In his sweet voice and continually repeated "dear sir," the *gendarme* recognized a hidden mockery.

—"Do you often steal things in the villages?"—he proceeded

—"No, dear sir, we do not steal anything. Rom Paikush does not steal! Rom Paikush earns his living as long as he can! However, now that our horse died, we can not go on. We must stay here until the weather gets at least a little bit better."

The story ends like this:

The entrance to the cave was, like before, blocked up by logs and moss. There was just a tiny hole at the top for the smoke to come out. They pulled away from the log and entered. It was dark and quiet inside. Soon their eyes got used to the darkness, and they were able to see a dark object in the middle of the cave. It was the Gypsies, all huddled together and covered by moss and leaves—and dead—for a few days already. The last log was smoldering. Why did they die? Because of the cold? Hunger? Or, maybe, smoke intoxication? Their bodies were dark-blue, frozen, and cold. Moving

MOBILITIES 79

them apart, the *gendarme* saw no horse leather beneath the old man's body. Partly eaten pieces of it were found in the children's hands. The *gendarme* and the cartman remained near the bodies for a long while; shocked, and filled with fear and pity. They probably physically felt the sufferings of those poor ones, the cries and screams of the children, helplessness, and hopelessness, and the despair of the old ones; their universe of poverty and suffering, misfortune and endurance; and all that was left now were just several breathless, motionless bodies huddled together. Without uttering a word, both men left the cave and went out into the open air. They barricaded the entrance to prevent the birds from flying inside. The scout crossed himself and whispered a prayer with his face turned to the cliff, returning back on the sleigh. The *gendarme* began to think what he would write in his report about the accident.[3]

This story speaks volumes to the tragedies that Roms have endured in the Carpathian region due to exclusionary discrimination and brutal state policies. The damp, cold living conditions, forced upon Roms through economic realities rooted in racist attitudes, contributed to their inevitable death. The cave offered shelter from snow and wind but could not alleviate the pain that comes when the body is hungry and chilled to the bone. Such winters have not ceased in this region, and the living conditions in Romani *saman* houses without much heat and insulation are similar in terms of dampness, darkness, and cold to that described by Ivan Franko more than 150 years ago.

Musical Research in Transcarpathia

Transcarpathia is home to 60,000 of the approximately 350,000 Roms in Ukraine.[4] *Tsyhany*, as Roms are still referred to in Ukrainian media (*Cigány* in Hungarian; *Zigeuner* in German),[5] live in 168 of Transcarpathia's 530 towns and villages in groups that number from 200 to over 2,000 people. Radvanka, home to approximately 2,500 Roms and an equal number of non-Roms, was a village incorporated in the mid-twentieth century within the city limits of Uzhhorod, the administrative capital of Transcarpathia and a provincial city with a population of 122,000. The lands surrounding Radvanka were part of the Austro-Hungarian Empire and were known in Hungarian as Ungvár-Radvánc. Ungvár-Radvánc once belonged to Hungarian poet István

80 RESOUNDING POVERTY

Gyöngyössy (1629–1704), who had allowed Roms to live on his land, and today the Romani school in Uzhhorod stands next to his Baroque mansion. According to the 1691 census, one of the nine streets in Uzhhorod was named *Tsyhanska*, Gypsy (Malik et al. 1991, 3). Documents show that this street was on the opposite side of the Uzh River than the town proper and, due to frequent flooding, was not a desirable place to live. The 1691 census reveals that Roms found work in Ungvar's castle stables, armory, and as musicians (Malik et al. 1991).

As the border region of kingdoms and empires, Transcarpathia was one of the most critical sites for ethnographic and musicological research in the early twentieth century. Austro-Hungary, which governed Western Ukrainian lands until World War I, promoted the study of folklore by scholars from the Shevchenko Scientific Society in Lviv.[6] With funding from the Austro-Hungarian government, Ukrainian music scholar Filarett Kolessa (1871–1947) and ethnographers Volodymyr Hnatiuk (1871–1926),[7] Juriĭ Zhatkovych (1855–1920),[8] and Fedir Vovk (1847–1918)[9] published numerous volumes of material collected from the Carpathian region. Even the Hungarian ethnomusicologist and composer Béla Bartók (1881–1945), having spent his childhood in Nagyazöllös, later Vynohradiv, Ukraine (home to one of the largest Vlax communities in Transcarpathia), researched the musical repertoires of ethnic groups living in the region. Unfortunately, few of these early twentieth-century studies, nor later ethnographical and ethnomusicological research in Transcarpathia, made a note of Romani musical culture or included transcriptions of music played by Romani musicians. Examples of musical transcriptions involving Roms like the one in a songbook published in 1938 by Kolessa are rare. In his folk song collection *Narodni pisni z pidkarpatsk'koï Rusi* (Folk songs from sub-Carpathian Rus), Kolessa makes a note of a Romani musician who accompanied a group of non-Romani wedding singers in Radvanka on the Ruthenian-language song "Eĭ, zahud my, hudachku [Play for me, musician]." Kolessa commented that the Romani musician who accompanied them refused to play when the scholar wanted to transcribe it.[10] Kolessa blames the Romani musician's lack of cooperation for his inability to complete the transcription. Kolessa's interpretation of the Romani musician's interaction with him points to the lack of understanding between Romani musicians and non-Romani music researchers. Kolessa was disappointed and frustrated that the Romani violinist refused to allow him to transcribe. However, such instances of ethnographic refusal often result from a lack of trust between researchers and interlocutors. As Audra Simpson reminds us, such refusal can often serve as an exercise of (limited) agency on the part of the interlocutor.[11]

Roms have many reasons to distrust non-Roms, and the most plausible explanation would be that the violinist did not want to share the details of his craft with strangers. We can infer that Kolessa interpreted the Rom's unwillingness to cooperate as the Rom's inability to grasp the greater political and cultural significance of folk song collecting. Kolessa, the founder of Ukrainian ethnographic musicology, was most probably primarily interested transcribing the song's melody and text as sung by the female non-Romani wedding singers and not in the Romani violinist's accompaniment. While Kolessa's partial transcription includes a melody and two verses of text for "Eï, zahud my, hudachku," no extant sketch reveals whether Kolessa even attempted to transcribe the Romani musician's instrumental part.[12]

While Roms have been excluded from Ukrainian-led ethnographic research in Transcarpathia, Hungarian ethnographers, including those conducting research in Transcarpathia, Hungary's "near abroad" (to borrow Putin's colonial term for Ukraine), place an important emphasis on Romani ethnomusicological scholarship. For Hungarians, Roms serve as culture bearers of Hungarian musical traditions, and their interests in urban, more professionalized musicians are guided by historical interests in the preservation of Hungarian (as performed by Roms) musical lore. The argument over who "owns" such music, the Roms who play it or the non-Roms who consume it, has been documented as far back as the times of Hungarian composer Franz Liszt (1811–1886), who argued that the improvisatory elements infused into Hungarian music by Romani musicians makes them the culture bearers of a musical tradition they have created and with which non-Roms engage, socially, politically, and economically (Hooker 2013).

Because access to a significant number of historic folk song collections was limited in the Soviet Union, the systematic examination of nineteenth-century ethnographic texts has taken on a new priority. Ethnomusicologists from the Lviv region who participate in ethnographic expeditions today often review their findings in light of historic expeditions conducted in the same area more than a century ago. A parallel exists between contemporary ethnographers' efforts and ideological motivations and their nineteenth-century counterparts like Kolessa and Klement Kvitka (1880–1953), whose work was guided by a search for distinctly Ukrainian features in rural folk genres. In 2004, the year of Ukraine's Orange Revolution, Mykola Dmytrenko, the head of the Folklore Division at the Ukrainian Academy of Sciences, published a historical overview of Ukrainian folklore studies.[13] Dmytrenko drew attention to the national consciousness of Ukrainian ethnographers like Panteleimon Kulish (1819–1897), Mykhaïlo Drahomanov (1841–1895), and writer Ivan Franko. Dmytrenko's personal sense of Ukrainian consciousness informed his narrative style and subject presentation. In his study *Ukraïnska folklorystyka druhoï polovyny XIX stolittia: Shkoly, postati, problemy* (Ukrainian folkloristics of the second half of the nineteenth century: Schools, figures, problems), Dmytrenko argues that nineteenth-century folklorists worked for the good of the "Ukrainian nation." He points out that Kulish was the first ethnographer to publish scholarly works in Ukrainian,[14] that Franko was critical of German anthropological methods because they "blurred" regional ethnographic differentiations and "smeared them in a sea of theoretical generalizations,"[15] and that Kvitka succeeded in collecting the "true voice" of the Ukrainian folk traditions in his fieldwork expeditions.[16] Such statements reveal an emphatic push to incorporate folklore into the post-Soviet nation-building project in Ukraine and an awareness of how political and economic systems influence the transmission of knowledge.

Romani music is still omitted from studies published by ethnomusicologists documenting the traditional music of ethnic groups in Transcarpathia, and the causes can be traced to outright (though veiled) racism because the cultural purity or "authenticity" that ethnographers seek in Ukraine is not believed to lie among Roms. Ukrainian ethnomusicologists today still question whether Romani musicians are creators of their music or merely interpreters and appropriators of the musical cultures of the countries in which they live. Contemporary scholars believe that the true essence of any music is found only in rural settings. Urban musical traditions are assumed to be hybrid and, therefore, inauthentic. Such thinking contributes to the continued omission of Romani music from local ethnomusicological research.

Romani Musical Dynasties

In the seventeenth and eighteenth centuries, Romani musicians performed in Uzhhorod and Mukachevo castles and were financed by the Hungarian ruling class. Until the early 1900s, families of male Romani musicians were the only Roms who had the right to live in apartments in Uzhhorod proper. Other Roms were forced to live outside the city limits (today's Radvanka) and were only allowed entry into the town center on weekends to sell their wares. Because male Romani musicians enjoyed this higher social status, Romani Yag draws heavily on their image in publications. Captions under pictures of Romani musicians published in the *Romani Yag* newspaper stress the prestige of male Romani musicians and emphasize the glory days of these musicians in Uzhhorod (Figure 4.1).

Before the collapse of the Soviet Union, most popular restaurants in towns like Uzhhorod and Mukachevo employed male Romani instrumentalists. These restaurants were well known among non-Roms in other parts of western Ukraine. Indeed, conversations with people from Lviv, Ternopil, Ivano-Frankivsk, and Rivne confirm that many non-Roms living in the western regions of the Ukrainian SSR were aware of the Romani restaurant music tradition in Uzhhorod and Mukachevo (Figure 4.2). Most venues that once employed male Romani musicians (like the restaurant Skalia) went bankrupt in the early years of the post-Soviet transition, and newly established clubs and restaurants did not hire live musicians due to rising costs. Despite aid from NGOs, the widespread loss of Romani performance opportunities resulted in a staggering loss of musical traditions.

Figure 4.1 Romani musicians in Uzhhorod, early 1900s.
Photo: Courtesy of Romani Yag.

Pictures published in the *Romani Yag* newspaper emphasize the professionalism of male Romani musicians in the past. None of the musicians in these pictures is young; older age indicates skill, craftsmanship, and is a marker that those pictured are due great respect. In most historical pictures published by *Romani Yag*, Romani musicians wear matching vests and are smartly dressed. Their appearance signals education and refinement. Interaction with non-Roms is thus implied indirectly: it is understood that Romani musicians performed mainly for non-Romani patrons. Because non-Romani views of musicians are more positive than their opinions regarding other segments of the Romani population, Romani Yag utilizes the Rom-as-musician stereotype to help to negotiate ethnic and class tensions between Roms and non-Roms.[17]

Ethnic-themed restaurants like Moscow's restaurant "Budapest" featured Romani musicians from Transcarpathia who came to represent ethnicities living on former Hungarian territories that came under Soviet rule after World War II. The structure of the Romani restaurant band with *cimbalom* and violin, common for Romani restaurant musicians in Budapest, came

Figure 4.2 Aladar Adam's father Evhen Adam performing on violin at the popular Uzhhorod restaurant Skalia (Cave) in 1976.
Photo: Courtesy of Romani Yag.

to represent Hungarians, but not necessarily Roms. Alongside the tradition of Romani musicians engaging with Hungarian music, new generations of Roms growing up in the Soviet Union came to look increasingly toward Moscow for Romani aesthetics and repertoires. At the time of my initial fieldwork in the early 2000s, there were very few Romani restaurant musicians working in Uzhhorod, in part because restaurants were no longer supporting live music, but also because such musical traditions had fallen away by the late Soviet period.

Romani Musical Dynasties Today

The social stigma associated with Roms continues to keep most researchers away from Romani settlements, leaving ethnomusicologists to conclude that Romani musical practices are based solely on repertoires heard in non-Romani settings.[18] Ethnomusicologists in Uzhhorod have predominantly heard Romani musicians perform in restaurants, where the standard repertoire comprises non-Romani melodies played "*po-tsyhansky*" (in the Gypsy style, interpreted as passionate, improvisatory, and virtuosic). Hearing Romani music in such limiting contexts reinforces the popular notion among Ukrainian ethnomusicologists that *all* Romani music is hybrid and unusable in furtherance of the nation-building project.

There is a lack of Romani musicians in academic settings because the majority, while professional, have not been educated in Uzhhorod's music schools. As Kandra Josyp Horvath explains, "I was the son of the famous Romani violinist, Béla Horvath. During my first violin lesson at the music school, I was given *noty*, a musical score, and told to play. I had never seen written music in my life, but because my father was a violinist, the teacher assumed that he knew how to read music and had taught me."[19] Many Romani musicians, especially older male instrumentalists, do not read musical notation and learn by rote. They learn by playing with older musicians who encourage involvement with the craft from a young age. The musician relies on the ear alone, not on visual aids that might detract from an immediate connection to sound itself. Such musicianship might sometimes be considered more authentic by folklorists.

As part of a so-called *muzychna dynastiia*, musical dynasty, Horvath was expected to have learned the musical craft from his father, who had learned it from his father, also a violinist. The virtuosity associated with showman-style performance for non-Roms that shaped older Romani performers like Horvath's father recalls accounts of nineteenth-century Romani violinists in Budapest (Hooker 2013) whose styles were retained by Hungarian Roms who settled in Uzhhorod. Kandra, however, felt he had little talent for violin playing and returned to music in his late teens as a *popsa* (popular music) singer. The career he has built as a Romani-Hungarian *popsa* singer has allowed him social and financial capital. A self-ascribed crooner, his vocal aesthetics align with the melodramatic styles of *estrada*, popular music, in post-Soviet Ukraine. Holding on to the synthesizer accompaniments and drum beat machines popularized in the Soviet Union when the synthesizer was first introduced, Horvath represents the voice of modern Roms who have achieved middle-class status. He performs in a tuxedo (as pictured in the concert advertisement in Figure 4.3)[20] and is a sought-after performer at weddings and events sponsored by the upper echelons of Romani society in Transcarpathia and Hungary.

Kandra's father Béla Horvath was part of an Uzhhorod musical dynasty of Romani restaurant musicians. Béla's father, also a professional violinist, performed in Uzhhorod at the turn of the century when the city was part of the Hungarian realm. The violin repertoires, as common in Uzhhorod as they are in Budapest and among Romani musicians who play in restaurants in Pittsburgh, include "Gypsy" standards like the *Csárdas* by Vittorio Monti,

Figure 4.3 Concert for International Roma Day, Mukachevo, Transcarpathia, April 8, 2019, featuring Kandra Horvath (center), Dorina, Csík Laci, Tsino, and Friku.

MOBILITIES   87

written in 1904 and based on a Hungarian *csárdas*, a folk dance in 2/4 time, the name of which is derived from *csárda*, the old Hungarian term for roadside tavern and restaurant. With its fast, virtuosic runs and improvisatory, light-hearted crowd-pleasing melodies, Monti's *Csárdas* belong to the repertoires of an older generation. Once traditionally danced among Roms in Radvanka, the *csárdas* has been replaced with more individualized styles: young men and women take turns improvising and displaying intricate footwork in the center of a dance circle formed by their friends. At present, the *csárdas* is mainly danced at weddings, usually when the bandleader suggests the guests dance *po-romsky*, in a Romani style.[21]

In 1998, Kandra became a cook in the restaurant "Budapest" in Uzhhorod. At the time, the restaurant had no live music, but Kandra performed during his breaks for his pleasure, singing in a part of the restaurant with only a handful of patrons. A local music teacher heard him sing and offered to work with him. Kandra studied voice against his father's wishes since this went against tradition. The historical repertoires were predominantly in-strumental, and women sang the lyrics in such cases where they were not. By developing a reputation as an *estrada* singer, Josef broadened the genres and the musical opportunities for younger Roms. Singing in Romani, Josef is among a handful of musicians from Transcarpathia who have gained an international reputation, albeit predominantly among Hungarian-Romani audiences.

Kandra has also used his social and economic status to produce concerts, most recently a musical event commemorating "International Roma Day" in Mukachevo, a town approximately 35 kilometers from Uzhhorod and home to a Romani *tabir*, camp, with more than 5,000 people. This event, organ-ized by two Romani city councilmen in Mukachevo, "invites all willing, free of cost" and offers a welcoming space for those who may not have the eco-nomic means to participate otherwise. The inclusion of the Romani flag on the upper-left side and the Ukrainian flag on the upper-right side positions Romani rights events within a broader discourse on citizenship, inclusion, and equal rights in Ukraine.

This politicized event engages Romani youths by featuring popular Romani musicians from Hungary like Csík Laci whose musical aesthetics align with popular musical genres played in local discothèques.[22] Alaina Lemon makes a note of younger Roms in Russia who identify with an "attitude that they can detect in expressions and movements of American musicians that renders them like [Roms]" (Lemon 1995). Barbara Rose Lange, in her in-depth study

88 RESOUNDING POVERTY

of young Romani musicians in Hungary, Slovakia, and Austria, shares that in the 2000s, Romani musicians began to fuse poetry, local folk music, and other vernacular music with jazz, Asian music, art music, and electronic dance music (Lange 2018). Furthermore, Katalin Kovalcsik's analysis of Romani involvements in rap and hip-hop points to the wide array of global styles with which Romani youths engage (Kovalcsik 2010).[23] In Transcarpathia, Romani audiences draw connections with global musical genres primarily via music industries in neighboring Hungary.

Transcarpathian Romani Jazz

Among Uzhhorod's musical dynasties, the Pap family has been particularly influential in expanding the local repertoires. Villie Pap Sr. has led a musical organization called Lăutari, a Romanian word that denotes Romani musicians.[24] The term is derived from *lăută*, the Romanian word for lute. Lăutari usually perform in bands that use the Turkish etymon *taraf*, as in Taraf de Haïdouks, discussed in the Introduction. As director of the Center for Culture and Children (PADIUN), Pap has held a position of power to influence children's programming and cultural events at the Soviet-era structure that houses numerous rehearsal rooms and a concert stage. At PADIUN, I often came to see the group Rom Som (I Am a Rom) rehearse, a dance group run by a former dancer trained by the Pavlo Virsky National Folk Dance Ensemble. The numerous programs run for Romani children with the help of Villie Pap's brother Aladar Pap offered opportunities for involvement among Romani children with certain means toward involvement in cultural affairs. For more than twenty years, the Pap Jazz Fest has promoted jazz through an annual festival featuring Pap's group, the Pap Jazz Kwartet, as well as international acts (Figure 4.4).

The Pap Jazz Kwartet's latest hit, "Memory of Django," honors Django Reinhardt (1910–1953), whose musical style is discussed in relation to his health in Chapter 7. "Memory of Django," with its hard bop style, was featured on the online streaming website for JazzInUa.com (Jazz in Ukraine) as one of the top ten tracks for the site, voted on by listeners worldwide. "Memory of Django" references Django Reinhardt, the Gypsy Jazz guitarist popular in the 1930s. Perhaps this homage falls in line with the iconic worship of Django identified by Siv Brun Lie (Lie 2013; see also Lie 2017, 2019, 2020). Relationships to Django, not necessarily as widespread in the

Figure 4.4 Advertisement for the Pap Jazz Fest 2017, the 20th Jubilee International Roma Jazz Festival in Uzhhorod, Transcarpathia, featuring Villie Pap (Jr.), Eduard Pap, AMC Trio Unit, Villie Pap (Sr.), Erik Marienthal, Petro Poptarev, and the Pap Jazz Quintet. The concert is sponsored by the Carpathian Fund, the International Renaissance Foundation, the American Embassy in Ukraine.

90 RESOUNDING POVERTY

former Soviet Union as they were throughout Western Europe, are coupled with politicized Soviet relationships to jazz (Starr 1983). S. Frederick Starr argues that jazz entered the Russian Empire through its higher classes and their engagement with globalized musical genres (via France especially, where jazz was proliferating). By the 1930s, at the height of Stalin's terror, jazz had trickled to the public. Communist leaders were determined to censor it for alleged musical and social improprieties, as would the Nazi regime in Germany a decade later (Von Eschen 2006). The decadence, improvisatory nature, and the individualism that the genre made room for would cast it as a genre targeted for censorship in the USSR.

With its elements of improvisation, jazz made room for discourses regarding the performer as composer akin to arguments popularized by Liszt in the nineteenth century regarding Romani ownerships over the (Hungarian) music styles they performed and improvised upon. The distinction between performer as a composer, as analyzed by Starr, undermined the Soviet school of composition, which, with its strict rules of harmony, its distrust of dissonance, allowed for very narrow understandings of music deemed appropriate for Soviet audiences.

Kalo Rom (Black Gypsy), the Musical

The Uzhhorod National Romani Theater was founded in 1999 by Villie Pap, a professional Romani musician who had once earned his living playing in Uzhhorod's restaurants. As the director of PADIUN, Pap produces musicals for the Uzhhorod National Romani Theater. The musical *Kalo Rom/Chornyĭ Tsyhan* (Black Gypsy) (2001) was produced with grants from the Open Society Institute and composed by Pap family members to highlight the history of Roms in Uzhhorod.

Black Gypsy features the story of Villie Pap Sr.'s great-grandfather, who in the 1920s joined the Romani settlement in Uzhhorod on the opposite side of town from Radvanka. The Mocharky camp, as the settlement was known, took its name from the swamplands (*mochary*) upon which it was built. As Uzhhorod's city limits grew, the area's name changed to Shakhta, meaning coal mine. The Mocharky/Shakhta camp has the most extended history of all Romani settlements in Uzhhorod. When Transcarpathia became part of Czechoslovakia during the interwar period, the Czech government built a school for the Romani population in the Mocharky camp. The school served as a marker of prestige among Mocharky dwellers concerning Roms living in other settlements like Radvanka. Many Romani musicians and Uzhhorod's Romani leaders went to the school, which today is a (quasi-segregated) school for Roms within the Uzhhorod public school system. Non-Romani teachers in the original school emphasized musical instruction rather than academic instruction. Each day the male students had music lessons while girls received instruction in hygiene, sewing, and household chores.[25] Though girls did not learn to play instruments, they participated in plays put on in the school by non-Romani teachers. The theatrical troupe in the grammar school considered itself a "theater" and performed plays like *Cikáni* (Gypsies) written by Czech playwright Karel Hynek Mácha (1810–1836). The Uzhhorod National Romani Theater claims historical legitimacy by marketing itself as the offshoot of the theater that existed at the Romani school in Uzhhorod in the 1920s (Crowe 1994, 46–48).[26]

The emphasis on the past dominates the discourse that informs performance practices in the Uzhhorod National Roma Theater. As one actor states: "The Theater will help us live forever—our ancestors left us very little history because nobody wrote about us—we are creating history for the future generation of Roms in Uzhhorod." A second actor concurs: "The Ukrainians celebrated a Millennium of Christianity (988–1988), but we have no history—Roms have lived in Transcarpathia for over 300 years but the oldest stories I know are of my grandfather." Though some Roms believe they have no written history, they have become increasingly conscious of capitalizing on their unknown past because of the funds awarded for such projects through NGOs. The question is what aspects of the past come to be represented and reinterpreted in the context of theatrical performance. To answer this I turn to a brief analysis of music and dance styles utilized in the musical *Chornyǐ Tsyhan* (Black Gypsy).

Chornyǐ Tsyhan serves as an illustration of the fluid imaginings that inform historical narratives. They also imbue more negative stereotypes with a positive agency. The protagonist, the Black Gypsy, once the source of everything bad in the camp, is redeemed through the love of a woman. He mends his ways and repents before he is stabbed in punishment by the camp elder or *baron*. The theme of redemption strips "blackness" of its implied negativity and, in such fashion, follows tropes familiar to depictions of Roms in Russian literature, including Alexander Pushkin's Aleko, banished for killing Zemfira and her lover in the narrative poem *Tsygane* (The Gypsies, 1824), and Maxim Gorky's short story *Makar Chudra* (1892) and its rendering in the Soviet film *Tabor ukhodit v nebo* (1975) in which Loiko Zobar kills the unfaithful Rada and is killed by her father in turn. The redemption of the "noble savage" motif frames much of Romani-themed nineteenth-century literature and continues in the NGO-sponsored cultural productions like *Chornyǐ Tsyhan*.

In many ways, the Romani audience members who saw the production of *Chornyǐ Tsyhan* in the spring of 2002 did not connect with many aspects of the music and dance. The music was a fusion of jazz, Russian pop aesthetic, and popular Transcarpathian Romani songs. The remaking of traditional songs in a jazz style disappointed many audience members because they had come to hear traditional violin, *cimbalom*, accordion, and double bass in a musical that had been advertised as a representation of Romani life in historical Uzhhorod.

Tensions regarding aesthetics, instrumentation, style, and the like are not uncommon to Roms in Uzhhorod. They do, however, point to the complex ways that music engages with identity politics. It also shows that the musical events in the town are rooted in deep history and are influenced by the personal choices of a relatively small group of male musicians who draw on family lineage to shape musical productions and tastes. As Roms gain access to broader repertoires, popularized on television, radio, and in the sale of CDs and compressed pirated MP3s at Uzhhorod *bazaars*, and, more important, gain economic access to musical playback equipment, the styles will expand and grow. The emphasis on Romani education, with a push to enroll Romani students into the Romani schools and integrate them further into non-Romani society will broaden such aesthetics. To date, however, the dominant Romani music events are closely tied to the funding structures that have solidified the impact that organizations like Lăutari, Rom Som, and Romani Yag have on urban music-related events in Transcarpathia.

5

Networks

In Transcarpathia, people keep time in unusual ways. Some set their wristwatches to Moscow time, two hours ahead of local time. Some set their clocks one hour ahead of local time, according to the time in Kyiv, the capital of Ukraine, the country whose westernmost border Transcarpathia now constitutes. Others live according to local time, referred to by some as Hungarian time. People's relationships with time—Russian, Ukrainian, and Hungarian—offer insights into parallel lives guided by efficacy and immediacy. In Transcarpathia, on the outermost reaches of former empires, time is not arbitrary. It is stubbornly realigned and bent to serve the needs of locals.

Such personal relationships to perceived structures play with normative life cycles some take as a given. They remind us that everything is in flux, ever changing, dependent on the individual's perception of the world around them. However, it is not concepts of time that are fluid. Instead, the state structures that organize time are perceived as so arbitrary and ineffective that locals privatize their response to them through various negotiations. In a post-Soviet border region, time is constructed through networks of government that engage with the past-past (Austro-Hungarian Empire), the past (Soviet Union), and the near-past, the period of *perestroika*, restructuring, that throughout the 1980s moved the USSR away from central planning through a restructuring of labor and capital production, eventually leading to the dissolution of the socialist system. Soviet-era ineffectiveness has retained its grip, and even the simplest tasks involve a significant number of steps to perform. As much cultural as it is political and economic, it is perhaps the perceivable *waste* of time that serves as its most unnerving yet reassuringly unifying feature in this part of the world. Bus schedules, delayed by breakdowns en route across the mountains, tedious lines to cross the borders into neighboring Poland, Slovakia, Hungary, and Romania, pension payments (*pilhy*) delayed in processing, especially by the ever-expanding bureaucracies that complicate efficient payouts, all reinforce common images of a region that circuitously perpetuates its entrapment.

ReSounding Poverty. Adriana N. Helbig, Oxford University Press. © Oxford University Press 2023.
DOI: 10.1093/oso/9780197631768.003.0006

On Doing Nothing

In this region, doing ethnographic fieldwork sometimes means "doing nothing." One waits: for the musicians to return from performing for a wedding in another town, for the one Romani family that has not abandoned the village searching for work in other parts of Ukraine to return from working in the fields. One waits for the snows to melt or the rains to subside to be able to reach an inaccessible village, made to seem even more remote than it is by the sheer impassability of a road riddled with potholes or washed out in yet another of the spring floods that plague the region as a result of the environmental destruction to the Carpathian forests, first by the Soviet government and now by corrupt local government officials who turn a blind eye to illegal logging (Kuemmerle et al. 2009). One waits for the woman who has traveled to another town to visit her son in prison, unfairly charged, beaten, and forced to sign a paper in a language he cannot read, inadvertently admitting guilt to a crime not committed.[1] Then, though, one listens, for long hours, to the cries, laments, and stories of better times past, of complaints against the present government for turning their backs on Roms, and one takes responsibility for the hope the presence of an ethnographer has brought to the house, that perhaps, finally, someone might be able and willing to help.

In Transcarpathia's Romani villages, time, like so many other resources, is limited. It takes time for the *saman* out of which many Romani houses are made, to set. It takes time to walk to the river for water because many houses have no indoor plumbing. It takes time to gather twigs to fix the brooms with which many Roms are paid to sweep city streets. It takes time to travel the many kilometers from the villages to the nearest town with an office of a Romani NGO to file paperwork for Holocaust reparations, to ask for judicial advice in handling interactions with the police, or to seek sources of financial help for medical care of a sick family member.

To date, scholars researching the lives of the poor have focused on the lack of time with which economically disadvantaged members of the population struggle. Referring to this concept as "time poverty," they focus on the lack of control that more impoverished people have over their own time. Scholars generally agree that time poverty is gendered: women in impoverished situations, with the additional burdens of caring for households and child-rearing, have even less control over their time than most of their male counterparts (Walker 2013). In analyses of poverty time, scholars differentiate between the various types of labor, including time spent working for pay and the amount of time spent on domestic work (Bardasi and Wodon 2006). Few, however, factor in the time spent on nurturing relationships between family, friends, and acquaintances or the time spent on musical entertainment and emotional release.

Such realities push back against the stereotype that impoverished Roms "do nothing." Non-Roms are increasingly blaming Roms for their own poverty and for their own lack of economic advancement. It is, however, challenging to increase financial growth in a situation where one must choose between buying medicine, clothes, or food. To use large families or a lack of education as an explanation for this only shows a partial understanding of the issues. When we speak of poverty, we speak of a system that is structured in ways in which some people have more and others have less. That Roms consistently find themselves among those who have less can only be explained through a thorough understanding of the paramount discrimination that exists toward Roms among the non-Romani majorities. In writing about discrimination, however, I follow Emanuela Ignățoiu-Sora, who argues that an overemphasis on discrimination clouds encounters and relationships that Roms have with non-Roms on a local level (Ignățoiu-Sora 2011). The rhetoric of discrimination, Ignățoiu-Sora explains, became common concerning Roms in the 1990s through the help of NGOs and the European courts, through which they helped argue specific cases of profiling and racism. She points out that an emphasis on the historical context is necessary to counterbalance an all-too-common view that Roms are *solely* a discriminated group that *only* needs legal protection against discrimination (emphasis Ignățoiu-Sora 2011, 1714).

The Specifics of Post-Soviet Poverty

Roms from Transcarpathia have, perhaps, received the most significant amount of negative backlash in politics and in social standing. Living in 168 so-called *tabory*, camps, they make ends meet through petty trade. Many collect scrap metal, clean the streets, and perform other menial jobs. Many also travel abroad to work in the forestry industry in the Russian Far East. The majority who travel for work head to central, eastern, and southern Ukraine to work as seasonal agricultural laborers. They camp by the side of the road or in the woods and are quite visible to passersby. The images of Romani encampments evoke stereotypical images of nomadic Roms and bring forth

96   RESOUNDING POVERTY

the historical wrath against and disgust with nomads. They symbolize the failure of the post-Soviet state to integrate Roms into society in ways that respect their distinct culture as both separate from and a unique part of the history, polity, and very fabric of East European life; they also serve as a simulacrum of the *bezladdia*: the lack of (social, political, economic) order, in independent Ukraine, marred by corruption illuminated the failings of the state to ensure the economic security of its citizens.

Poverty, once viewed as a natural extension of the backward peasant-serf in the Russian Empire, was the rallying cry of Vladimir Lenin's worker-instrumentalized revolution. Poverty in the Soviet Union was cast in the rhetoric of equality, with everyone allegedly having an opportunity for an equal share of economic goods. Indeed, people had jobs and housing, and food was available. Roms, benefiting from affirmative action plans at the expense of forced assimilation, were molded to become Soviet citizens, serving in the army, attending school, and being offered housing and opportunities to work. Soviet citizens and Western powers like the United States blamed any degrees of poverty experienced by people in the Soviet Union on the Soviet state, which, in turn, vehemently denied the existence of poverty as this would have revealed the failures of the Soviet state (Matthews 1986).[2] The Soviet ruble did not function as a currency in a market economy because prices had no relationship to true manufacturing cost. While certain goods were priced very low, others were inaccessible due to manufacturing shortages. The black market economy functioned as a supply chain for Western goods, jeans, music, and the like.

The dissolution of a non-market currency and the emergence of a market economy in 1991 brought about the devaluation of the Soviet ruble and spiraled the post-Soviet sphere into an extreme economic crisis.[3] By the time I had begun my fieldwork in 1999, hyperinflation had contributed to the extensive widespread poverty I was witnessing across the country. Many were immigrating west while others were resorting to extreme measures to make ends meet. During this time, the Romani musicians with whom I had intended to conduct fieldwork sold their instruments, marking the beginning of a silent decade in many Romani villages.[4]

The two little Romani girls on this volume's cover photographed in Kyiv in 1995 hold batches of *kupony*, the intermediary currency, in their hands. *Kupony*, akin to Monopoly money, were stamped with the word "Kupon" and were essentially cut out pieces of white, green, blue, or pink paper; they were given in stacks because eventually even a large handful, like the one held by the little girls, became worth less than one ruble. The price of jeans would eventually jump to a few million *kupony* before the Ukrainian *hryvnia* was introduced in 1996. Such economic instability led to suicide, depression, and a host of emotional traumas and physical illnesses. It also set up the new Ukrainian state as untrustworthy (Senders and Truitt 2007). The move toward liberalization, privatization, and internationalization, as guided by US economic strategies, solidified a context for widespread corruption among politically connected entrepreneurs (Dudwick et al. 2003; Hann 2002). The haphazard privatization of property that had once belonged to the Soviet state and came under the ownership of a select few, known generally as *oligarchs*, corrupt businessmen with political ties, plunged the population into degrees of destitution (Orenstein 2008). Ukraine's 2004 Orange Revolution and the 2014 Revolution of Dignity were cries against criminal actions such as voter fraud that exposed the deep-rooted relationships between the post-Soviet criminal underworld and the new political elites. These events reshaped attitudes regarding people who have money and those who do not.

Time and poverty seem to be cyclical when it comes to Roms in post-Soviet Eastern Europe. Time frames international approaches to helping the Romani poor, and life among the poor now rises and falls within cycles of funding. Many of the grants that helped to sustain Romani communities came to fruition during the Decade of Roma Inclusion (2005–2015), an initiative of twelve European countries to improve the socioeconomic status and social inclusion of Roms in Central and Eastern Europe and the Balkans by focusing on education, employment, housing, and health.[5] Projects organized by NGOs were funded for various lengths of time, often with temporal stipulations put in place by donors. Life cycles were altered based on when projects began and ended, varying from a few months to a year. These projects included rebuilding schools, offering scholarships to Romani students for higher education, health monitoring programs, media monitoring for anti-Romani discrimination, and community technology initiatives. The Decade has passed, and anti-Romani discrimination is at an all-time high. European governments have initiated another program similar to the Decade called Roma Integration 2020. It aims to support Romani integration within the EU member states in the enlargement region (Brüggemann and Friedman 2017; see also Friedman 2002).[6] This book, through ethnographic accounts among Roms living in a region just beyond the border of the European Union, argues that such programs, while originating among well-meaning non-Romani and Romani leaders at the top, trickle down to the villages through interventions that often cause great emotional stress for those people whose lives they are meant to improve.

The Un/Deserving Poor

Serena Romano reminds us that global discourses on poverty are cast in moral terms, within a binary of *deserving/undeserving poor* (Romano 2017). She elucidates that the notion of the *undeserving poor* and those considered *worthy poor* are ways in which societies determine whom to aid. The *undeserving poor* in this sense are those who are considered *responsible* for their poverty, while those qualifying as *worthy poor* have historically been those who can be "morally excused from work" on account of their assumed vulnerable status or condition, including the aged, sick, and infirm—together with children and widows—while all able-bodied adults would belong to the latter group (Romano 2017).

The emphasis on family makes Dorothea Lange's photograph "Migrant Mother" such an effective testament of the Great Depression following the Wall Street Crash of 1929 (Figure 5.1). When farmers fell into poverty due to a string of natural disasters, including floods and dust storms that devastated their crops and destroyed their livelihoods, thousands of poverty-stricken families migrated to the agricultural fields of California in search of work, only to find that life was not much better there. The Resettlement Administration (later the Farm Security Administration), one of the agencies established by Franklin D. Roosevelt's progressive social policies, employed a team of photographers to document the lives of these migrant workers. The object was to demonstrate the need for federal assistance and justify legislation that would make it possible. Lange was among the agency photographers who documented the experiences of destitute farmers living in poverty, hunger, and disease.

Dorothea Lange's 1936 documentation of the "Migrant Mother" humanized the face of Depression-era white poverty, serving as a call to the US government for its moral obligation to help. Cheryl Greenburg's study on Depression-era race relations in urban contexts, focusing on Harlem, argues that the Depression hit African Americans twice as hard. African Americans struggled to gain employment because in the era of scarcity, any job, including porter and domestic, became a "white man's job." African Americans were the first to be fired and the last to be hired, contributing to creative ways

Figure 5.1 Dorothea Lange's "Migrant Mother," Nipomo, California, 1936. Getty Images.

that Black churches engaged Black social and political networks to provide security for those for whom the government and philanthropic programs did not adequately provide (Greenburg 1991).

Such has been the case for certain segments of the Romani population on the territories of the former Soviet Union. Non-Romani narratives about Roms frame them as unable or unwilling to work and at fault for the poverty that stems from their unemployment. Their attempts to make a living positions them as economic Others whose modes of procuring economic security are viewed as suspect, undignified, and oftentimes illegal. My own experiences as a scrap metal collector among Roms illustrate this case in point. During much of my fieldwork, I attempted to work and to be alongside as many groups of Roms as possible to experience the varying ways people with varying economic means experience everyday living. Much to the chagrin of my more affluent Romani NGO affiliates, I spent time among the street cleaners, beggars, and scrap metal collectors in Uzhhorod. I rode with a Romani on his wagon around town to pick up metal that was then sold to local dealers. One day, we were stopped at an intersection when a group of tourists emerged from a bus. I recognized the bus company and the tourists— they were part of a group traveling through my mother's (New Jersey–based) agency that organizes tours to Ukraine. The tourists, clearly not recognizing me in my local clothes sitting next to a Romani man on a wagon pulled by a horse amid a heap of scrap metal, began to point and shout, "Tsyhany!" (Gypsies!) and quickly began to move away from us. The reactions of these tourists, perhaps warned about the dangers of Romani beggars, illustrate the exotification and the abhorrence and fear that the poor, associated with dirt, disease, and activities deemed suspect and illegal, experience.

The In/Audibility of the Poverty Gaze

How does the picture of the "Migrant Mother" relate to the picture of the two little Romani girls on the front cover of this book, playing music for money? For one, the stereotype of Roms performing in public for alms is so inherent that hardly anyone takes notice of the Romani poor who sing while begging for money. Romani children do not evoke the pathos that representatives from other groups might simply because they are Romani and have held the status of beggars for generations. Very few non-Roms stop to think why Roms beg, let alone allow themselves to feel any responsibility toward a system that systematically excludes Roms from the very social, economic, and political fabric that would allow them to "pull themselves up by their bootstraps," so to speak.[7] A growing number of state-funded programs are geared toward helping those in need. These, however, fall beyond the reach of most Roms, because they either lack access to information about the programs or are based on deeply rooted discriminatory attitudes regarding Romani labor and the fraught histories of Romani and non-Romani economic exchange.

Roms carry the burden of their own economic disparity and are punished, as evidenced by the rise in attacks against Romani migrant workers from Transcarpathia who travel to cities like Lviv and Kyiv in search of work. As Halyna Yurchenko, coordinator of the NGO Roma of Ukraine—Ternipe, states: "Most of the attacks [in 2018] were conducted on vulnerable groups quite below the poverty line and on those who live a traveling lifestyle. This traveling lifestyle is not a tradition but a forced labor migration because of their difficult socio-economic situation."[8]

Jan Grill describes music-begging performances and busking as a migration tactic among adult Romani men from the Slovak-Hungarian-Ukrainian borders who have migrated to Geneva, Switzerland. They play with the Rom-as-musician stereotype and perform on accordion and violin for passersby. Grill observes that practically none of them possesses any musical skills or formal education. They play a limited repertoire and employ a few catchphrases in French and perform in public places like parks and gardens in heavily populated areas. Some Roms perform on trams or try to perform for restaurant patrons, only to be chased away by serving staff (Grill 2011). He recounts:

> From the reactions of the restaurant guests and passersby it was clear that people were variously entertained, moved, indifferent or annoyed by the begging musicians. Some of the restaurants' guests pitied them. Their attention was caught by these seemingly exotic and unknown musicians who, in a thereto unknown way, came right up to the table asking for money and performing. But some of the guests and passersby were also annoyed, ignored their playing, and became offended by the begging migrants. This potential for ignoring reveals something about the social position of these actors in the social hierarchy of Geneva society—poor playing-begging migrants wait, long-suffering, for the non-Roms, and richer, residents of Geneva dining in the restaurants to give them some relatively merciful trifle. It also highlights the clear limits to and paradoxes in their own imaginations. On one hand, through busking the migrants try to reinvent their positions vis-a-vis the dominant societies. They leave homes to escape their position in Slovakia at the bottom of society. On the other hand, it is this clearly asymmetrical relationship between the guests and Romani musicians that seems to reproduce a very similar dependence of Roms on the mercy of the restaurant guests. And yet the Roms choose to migrate with a hope of actively improving their lives. (Grill 2011, 80)

Post-Soviet Villainization of Poverty

In 2012 a young Romani child who was singing for money in a Kyiv metro station was picked up by the police and sent home on the train to

102 RESOUNDING POVERTY

Transcarpathia, his place of origin identified by the song he sang. A child of Romani laborers working as field hands in the agricultural landscapes where large Soviet collective farms once stood, the Romani boy's song was a cascading prayer "*Paniko, pozhalijte mene*" (Dear lady, pity me). A repetitive evocation of pathos and emotion, the boy's song tried to play to the emotions of passersby, the majority of whom ignored him and was framed in narratives of hope. His presence, much like that of most Romani poor, was transitory. He moved from place to place, hopping trains from station to station, in hopes of a coin for his efforts.

Easily dismissed, his song was the public manifestation of private Romani realities at the time. Unable to find jobs in a collapsing and increasingly racist economy, Roms from Transcarpathia were traveling hundreds of kilometers eastward to pick strawberries and sugar beets. (Only a few were able to travel westward into Europe since, unlike neighboring Slovakia, Hungary, Poland, and Romania, Ukraine would not be part of a visa-free travel regime with the European Union until 2019.) Bent over in the hot sun, they stayed away from home for weeks at a time, camping near the fields with their families, only to be paid not in the promised cash but in a portion of the food products they picked; they were forced to be twenty-first-century sharecroppers, much like Lange's "Migrant Mother." Loaded with heavy baskets of strawberries, with their large families in tow, they settled in on the floors of the cheapest railcar, *platskartnyi vahon*, the last car on the train, to sit on old wooden benches, moving into other cars only to sell strawberries to other passengers on the train. It was known to all that no other food was sold on the trains except brewed tea. The sharing of food prepared at home while on the train with neighbors and strangers alike was an expected form of cultural exchange. The songs of Romani children with their hands outstretched for coins were as much part of the soundscape as the deafening rattle of the old Soviet trains, painted blue and yellow in the colors of the flag of the now independent Ukraine.

At the mercy of programs initiated abroad to help Roms via international development programs, the Romani poor, lacking marketable skills, education, and economic agency, are forced to live as invisibles, scapegoats for all that is wrong with the post-Soviet state. Romani homes, often situated on the lower less-desirable ground, are washed away in torrential mud-flows in springtime. Some villages are, in fact, entirely inaccessible in the spring, the roads drowned out beneath them. Wet, muddy, cold, and miserable, Romani realities beyond the mountains ask the question, how much of this can people stand? The songs of begging children depict such images and ask passersby not to ignore their pleas. Gruff answers and a wave of the hand are the most common responses. Children move to the next person and ask again.

The racialization of post-Soviet class identities sheds light on Romani realities in which the Romani poor are villainized. Viewing poverty through the lens of morality fosters rhetoric of victim-blaming that casts life choices into categories of right and wrong, good and bad. Roms, historically stereotyped as wrongdoers throughout centuries of impoverished existence because of their exclusion from local economies, are inherently denied opportunities to advance within a cycle of discrimination that excludes them because they are poor. In other words, Roms, perpetually chided by non-Roms for smelling different, looking different, not studying, not mobilizing economically, not caring for their families, and not living, acting, working the "right" way, have significantly fewer options for altering aspects of their realities because of rhetoric that prevents the establishment of a Romani middle class. Readers may point to the existence of a handful of very wealthy Roms whose materialist gains in the post-Soviet era have been featured in English-language magazines like *National Geographic*.[9] This opulence, however, is exoticized and stigmatized as much as is Romani poverty; racist rhetoric casts doubt on the legality of how such wealth was amassed. Thus, the roots of anti-Romani discrimination lie, in part, in economic exchanges between non-Roms and Roms.[10]

In postsocialist economies, NGOs inadvertently represent the Romani poor as a commodity, one to be consumed by Others through the so-called poverty gaze. This generally uninformed engagement frames perceptions of a person who is assumed to be struggling, a person who is to be pitied, if only for a fleeting second, viewed through scrolls on the Internet, a click away from less emotionally jarring or guilt-evoking feelings. The pictures from the Great Depression heralded the beginnings of classist American engagements with poverty, with relatively new media at the time (photography) used to delineate between the haves and have-nots. It was, after all, those who could afford such technology, or allotted monies for such technologies from the US government, to take pictures of the poor. The poor have had little opportunity to not only document themselves but have been positioned to serve as an inspiration for others. Such forms of objectification, highly critiqued in disability circles of late for parallel exoticizations of people with visible physical handicaps achieving goals, often accompanied through rhetoric that implies that in spite of or despite their handicap, they do what able-bodied persons do.

104   RESOUNDING POVERTY

Such was the common rhetoric at the Conservatory of Music in Lviv where a Romani piano player was studying and her successes acknowledged *in spite of* her ethnic background. As irritatingly racist as such rhetoric may be, it is still the norm and is now countered on a psychological level in Romani families and the classroom of the predominantly Romani school No. 13 in Uzhhorod. Romani students are also now given increasing opportunities to represent themselves through art, sports, and other NGO-sponsored programming. The explosion of the Internet in Ukraine in the last five years has created immeasurable opportunities for new self-narratives, and Romani schoolchildren accessing social media through computers donated by philanthropic organizations now send friend requests worldwide, following the networks of older Roms involved in Romani rights advocacy. The most unique fieldwork aspect of social media usage is perhaps when I, as a forty-something non-Romani professor in the United States, receive friend requests from pre-teen Roms who are encouraged by local Romani leaders to forge international connections.

Such reclaiming of agency falls in line with projects among anthropologists who distribute cameras to children in developing countries to document themselves rather than documented by scholars with means, especially researchers from the West (Grimshaw and Ravetz 2004). I, too, have myriad pictures of children by children who post with hip-hop hand gestures. Letting go of my technology into children's hands has been easier with the advent of smartphones. In the past, my Nikon and Canon cameras, for which I could only purchase the film in the United States (Kodak film was not readily available for purchase in Ukraine during most of my time in the field), were too heavy and too expensive to lend out.[11] Members of the community where I lived knew that I kept my equipment in the Soviet-era refrigerator in the cement-block house I rented from a Romani man working as a migrant laborer in the forestry industry in the Russian tundra.[12] The refrigerator, unplugged, served as the safest place to store my IBM ThinkPad laptop, Sony Hi8 video camera, and Nikon and Canon cameras with telephoto zoom lenses.[13] The roof leaked and the neighbor's emaciated horse often stuck his head through the window of my one-room home, chewing on what he could reach. The refrigerator became the most consistent storage space. I also kept my home unlocked, as was the custom in the community. I was, admittedly, unnerved by the prospect of leaving such equipment in the home when I was away, but Romani neighbors kept watch and often came into the house to bring food they had cooked in exchange for a constant supply of sugar that was a luxury few could afford.

Changes in Romani-related documentation are reflected in the materials produced by Romani NGOs as well. The European Roma Rights Center (ERRC) has expanded its reporting from pictures and text to online videos that allow us to hear the stories of Roms in their own words. Narration in English now allows these videos to reach larger audiences. In Transcarpathia, a Romani-oriented television program *Romano lav* (Romani Voice), once broadcast in Romani and Ukrainian. Once led by Myroslav Horvat, now an Uzhhorod city councilman, *Romano lav* was taken over by Victor Chovka, a Romani journalist who creates videos for the program about events in Transcarpathian Romani communities. Chovka has featured segments on the establishment of Romani youth soccer teams by former professional Romani soccer player Yuri Mandych and the annual Romani jazz festival in Uzhhorod put on by Villie Pap Sr. and Villie Pap Jr. Chovka also creates segments on aspects of Romani cultural traditions and ways of life in Romani communities throughout Transcarpathia, uploading these to social media where they are circulated by Roms with access to the Internet throughout Ukraine. Recently, the videos are reaching an increasingly international audience.

The reclaiming of media narratives about Roms by Roms is central to claims for agency and self-representations. Romani leaders and intellectuals continue to work through various forms of narrative building to represent Roms in a positive light. They are tasked, however, with documenting the realities of those who have suffered for centuries from systemic discrimination. As this chapter has aimed to illustrate, representations of Romani poverty in musical productions, film, photographs, and written text are central to the broader context in which Romani cultural production circulates.

6

Tuning In

"Does it sound in tune?," asks Gogol Pasulka, a middle-aged Romani man in the village of Bilky, Transcarpathia. His eyebrows raised, he leans his body into the guitar and raises it to his left ear. I peer over my video camera, indicating that the video is recording. I zoom the camera onto the guitar. Like the fingers of the man holding it, it too is cracked and worn. The tuning pegs are loose and unable to hold tension in the strings; like errant threads escaped from a hem, they hang limp and slack across the instrument's body. Gogol's emphatic strum emits a twang that sounds like a bang on a can. He takes a wooden match, the tip of which he has been chewing, and sticks it where the upper fret should be. The match moves, and he carefully readjusts it. He strums the guitar again. The instrument sounds loudly, like a clash of cymbals, rich in timbre, but with no discernible pitch.

As the guitar sounds, the children dance, and the women hold each other in pairs, touching upper arms and move four steps to the right, to the left, to the right, to the left, their hips following the direction of their shoulders that twist. The voice of Pasulka, raspy and guttural from years of smoking, soars above the crowd that gathers and a big grin crosses his face. His favorite song is a well-known Russian-language *chastushka*, a ditty with a repetitive melody he learned while serving in the Soviet army. He had bought the guitar while stationed in Vladivostok.

The singer enjoys himself, and his family surrounds and supports him with clapping. *Pidtrymujte, liubit, ne zhalujte!* "Support me, love me, do not hold back," he hollers. Other male musicians join in, on violin, accordion, and a bass drum with an attached cymbal, and the full band is set up the entrance to the brick house, which stands as a reminder of better times when Gogol was employed and earned a steady income under the Soviet regime. Today, he is barely able to scrape by, the deteriorating objects around him connected to the lifestyle he once led.

By now, a crowd of more than fifty people has gathered, especially women and children who are near the houses on this Sunday afternoon.[1] The boys slap their upper arms to fast-moving feet that they bring high into the air,

ReSounding Poverty. Adriana N. Helbig, Oxford University Press. © Oxford University Press 2023.
DOI: 10.1093/oso/9780197631768.003.0007

RESOUNDING POVERTY

snapping their fingers before slapping their shins and thighs to the rhythm. Live music, not often heard in this village, offers a sense of joy and release and bonding, reinforcing relationships with family and neighbors. As the children take over the dance space, crowding out the older dancers, the women retreat to the sides to watch, standing close to one another. One pulls out a pack of cigarettes, and they look on, surrounded by smoke. I pay the musicians for their time, the exchange of money in return for music a relatively infrequent transaction in the village since the fall of the Soviet Union.

Instrumental Identities

Musicians identify closely with their instruments. The instrument can serve as a stand-in qualifier for what the musician does and for who he is— violinist, an accordionist, or *barabanschyk,* drummer, because musical instruments are so central to professional and, by extension, personal identities. Musicians go to great lengths to care for their instruments. Some name their instruments or speak of them as they would to a person they love. The instrument is not only a source of potential income; it is an extension of status, family name, and personhood.

Musicians invest money in the upkeep and tuning of instruments, adding to what the instrument needs to produce music to the extent that the musician can afford to do so. Keeping instruments in playable condition requires time and money for upkeep. It also requires a living or storage space that ensures the elements will not damage an instrument —that it will withstand heat, humidity, dampness, and raw living conditions.[2] Instruments that are kept under less-than-ideal conditions are in danger of undergoing a slow process of degeneration, becoming brittle, cracking, breaking. Like bodies that age and move into different states of ability, instruments have lifelines and sound worlds that are (in)accessible at various stages. The instrument emanates what it soaks in. It takes on the harshness of the environment, the heat of the summer and the dampness of winter cold, having also marinated in that which makes old bones creak. It breaks and snaps and bellows and sighs. Its shape altered by forces beyond its control, it is unable to fend off the forces that unwind its screws, cracks its belly, and peel off its lacquer finish, strip by strip. It is saved from discard because it cannot be replaced, not necessarily because of what it is or what it means to the player, but by the owner's sheer lack of ability to purchase a new one. Unable to be refurbished, sold, or substituted by a newer, better, more precise instrument, the worn guitar sticks around, emoting what it can, offering, patching, engaging how it can. It serves as a metaphor for life in this region where people go without and put to creative reuse. A concern of all musicians who use instruments to produce sound, the fate of instruments is of *central* concern in conditions of poverty wherein the physical bodies of both instrument and performer change in response to the lack of adequate care.

The challenge of producing sound on instruments that are broken, cracked, infused with humidity, or suffering from dryness is familiar to anyone who has inherited an instrument from a family member or friend who had not kept the instrument in optimal conditions. This chapter gives voice to such experiences and shares the feelings that musicians have about their instruments as they go through various stages of disrepair and discard. It engages with ongoing conversations in organology by asking us to consider our imaginings of instrumental ideals (Rognoni 2019). Through the lens of anticipation, failure, and desire, this chapter engages with ideas of the attained and the unattainable in music through an emotionally rich discourse on what it means for an instrument to be tuned, untuned, or out of tune. Using the trope of "tuning in," it focuses metaphorically and ethnographically on how musicians relate to instruments in disarray, brought to such a state, in part, by the economic difficulties they face every day. With what state of an instrument's existence do we engage when we speak of an instrument being in tune? Instruments, as objects, embody characteristics that parallel human body conditions. In contexts in which health issues guide engagements with the outside world, the dis/abilities of instruments to produce sounds take primary precedence over the types of sounds they produce. In other words, this chapter focuses on how musicians and their listeners alter realities of listening within broader performance aesthetics to hear possibilities of sound in contexts that silence the Romani poor, whether physically through processes of marginalization and metaphorically through physical destruction and decay. It uses musical tuning as a metaphor for development discourse and gives space to the anxieties that surround the production of sound in contexts in which producing sound is not easy. This analysis sets up the narrative for Chapter 7, where such discourses are extended to the physical body and highlight how illness shapes Romani voices. Chapter 8 gives space to (re)sounding emotional (in)abilities to engage with the constant stress of living under such conditions.

Sounds of Silence

Saman houses have little insulation and no heat. The wooden roofs, with gaping holes, let the bitter drenching rain seep onto the cold, muddy floor. The windows have no glass—they are covered with cellophane or plastic. The bricks, cracked and settled, let the howling winds through the one-story, one-room dwelling, often a home for more than twenty people. In households that can afford it, big machine-spun carpets purchased at the *bazaar* hang on the walls to block out the Carpathian cold. The bitter dampness chills to the bone, with only brief respite offered by the fire at the center of the home: the fire that fills the home with heat and smoke.

Guitars, accordions, violins, and drums live alongside the people who own them. Instruments are susceptible to fluctuations in weather. A rise or drop in humidity warps wood and affects an instrument's ability to hold tension. Instruments are stored out of the way, alongside walls, often absorbing even more humidity than they might if they were closer to a consistent heat source. Others, especially violins that are exposed to the elements, not protected by cases, hang on the wall. Violins are especially vulnerable in such contexts because the strings, much like that of the guitar that begins this chapter, must be tuned with pegs.

Similarly to the guitar, they cannot hold the tension, leading to multiple stops to tune during moments of play. The vast majority of Roms in the Transcarpathian region do not have the expendable income to rent halls for events; consequently, the vast majority of activities that include music takes place outside, at least in the summer months. Thus, the state of the instrument becomes worse and worse, falling more deeply into disrepair and, states of disability. Rarely are such instruments thrown out, however. Instead, they are held, as if in remembrance of their imagined sonic past. Their sounds are referred to through their imagined beauty and the emotions associated with playing it and hearing it performed.

When did such instruments enter circulation among Roms living in such difficult conditions? Much like the carpets that hang on the wall, they were purchased during Soviet times, when objects considered today to be unattainable luxuries were once produced cheaply and could be traded or purchased in the outdoor markets that were once the center of rural trade.[3] To buy an instrument today would involve traveling to a town with a Soviet-era music store that was privatized and managed to stay in business through the sheer monopoly of having been the only musical instrument store in town. Specific instrument-making factories have managed to transition from socialist to postsocialist economies successfully.

The quality of Soviet-era instruments was never good, to begin with. Soviet instrument makers produced massive amounts of budget instruments that made ownership feasible for even those with the most meager jobs. In an economic system that touted employment for all, musicians could afford to buy the instruments they wished. The most commonly circulating instruments in Transcarpathia were accordions, violins, and guitars. Romani men from rural areas served in the Soviet army and, like Gogol Pasulka, brought back instruments upon their return. Some inherited or received instruments from older family members or community members who were no longer playing them. The passing along of instruments was, in large part, a way through which musicians learned, entertained, and taught others in their community. In the first harsh years of the post-Soviet transition, many Roms sold their instruments at *bazaars*, often, sadly, to non-Roms, to make ends meet. This action took a particular instrument out of rotation and stopped a specific repertoire from being heard or performed, effectively preventing it from being passed on to the next generation.

The grinding halt to which the collapsing Soviet economy was brought affected even the most mundane aspects of life. Even the replacement of a broken guitar string became a near-impossible feat that, if attempted, usually involved numerous failed attempts over long periods. Since music stores had been owned by the state and had retained that status in the first years of independence, the supply chain became unreliable, the goods scarce. If a store owner had a package of strings to sell, they were willing to sell only one string at a time, knowing that this was the upper limit that most customers could afford. The sale of one string, however, meant that a complete package of strings was rarely available. Travel between rural and urban areas became increasingly difficult as well. Soviet-era buses were beginning to break down, so a full day of travel to purchase that single string could result in no string at all because it had already been sold as a single string from an already-opened package to somebody else.

Traveling from place to place, either by train, Soviet-era car, bicycle, or on foot, I traveled across Transcarpathia, moving from place to place searching for musicians.[4] I often arrived at a Romani village early in the morning, my sneakers caked in mud, carrying a backpack with cameras and video equipment and some food gifts, with hopes of meeting musicians before they left the village to run errands or to work in the woods or fields, to catch fish, or to

112   RESOUNDING POVERTY

sell wares. It often took more than an hour to walk from the local train station or bus stop. Sometimes I hitchhiked, only to be scolded for hitchhiking by the person that offered me a ride. Everything took time. My efforts often resulted in dead ends. Many Romani houses stood empty, and I found few people with whom I could speak. Villagers would share that local Romani musicians had died but that perhaps the Romani musician is still alive in the neighboring village. Arriving, in one case, minutes before a Romani musician's death, I came to realize that I was bearing witness to an end of an era of music-making in the villages. Younger family members were not learning the songs because in a time marked by hyperinflation, music, and entertainment stopped being a viable way to make a living. Many older musicians were too ill to play their instruments. Often I was encouraged to move further, to the next village higher in the mountains, even more inaccessible, only to find that there had never been any instrumental musicians in that village and that those who had played for a wedding there a few years ago had come from yet another village further away. I would move on to the next village, and the process would begin anew. After months of such attempts, I came to realize that I would not find that which I had hoped, groups of musicians in each village that I could interview and record. It was only through the revisits of my ethnographic material years later that I realized that the story was more about the absence of music or about the memory of music that was. Thus, the imagining of music and the acceptance of musical realities, like the match stuck in the broken guitar to retain pitch, forms a central tenet of the second half of this book, one that associates the sounds of music with the potential for an emotional release that they bring.

Field/work as Failure

Engagements with broken instruments and the inability to tune them shape ways of being that allow for feelings of anticipation, desire, and disappointment. In contexts where so few things "work" in terms of everyday infrastructures, how people allow themselves to engage with failure directly impacts their health and well-being. To allow oneself to feel disappointment when something does not go one's way is to acknowledge that one dared to believe in a reality beyond that which might be possible. That hope of achieving something is both a tantalizing dream that drives people to alter realities as much as it reinforces and augments feelings of frustration and anxiety. In a postsocialist system, where the success of outcomes depends not on a person's work ethic but on a person's ability to network through a complex system of corruption reinforces feelings of relief when something works the way it should but keeps people in a state of not getting their hopes up. This feeling of constant stress and anxiety, a difficult context to work in, let alone live in every day, gets compounded by a never-ending cycle of daily hardship. It is only through kinship and friend networks that people survive in a system of reciprocity, known commonly as *blat*. To achieve or receive something *po blatu* means invoking a system of favors through a broad network of people who are constantly and consistently involved in helping each other with access to food, medicine, cash, and other necessities. This network, the primary way people were able to procure much-needed goods in the Soviet Union where products and wares were often scarce, has continued to serve as a primary exchange network in the post-Soviet era. This system, albeit effective, sets into play a system of favors upon which the economy rests. In other words, favors, akin to bribes, create similar ways of being and doing and keep the flow of goods moving in good faith. The *oligarch* culture, albeit operating on a much larger scale, is rooted in the *blat* system that led certain groups to exploit the economic vulnerabilities of the failing Soviet and fledgling post-Soviet state and forced the majority to rely even more on *blat* as a way to maintain access to basic human needs. That Roms have been increasingly pushed into an ethnic corner of the *blat* network that once transcended ethnicity reveals that high corruption has contributed to increased divisions of post-Soviet society in terms of ethnicity and race.

The inability to alter one's material realities within a broader system marred by political and economic corruption is perceived as failure. People who perceive the system at face value are recognized as not being able to move forward. The system offers possibilities for advancement only if a citizen acknowledges that it is corrupt and engages with the corruption. Black market dealings, bribes, and entrepreneurial law-bending activities are the norm, and one's choice to engage in such dealings delineates those who can move beyond the realities that the system sets up. For Roms, the danger in dealing with the system is framed by the realities of blame, where corruption, when caught, is attributed to this group first. Thus, the responsibility is doubled for Roms, to engage with corruption and not get caught and, additionally, to not carry the burden for others engaging with corruption.

Queer theories on failure, as perceived within capitalist, heteronormative context, imply that systems are porous and not all-consuming with power—there are ways to work around and through them (Halberstam 2011, 88). In other words, queer theories of failure allow for alternative narratives to conventional narratives of success. Augmenting Halberstam's theory of failure to consider contexts where failure is deemed inevitable for everyone in a narrative of a "broken" system, the post-Soviet context repositions failure as the norm. Failure is ground zero in a system where everything is perceived to work against the wishes of the people. The goal is less to succeed but, instead, not to make things worse for oneself than they already are. This key difference goes against the Western ideology that frames discourses of development. The Western way is to rebuild, improve, push forward, and achieve. The Western way is to "fix" a broken system rather than merely accept realities and attempt to survive in it. However, in a postsocialist frame of mind, we have just that—an acceptance of stark realities, especially among the poor who do not engage with system-altering discourses that have framed political upheavals of late. The peaceful protests, cyber-based social movements, and violent revolutions have not followed romanticized overthrows of governments by the most marginalized. Revolutions are charted by the political, economic, and cultural elites who work with Western governments, NGOs, and cyber-connected actors to place demands on the "broken" system that allow their interests to move forward.

Ukraine's postsocialist revolutions, including the 2004 Orange Revolution and the 2014 Revolution of Dignity, reinforce the notion that the post-Soviet system remains broken. It continues to serve the interests of those in power aligned with the state. The main difference is that while the state is still perceived as not working for the better good of the people, the people believe they have the power to change it. While common among Soviet citizens, this belief was not articulated as clearly beyond the small group who indulged in a postcolonial dream of independence from the Soviet Union. Herein lies the crux of development shortcomings. The post-Soviet revolutions, romanticized online as pushing forward the will of the people, are movements that push forward the interests of those in power. The marginalized do not travel to the capital city to protest; in fact, they do not participate in the political process at all. Few Roms, for instance, have passports and documents with which to vote and have few opportunities to connect to broader narratives that frame their realities. This failure is systemic and entraps the Romani poor in a cyclical renewal of disenfranchised realities.

As systems change and market forces are introduced in formerly socialist economies, the poor are left to fend for themselves in both contexts. Already vulnerable in a socialist state, despite alleged access to free healthcare, housing, and employment, the Romani poor cannot leap into postsocialist market economies because postsocialist transition "succeeded" based on skewed principles of privatization. The goods people used during the socialist era became theirs to own in the postsocialist era. In other words, the dwelling people had in the socialist period became private ownership (to use or to sell) under postsocialism.[5] This imbalance brings forward the issue of equity with which one entered the burgeoning market economy. Because the socialist system was not as equal as it purported itself to be, many Roms were introduced to the system with significantly fewer advantages than non-Roms. Romani villages, especially in regions under former Austro-Hungarian rule, were established well before Soviet rule. Many are on arid soil and in floodplains, land deemed undesirable by local populations. The villages are also far away from larger towns and are not connected through infrastructure. The lack of electricity, running water, and the lack of access to transportation networks bring the question of equity center stage. In other words, postsocialist housing privatization processes were guided by the thought that the housing people were given to alleviate the housing shortage after World War II would become theirs rightfully following the collapse of the state to which everything belonged. Roms became owners of low-income housing in out-of-the-way regions, similar to what was described in the excerpt described by Ivan Franko in the short story *Tsyhany* (The Gypsies) (1882) in Chapter 4. Development programs allegedly offer a step in class advancement, allowing, in theory, for people to use the structure to improve their financial standing through access to education, healthcare, and political representation. However, considering the centuries of inequity that still determine Romani realities today, it is not possible to resolve such structurally predetermined systems of failure with development grants alone.

A closer analysis of tunings sheds light on how such inequities play out in musical terms and how a closer listening to the language of in-tuneness offers insights into broader social and political framings of inter-ethnic exchange in the post-Soviet context. The latter half of the chapter focuses on how the Soviet state worked to tune the ethnic makeup of the republics and how the language of in-tuneness foregrounds itself in post-Soviet politics. Examples ranging from Putin's music-laden political discourse to the tuning of instruments on the stages of politically framed folk revival festivals reveal

116   RESOUNDING POVERTY

that the anxieties surrounding pitch and tuning, as well as an instrument's ability to stay in tune, are closely tied with discourses of class fluency that frame sociocultural, economic, and political negotiations for power and influence in the post-Soviet sphere.

The Politics of In-Tuneness

On May 14, 2017, while waiting to meet with Chinese president Xi Jinping, Russian president Vladimir Putin was filmed playing two melodies on a grand piano: "Evening Song," a popular melody in St Petersburg (the song's lyrics refer to the city by its Soviet-era name, Leningrad), and "Moscow Windows," a song about friendship. When Putin was ridiculed for his renditions in the Western media for their technical inadequacy, he responded by saying, "It is a pity that the piano was out of tune."[6]

Putin has been known to express political ideas through music. He participated in the hip-hop "Battle for Respect" on Russian television in 2009. Since then, the government has initiated crackdowns on hip-hop musicians, detaining a rapper named Husky and canceling concerts across the country.[7] He also spoke in support of Russia not participating in the 2017 Eurovision song contest hosted in Kyiv after a Crimean Tatar singer, Jamala, won the 2016 contest with her song about the 1942 Soviet expulsion of Crimean Tatars from Crimea.[8] In light of a history of comments on music, Putin's remark on the Chinese president's piano could be seen as more than a justification of his poor piano-playing skills, especially since a piano can be played even when out of tune. More than other Western instruments, the piano draws on a long history of political use in the Soviet Union. At the height of the Cold War, the piano served as an essential symbol through which Soviet cultural policy engaged with the West (Tomoff 2015). It was, after all, on a piano that, in 1959, US-born pianist Van Cliburn won the inaugural International Tchaikovsky Competition in Moscow.

A tempered instrument, the piano constitutes the twelve pitches and intervals to which the myriad of musical folk traditions practiced throughout the vast Soviet empire were tuned (Olson 2004). Newly formed folk choirs practiced to piano accompaniment, altering pitches that had once formed the basis of local identities. Tempered tunings signified the Soviet modern and served as a way to gain cultural status in a world that, at the time, engaged primarily with the Western tempered tuning imposed by colonial networks. Russian émigrés fleeing the fallen Russian empire had augmented the piano's upper-class sensibilities in Chinese society (Kraus 1989). Under Mao's Cultural Revolution, Western instruments like the piano were recast as bourgeois and forbidden (Xiao-Mei 2012). Thus, the piano in President Xi Jinping's residency is not merely an instrument for playing pleasure. It functions as an intentional symbol of power, status, modernity, and Westernization. Putin's comment about the piano's alleged out-of-tuneness could thus be interpreted as an intentional power move infused with political critique.

An instrument's ability to sustain Western tempered tuning carried political connotations in the Soviet Union. Consider Vladimir Vysotsky's (1959–1980) out-of-tune guitar. The bard accompanied himself with a sharp strumming style on an out-of-tune *semy-strunnaya gitara* (seven-string guitar) at performances in universities, in apartments at private parties, and open spaces. His music, a metaphoric critique of the Soviet system, circulated among the masses via homemade reel-to-reel and cassette tape recordings called *magnitizdat* (Kind-Kovács and Labov 2013). The hoarseness of his voice and the dissonance produced by his guitar carried his message of opposition. Vysotsky used the boundaries of tonality and tuning to vocalize his distrust of and disgust with the political system (Tsenova 1998).[9]

The push to modernize sound production led to new musical instruments like the ANS synthesizer (Schmeltz 2009b).[10] Synthesizers were analog and built from materials found in Soviet nuclear power plants or procured from KGB agents that worked in communications.[11] These synthesizers played an essential role in pushing forth Soviet-era popular music, broadening timbral aesthetics, and allowing musicians and composers to experiment with pitch variation. Dissonance, intentional or accidental, was disapproved by Soviet cultural elites. The Soviet Composers' Union was tightly monitored, and musicians took great risks when incorporating new techniques and aesthetics of dissonance. The scholarship on dissonance, however, has omitted one crucial factor—an analysis of the physical state instruments upon which music in the Soviet Union was performed.

Instruments that could produce dissonance were hailed for their modernity but viewed as suspect for their alleged role in facilitating anti-state cultural expression. Musicological literature overstates Soviet state's disapproval of dissonance in composing music because it does not consider dissonance the dominant aesthetic that framed music-making. The low quality of Soviet instruments produced the out-of-tuneness they intended to regulate. As the

118 RESOUNDING POVERTY

analysis in the following section shows, it was the dissonance, the out-of-tuneness of rural music-making, that the Soviet state found distasteful and woefully unmodern. Moreover, it was the angst of the village and all that it symbolized—close ties to the land, to community, and local identities—that the Soviets aimed to uproot. In other words, in the Soviet imaginary, the village needed to be re-tuned.

Re-Tuning the Village

The Soviet government instituted Houses of Culture in rural areas to draw in rural musicians to participate in choirs and ensembles associated with local factories, communal farms, schools, and village centers (Noll 1994; Slobin 1996). The first among the instruments to be reappropriated was the *balalaika*, a triangular plucked lute with three strings once used by peasants in the Russian Empire to accompany songs against the Tsar (Chlebak 2015). It was, in fact, illegal to own a *balalaika* because of the instrument's anti-Tsarist connotations. Those who performed on it risked punishment by authorities, whereas the *balalaika*'s anti-Tsarist associations were welcomed by Soviet leaders who came to power after the 1917 Russian Revolution. The *balalaika* became an instrument of Soviet unification, and schoolchildren were encouraged to learn to play it and its accompanying melodic counterpart, the *domra*, a rounded plucked lute. In such a way, top-down musical policies emanating from Moscow reshaped and reframed the musical aesthetics of the new Soviet collective (Olson 2004).[12]

Among Ukrainian peasants, instruments like the *bandura*, a plucked lute associated with epic singing, were censored in their traditional modes but were remodeled for the Soviet stage. A complicated system of tuning restructured the *bandura* from the twenty-stringed diatonically tuned *starosvitskaya* (old-style) *bandura* to the chromatically tuned concert *bandura* with sixty-eight strings (Mishalow 2013). The inability of a folk instrument to retain chromatic pitch and to match pitch with orchestral sounds rendered it useless in the Soviet system. The Ukrainian *bandura* was reconstructed and rebranded as a stage instrument. Its original repertoire of religious epic songs was forbidden, and the instrument served to accompany light-hearted repertoires composed in a Western tonal language (Kononenko 1998, 2019). While instrument makers were successful in their reconstruction of the *bandura*, albeit rendering it a physically heavy instrument that required years of professional training to master, Russian folk instruments like the *domra* and *balalaika* were constructed in various sizes—the emphasis on chromaticism allowed for classical repertoires to be performed. The tuning process was made difficult by the complications placed on instruments not structured to handle such a range. For instance, the diatonic *bandura* is tuned by turning individual wooden or metal pegs at either the top or the bottom of the instrument. Some *banduras* also have switch mechanisms that can be used to alter the instrument's tuning chromatically during a performance. These instruments are very susceptible to humidity and do not keep their pitch for long. They are constantly re-tuned during performance.

Tuning charts, such as those that accompany the Hungarian-style *cimbalom*, emphasize a folk instrument's ability to maintain standardized tunings.[13] Concert versions of folk instruments emphasized a broader range of pitches and a chromatic scale that allowed Soviet musicians to perform classical repertoires. *Cimbaloms* were so popular that they were produced in factories in Chernihiv and Kamianets-Podilsky, Ukraine, and Kişinău, Moldova, from the 1960s to the late 1980s.[14] The concert *cimbalom* developed by master piano maker Jozsef Schunda in 1874 in Budapest, Hungary, was closer in its range of pitch, dynamic projection, and weight to the proportions of a small piano than to the various folk hammered dulcimers that had been ubiquitous before the *cimbalom*'s arrival on the scene. The Schunda *cimbalom* was equipped with a heavier frame for more stability and dynamic power. It included many more strings for extended range and incorporated a damper pedal to provide more dynamic control. Four detachable legs were added to support this much larger instrument. The concert *cimbalom* became popular within the Austro-Hungarian Empire and was used by diverse ethnic groups within the country including Hungarian, Jewish, and Ukrainian (Hutsul) and Romani musicians. The emphasis on notation reflected the push to move the instrument out of the realm of the folk into the realm of the classical. Music conservatories offering parallel instruction in classical instrument performance and folk instrument performance reflected such politics of sound.[15]

Tuning Anticipation

Instruments hold the promise of sonic potential, with some offering promise of better sounds than others to the musically and culturally trained ear.

120 RESOUNDING POVERTY

Their pitches elucidate a sonic framing of the physical status they embody. Instruments call attention to themselves as objects of artistry that carry various meanings—whether as a remembrance of function in original context or as an appropriation of new intentions. Whether on stage, on display in a glass case, or as simulacra of themselves in scholarly publications, musical instruments evoke an embodied anticipation of sound. Anticipation understood as a chain of complex socioemotional and psychological projections and feelings triggered concerning encounters with familiar and unfamiliar signs is overlooked as a subject of sonic research.[16] How, though, can we disregard those feelings of excitement when we watch a performer tune an instrument, readying it to make music for our listening pleasure?

Phenomenologist Edmund Husserl accounts for feelings of anticipation. Even if we do not know what is going to happen, we develop expectations. Instruments, as signs, carry the promise of sonic beauty, and that it is this potential capability (i.e., the memory of an instrument in our previous experiences as well as our imaginings of what it might sound like) that causes us to relate to the instrument as the potential sound object in a particular way. If we accept the premise that all instruments can produce sounds, how might we begin to think about instruments in disarray—old, broken, or improperly cared for and mishandled? What might be gleaned from the discourse surrounding such instruments and the sounds they produce among musicians and their audiences? To what extent does an instrument's potential to produce one sound but, in fact, make another (or to make no sound at all) destabilize expectations of the instrument as a potential sound object? As cognitive psychologist Alexander Riegler explains, "Rather than get overwhelmed by the details of a new situation, humans seek to replace them with familiar activity and behavioral patterns that show a high degree of predictability to putatively gain control again, to be able to anticipate the outcome" (Riegler 2003, 12). In other words, whether we encounter a guitar, an iPod,* or a sound mixing board, our imaginations anticipate the potential of sound. The physical parameters and limits of the instrument as an object determine how and what kind of music will be made. We anticipate the sound that has yet to be produced.

This type of acoustic conditioning has been explored in numerous ethnomusicological studies. In analyzing cassette culture in India, Peter Manuel shares how his interlocutors prefer the sound of old, worn-out analog cassette recordings to more acoustically pristine recordings of the same music (Manuel 1993). Such is the case now with the return to vinyl recordings in the

United States. The process of acoustic degeneration is gradual. Through years of wear and deterioration, the listener is conditioned into a state of sonic acceptance; the recording was clear and crisp when the cassette was purchased (or when the mixtape was made), and the wear that produces the degeneration of the physical medium of the tape itself is indicative in itself of the fact that the owner listened to it, rewound it, fast-forwarded it, and listened again countless times.[17] Analyses of instrumental tunings and timbres tend to speak of the instrument in its optimal condition, rather than considering the nostalgia that imperfections can evoke in recordings. All sound-producing mechanisms are incorporated into performance because of their abilities to produce the desired sound.[18]

When used by musicians in the West who play Romani repertoires, older instruments imply that the instrumentalist, like the instrument itself, is experienced and brings some cultural and musical knowledge and prestige to the stage. Likewise, as in the case of an old Stradivarius violin, there is a cultural anticipation on the part of the audience; there is a sense of nostalgia, a reverence for the history, a connection to "the old country" that might have nothing to do with the actual provenance of the instrument or its player.

An old instrument differs significantly from a broken instrument. A broken instrument tends not to be the *desired* instrument. It would be extremely rare for repertoires to require to be played on a broken instrument. A broken instrument is approached with hesitation and guessing. It is not known what type of sound a broken instrument can produce. There is no way a performer or listener can tell what the instrument will sound like without, perhaps, recognizing what part of the instrument is not in optimal condition. A broken instrument can also become broken in a time of war. We relate differently to such an instrument, holding on to it as a way to remember, its silence a way to connect to the sounds of the past. This may be similar to holding on to outdated technological music media that one no longer has the means to play.

Some instruments can be readily identified as being in disarray. A cracked reed on a clarinet, for instance, is a sure indicator that the instrument will squeak and honk like an asthmatic goose. The worn paddings on a saxophone may draw the player to recognize that the instrument may not cooperate in pitch production. An open seam at the back of a violin, viola, cello, or bass will keep the instrument from projecting. However, it is not until the player uses the instrument that any assumptions are actually contradicted or confirmed.

122   RESOUNDING POVERTY

An instrument can also gradually lose its ability to work as the player wishes. In the case of a piano that loses its tuning over time, a musician may become accustomed to the sound and work with what the instrument can produce. A few years ago, a colleague teaching at a conservatory wished to improve her economic situation by collecting glass bottles and submitting them to recycling points throughout the city for reimbursement. One evening, too tired to take the bottles home, she hid them in the base of an upright piano. Forgetting about them the next day, she was horrified to find the piano being used in a concert rehearsal. The students were so conditioned to the sounds of the piano that nobody opened the piano to see why the timbre of the piano had changed. Since the piano was known to be out of tune and with a hollow sound that often results from a cracked soundboard, the relatively worse-sounding tones that emanated from the ersatz recycling bin were assumed to have signaled the next step in the instrument's degeneration.

The Emotions of Tuning

Instruments are referenced through languages of love and imageries of the soul, believed to be an extension of the person who plays it.[19] The search for the ideal offers a glimpse into sonic desire, the search for that which fulfills and brings satisfaction upon attainment. As instruments are known for going out of tune, this continuous search for that which is always a step away moves one forward in the search for fulfillment. The brief attainment of what sounds pleasing and good adds to pleasure dimensions when an instrument is played. Knowing what was and the ideal that is accepted, held, and produced offers reprieve and release, both aural and emotional.

All instruments need tuning. From adjusting a mouthpiece to turning a peg, the tuning process is as vital to the performance as the talent, training, and dexterity to play the notes the player intends. Much emphasis is placed on achieving and maintaining desired tunings, including tuning devices and apparatuses such as humidity cases believed to help maintain an instrument's pitch. The whole business, one might say, of achieving and maintaining tuned pitch focuses on the attainment of an ideal and of something that involves work to create. There is a belief that such a state is, in fact, achievable, and this establishes the frame through which sound relays meaning. According to the system in question, so much is tied into the state of tuning that something that is out of tune is perceived to be incorrect, irritating, and indicative of a lack of training or talent on the part of the musician. The Ukrainian word *rozstrojena*, meaning un-tuned, or having lost tuning, is the same word used to describe the emotional state of disappointment. Such examples show that something being tuned or un-tuned is akin to an altered state of physical or emotional being.

We tune into and out of perceptions of pitch through our expectations for particular sounds. At what point do we accept the limits of an instrument's in-tuneness and accept degrees of pitch variability? Are such decisions cultural, or are they accepted out of necessity? On a piano, for instance, where the player cannot tune the instrument "on the fly" and without professional training, the musician might choose to play on an instrument in its present state with the idea that the pitch variation is not a reflection of skill and that the audience will know this. The piano and pipe organ are perhaps the only exceptions in terms of our ready acceptance of untuned instruments since, unlike most other musicians, pianists and organists cannot transport their instruments to every performance. The player knows that their playing will sound better on a better instrument in the future, thus perhaps ignoring some of the inaccuracies endured on an instrument in disarray. A particularly poignant example of this type of case is the scene from Roman Polansky's 2002 film *The Pianist* based on the memoir *The Pianist* (1946) written by the Polish-Jewish pianist and composer Władysław Szpilman, a Holocaust survivor. Szpilman had worked as a pianist on Polish Radio until the Germans invaded Poland in 1939. Saved from the train to Treblinka, Szpilman survived in increasingly destroyed Warsaw, moving from one bombed building to another. In the winter of 1945, Szpilman, who is played by Adrien Brody in the film, is discovered in an empty building by an SS officer who asks him his profession. Szpilman answers, "I am . . . I was a pianist." The SS officer takes him to the dust-covered grand piano with a visibly broken key. To save his life, Szpilman knows he must perform, the terror of the moment framed in the irony of playing the piano for a Nazi after hiding in silence for so long. The perception of pitch and ability to play is critical in this moment because they will determine whether the officer will let him live. The pianist must "move" the listener to an emotional state that will rekindle his human spirit amid the cruelty of war. The perception of in- or out-of-tuneness in this scene for Szpilman's audience (the SS officer), and the viewing audience, is couched in anxiety and surprise because we can only hope that Szpilman, emaciated, can still play after three years of traumatic survival. In the beginning of the scene, the pitches sound tentative and contrast with the confident style that characterized his playing in earlier parts of the film. To authenticate the experience, the piano's pitches sound hollow and flat. This contrasts with the official soundtrack, which features a precise rendition of music by Polish composer Frédéric Chopin (1810–1849).[20] Thus, while watching the film, our visual and emotional cues associate the potential playing with a sense of potential failure, that it will not live up to specific standards, and we are relieved when it does. When it sounds "good," we know that the pianist will live. Our aural and visual associations influence our perception of the instrument's physical state, and we hope for the best.

Tuning as Agency

To return to the ethnographic vignette that opened this chapter, Gogol Pasulka, the Romani guitarist who tuned his broken guitar in front of me, knew how to work with it. The guitar was *semy-strunnaja* (seven-stringed), tuned, in theory, on an open G—DGBDGbd—similar to the guitars that have accompanied Romani singers throughout the Russian Empire. He stuck a match where the missing fret should be. As he strummed, the match moved, creating warbling sounds. The musician moved the guitar up and down, rubbing it against his stomach to soften some additional twang. He had played it many times before and met the instrument at its present condition. Was his concern regarding tune-ness for my sake? Did he want to be sure I could understand the pitches of the melody as he intended it, meaning as he heard it in his memory, more than how it sounded in the sonic reality? For Gogol, sensitivities to audience response tend to guide interactions with tunings. Audiences draw on prejudices about nomadism and assume (incorrectly) that since Roms have (allegedly) not stayed in one place long enough to enroll in school, they have neither education nor training. They think of musical skill as a natural trait, passed down genetically from father to son, and not one learned in school. However, those who have completed the rigorous training of the rural Soviet-era music schools read musical notation. They are also fluent in Western music theory and use Russian terminology to describe chord progressions, rhythmic patterns, tempo markings, and aspects of performance practice. These terms signal a language replacement among Romani musicians, from an *emic* (insider) communication style to one now framed by non-Romani musical sensibilities.

In the Soviet Union, great emphasis was placed on altering rural aural aesthetics to reflect the musical desires of urban populations. Musicians were trained in classical repertoire in *muzychni uchylyscha*, musical high schools, that specialized in artistic performance, music education, and music theory. Following Khrushchev's decree of 1956 that made nomadism illegal, large numbers of Roms were moved into urban housing projects at the edges of towns.[21] Though the provision of educational opportunities for Roms was not a high priority within the Soviet school system, a high percentage of male Romani children were accepted into music schools based on talent. Romani children received musical education that included theory, composition, arranging, and performance. A curricular division between rural traditional and urban repertoires set the stage for Romani musicians graduating with knowledge of classical repertoire rendered on instruments deemed proletarian. The training of Romani male children in such schools also stemmed, at least in part, from historical and cultural stereotypes of Roms as natural musicians. Unfortunately, even those who would have wished to study other topics in more depth were sent to music classes; even those with inclinations toward the sciences were assumed to be capable "only" of music. In some village schools, even as late as the 2000s, where teachers either lacked the resources or simply did not want to put in the effort to bring Romani students up to the same level of academic work as other students, Romani students were placed in separate classes that focused on music and dance. Musicians like Gogol who received such formal musical education (*muzychna osvita*) take this professional training very seriously and reference it to highlight their level of education. The idea behind such schools was to make the musical tastes of the *bourgeoisie* accessible to the proletariat. Young men from rural Romani communities enrolled in rural music schools learned extensive music theory, educated in Soviet performance aesthetics that emphasized professionalism, skill, and virtuosity. This very significant difference between rural and urban Romani musicians flips the narrative that one might assume regarding the skills that emerge from rural/urban musical training.

The *Gogol Bordello* Factor

In the 2006 documentary film titled *Pied Piper of Hützovina*, featuring Eugene Hütz from Gogol Bordello, American filmmaker Pavla Fleisher captures moments of Hütz's symbolic "return" to his sonic inspirations in Transcarpathia. Hütz presents himself in interviews as having come from a *Servy* family near Kyiv, Ukraine. Through the depictions of his "return" to

126 RESOUNDING POVERTY

Romani settlements in Transcarpathia, home to groups of Roms that differ culturally, musically, and linguistically from *Servy* in central and eastern Ukraine, his musical upbringing did not include Romani-influenced music making. Gogol Bordello's punk style might best be described as a form of postmodern cabaret that fuses the hard-edged, anti-establishment aesthetics characteristic of punk music with eclectic costuming that ranges from Soviet-era military hats to belly-dancing scarves and striped pants in the style of court jesters. Notions of the "Old World" are embodied in Hütz's persona—he speaks with an accent, has a gold tooth, and presents himself as a cross between a village bumpkin and the poster-child for the postmodern citizen of the world. One of Hütz's biggest draws is that he manages to diffuse the information about his exact ethnic roots. Born in Kyiv, Ukraine, he was displaced because of the Chernobyl catastrophe and lived with his family for three years in refugee camps in Austria, Italy, Poland, and Hungary before arriving in New York in 1999. He uses such stories for marking himself as a person who has no specific roots in any one place but feels and acts at home everywhere. In many ways, Hütz presents himself as an itinerant "Gypsy," a term he embraces and superimposes onto his immigrant identity in the United States.

In the documentary, Roms in a Transcarpathian village have gathered to welcome Hütz in their home, and Hütz plays for them on an acoustic guitar with a broken nylon string. The Romani host, eager to try the guitar, repeatedly states that one cannot "properly" play on a guitar with a broken string. On one level, his consciousness about "proper" playing positions non-Romani tonalities as normative. In this way, his talk about the inadequacies of the instrument highlights his understanding of music in a way that correlates with non-Romani understandings. His playing is virtuosic, and an unsuspecting listener might not recognize that the guitar was missing a string.

I focus on this exchange between the Romani host and Hütz because it brings us back to one of the themes of this book, namely whose repertoires constitute contemporary categories of Romani music? Hütz popularized the genre of "Gypsy-punk" music by fusing various traditional and popular musical elements. His musical interpretations of Romani music have returned to Ukraine via Gogol Bordello's performances in Kyiv and via connections with musicians who participated in the 2004 Orange Revolution and the 2014 Revolution of Dignity. His music has spurred a great interest among Ukrainian audiences in so-called Gypsy music and a growing number of non-Rom musicians are drawing on traditional Romani genres in folk-fusion repertoires. Additionally, this growing interest has brought Romani musicians to the stages of Ukraine. Macedonian Romani singer Esma Redžepova (1956–2016), the so-called Queen of the Roma who, in her lifetime, gave more than 8,000 concerts in over thirty countries, participated in the 2007 Krajina Mrij (Land of Dreams) ethno-folk festival organized annually by Oleh Skrypka, the politically active lead singer of the punk band Vopli Vidopliasova. Skrypka's vision for Krajina Mrij has helped legitimize the rural folk singing revival in Ukraine by offering the growing number of *avtentyka* folk singing ensembles a platform to perform. His festival has helped fuse this genre with other forms of popular music, as these are performed on other stages throughout the festival grounds near Kyiv (Sonevytsky 2019).

In 2009, Gogol Bordello helped organize BalkanFest in Kyiv, which featured Emir Kusturica, the famed Serbian filmmaker and musician. Kusturica made a name for himself by appropriating Romani music repertoires and popularizing them through Romani-themed films like *Time of the Gypsies* (1988) and *Black Cat, White Cat* (1998). Romani-infused Balkan music, already popular among folk-fusion groups in Ukraine, opened the floodgates on Romani/Gypsy punk-themed musical groups throughout Ukraine and among the Ukrainian diaspora in the West. Toronto-based Lemon Bucket Orchestra and Kyiv-based Toporkestra are among the many bands that have embraced Gogol Bordello's punk fusion style. There have also been strong influences in performance aesthetics among KlezFest participants, mirroring the overlapping aesthetics in scenes between Balkan, Romani, and Jewish music in New York, as brought together in Brooklyn every January for GoldenFest, a scene first described ethnographically by Mirjana Laušević (Laušević 2006). Gogol Bordello continues to serve as a strong draw for festivals in Ukraine, appearing most recently at ZaxidFest (literally, WestFest), a rural Woodstock-style outdoor music festival where audiences overnight in a tent city near Lviv. Romani-inspired punk now serves as a critical way of engaging with cosmopolitanism, nature, and community. Not lost is the irony that the festival had few Roms in attendance due to economic inaccessibility and safety reasons.

Tuning as Metaphor for Development

Among the most significant concerns for Romani musicians is the appropriation of their music by non-Roms and the claiming of local repertoires by non-Romani musicians. When the performance framework is dominated by non-Roms who instrumentalize Romani music in ways that diffuse original aesthetics, Romani musicians come across as too traditional, behind the times, and unmodern. The resulting points of exclusion are twofold: (1) Roms must compete with non-Roms for the "right" to play their music; and (2) Roms are forced to perform within a circle of stereotypes. Because music performance opportunities are so closely tied to economic and social mobility, such tensions are augmented exponentially among predominantly non-Romani global audiences drawn to the historical allure that frames music industry marketing of "Gypsy" music.

Development initiatives are sticky ventures. In striving to offer economic security for the disenfranchised, they help Roms capitalize on non-Romani musical interests. The cycle of production and consumption of Romani stereotypes continues with the assistance of development aid, with additional development aid allotted to undo (!) such stereotypes. Much like tuning an instrument, development interventions work to keep the damage of Romani cultural products in check while helping create additional demand through festival sponsorship and musical production.

7

Sound Health

Ukrainian ethnomusicology has relied heavily on the ability of older rural populations to remember the repertoires that had been forbidden and forgotten under the Soviet regime. This so-called usable past has steeped post-Soviet ethnographic disciplines in rhetoric of urgency to record and learn repertoires that had once been integral to village agricultural, religious, and kinship cycles (Knight 2000). Revived musical repertoires, now performed on stages at numerous folk festivals and incorporated into modern repertoires including rock, hip-hop, electronica, and others, have positioned the old at the heart of the new.

As practiced by scholars and musicians seeking such sounds, salvage ethnography brings the young(er) generations in proximity with older generations.[1] Couched in rhetoric of the so-called dying village, which alludes to the contemporary movements of younger people to the larger cities for higher education, job opportunities, and modern ways of life, the rural, once at the heart of the Soviet modernizing experiment, is now associated with death and decay (Allina-Pisano 2007). This chapter approaches the theme of salvage ethnography from the perspective of Romani musicians. Because non-Romani ethnographers rarely research in Romani settlements, the narrative unfolds with representatives from Romani NGOs who travel to rural communities to collect data for publications and reports. They document grievances against local police, medical personnel, housing authorities, and politicians. Most important, they help file Romani applications for Holocaust reparations. Such visits bring urban, educated Roms and non-Roms who work in the development sector in contact with ailing Romani bodies.[2]

This chapter's focus on Romani health pays specific attention to ailments that affect physical organs central to sound production, namely the lungs and throat. Moreover, this chapter takes the cough as the primary analytical frame and uses it to analyze discourses of musician bodies through frameworks of health and disease (Applebaum 1990). Drawing on the growing literature in disability studies and ethnomusicology (Koen and Lloyd 2008; Howe and Jensen-Mouton 2016), this chapter looks at how

ReSounding Poverty. Adriana N. Helbig, Oxford University Press. © Oxford University Press 2023.
DOI: 10.1093/oso/9780197631768.003.0008

diseases affect how people relate to their bodies through sound. Specifically, it focuses on diseases punctuated through coughing and positions discussions of the cough in the broader context of pandemic tuberculosis, which reached epidemic proportions in post-Soviet Ukraine, affecting the country's poor in staggering numbers. It also addresses the smoking habits of Romani musicians and analyzes how this deadly habit weakens tubercular lungs and affects musicians' abilities to make music. Written in memory of those whose lives were cut short due to the lack of availability of the expensive antibiotics that can cure this widespread disease among Roms in Transcarpathia, this chapter evokes the songs unsung due to physical exhaustion, weakness of the lungs, and coughing fits that convulse and control the tubercular body.

Poverty, Dirt, and Disease

Soviet approaches to citizen health targeted disease to "sweep clean" and civilize the nation (Starks 2008, 22). Stereotypes of Roms as dirty, and by extension, unhealthy were reinforced through intervention methods meant to eradicate the perceived threats of their presence onto non-Romani bodies. Such interventions aimed to transform villagers into modern citizens who complied with state-imposed ideals of the human body. Such interventions into the rural countryside were already commonplace in the Austrian Empire where ethnographers, working on an encyclopedia of ethnicities, alongside recording musical traditions on wax cylinders, also took measurements of peasant bodies.[3] Peasant heads were measured to make claims about intelligence and abilities based on physical attributes (Berner 2010). Race science, spurred on by growing nationalism and evolving scientific interests in genetic studies and eugenics, laid the groundwork for what was to come in these regions during World War II.[4]

Roms, viewed as unfit not just socially but also physically, were targeted for extermination during the Holocaust (Hancock 2002; Kapralski, Martyniak, and Talewicz-Kwiatkowska 2011; Segal 2016).[5] Nomadic Roms, undocumented by the state, were massacred by the thousands in Ukraine between 1941 and 1944, murdered by Nazi *Einsatzgruppen* and local collaborators (Kotljarchuk 2016b). Andrej Kotljarchuk places the number of known Romani victims at 73,000, with 113 places of extermination identified on the territories of Ukraine as of 2014 (Kotljarchuk 2016a). Never deported

SOUND HEALTH 131

to concentration camps, Roms on the territories Ukraine were shot on site (Wawrzeniuk 2018).

Long-closed archives have led to difficulties in writing down Romani experiences during the Holocaust. Few Roms receive Holocaust reparations because very little documentation exists, particularly for Roms who were nomadic at the time of the war.[6] It is known that twenty-seven families in a caravan of nomadic Roms had settled in a meadow called Natalkin Luh (Natalia's Meadow) near Babi Yar on the outskirts of Kyiv in 1937. The Kalederash families made a living in the area as blacksmiths and metalworkers. Nazis occupied Kyiv in September 1941 and the Romani families had no chance to escape. The eighty-four adults and 132 children in the camp were murdered at Babi Yar sometime in September 1941 (Wawrzeniuk 2018). The stories of Romani Holocaust victims are only now coming to light through family members and witnesses who, with the help of international grants, have begun to file paperwork for Nazi-era reparations. Alongside the menorah-shaped monument erected in 1991 to commemorate the 34,000 Jews who were massacred by Nazis at Babi Yar, a memorial in the shape of a Romani wagon was erected in 2016 to commemorate the Romani victims of the Holocaust.

Following the end of World War II, mandatory assimilation of Roms living on newly acquired Soviet territories was motivated by centralized control of the population. Minority groups within the new borders determined to be enemies of the state, either through political leanings or through their way of life, were subject to scrutiny and control. Crimean Tatars were deported from their home territories on the Crimean Peninsula in 1942 by the Soviets for alleged collaboration with Nazis. 200,000 were deported to Central Asia, with only a fraction surviving (Williams 2002). During and after the war, the mass mobilization of people came as a result of populations fleeing two opposing forces that moved back and forth across Ukraine, bombing and burning everything in their path so as not to leave resources for the opposing front. Between the Soviet armies and the Nazis, cities in Ukrainian territories were left in the rubble.

The sheer loss of population numbering in the millions resulting from Stalin's and Hitler's atrocities left Ukraine to enter the fold of the USSR with unequal population distribution. Many people had fled, particularly from western Ukraine, establishing postwar diasporas in the West. Those deemed enemies of the people were sent to the *gulag*, prison camps in Siberia, while others languished or were tortured and killed in Soviet

132 RESOUNDING POVERTY

prisons. New Soviet policies aimed at eradicating kinship pockets of political ideologies led to placements of graduating university students in
jobs far away from their hometowns. Graduating university students were
sent into villages to work for one year to help educate the countryside. The
war, which had uprooted ways of life on Ukraine's territories, led to further dispersal and movement of people across the newly formed USSR. In
this context, as a group that had already been targeted for their way of life
through interventionist decrees, Roms were forced to alter their ways of life
once again.

Socialist Population Control

The Soviet state emphasized physical health, embodied through placards and
monuments depicting strong, muscular Soviet citizen-laborers, paralleling
Nazi-era ideologies, stressing first and foremost use of the body for labor and
procreation. Abortion was illegal, and contraception was generally unavail-
able. Thus Romani women, following traditional patriarchal norms, were
encouraged to marry early, in their teens, and give birth to multiple children. However, Romani women did help each other terminate unwanted
pregnancies, with one woman confiding in me that she had twenty-seven
home abortions.[7] However, she died young, often complaining about pain in
her lower back, attributing it to problems with her kidneys. Home remedies
and solutions among Roms continue to be the norm, especially among more
traditional communities that consider it inappropriate for Romani women
to be treated by male non-Romani doctors. It is common in hospitals to see
multiple family members staying in their patient family member's room
when hospitalization is unavoidable.[8]

The mistrust toward state-associated healthcare and the post-Soviet aver-
sion to hospitals among Roms today is, to an extent, grounded in genuine
fears and mistrust based on Soviet interventions in Romani bodies. To this
extent, Slovakia serves as a case in point. In socialist Czechoslovakia, doctors
performed unauthorized surgeries on Romani women to render them unable to bear children (Sokolová 2005).[9] The unauthorized transgression of female bodies by doctors in state-run facilities reinforced the lack of autonomy
Roms have over their bodies vis-à-vis the state. Such interventions were jus-
tified to prevent the procreation of Roms, referred to among non-Roms as
parazyty, parasites.[10] The biological use of the term *parazyty*, reinforcing

an image of welfare citizens sucking the state dry, fell in line with Soviet-era rhetoric of cleaning up the state, cleansing through biological and health interventions, and cleaning up the countryside of illiterate backward citizens.

Following the loss of millions of lives during World War II, the Soviet state emphasized rebirth, honoring women for the children they raised. The state honored Hero-mothers, *Maty-Heroinia*, women who could give birth to eight or more children and raise them past infancy. This honor was contingent on the children surviving childhood. Romani women, whose parents had been nomadic, were encouraged to become good Soviet citizens, complying with state's wishes and raising their children as laborers. Many Romani families grew in size, encouraged by Soviet policies in support for mothers. These large families, already living in poorer conditions due to the transition from nomadic to settled life, inadvertently contributed to poverty conditions that were meant to be alleviated by the birth of new laborers by the Soviet state. The state, however, had few resources to contribute to Roms living along the furthest reaches of the vast Soviet Union, and the newly acquired territories faced population challenges. In the end, Roms had to fend for themselves.

After the fall of the Soviet Union, independent Ukraine faced a declining population, this time due to outmigration rather than to loss through death and disease, as was the case during and after World War II. Ukraine's population dropped by 10 million in the first decade of independence, with significant numbers of people moving West, both legally and illegally, to escape the economic hardships of the early post-Soviet years. While this outmigration has stabilized to some extent, with today's population of Ukraine stabilizing at 43 million, the death rate is still higher than the birth rate. For the last decade or so, the Ukrainian government has been giving substantial subsidies for every child born. A higher percentage of funds is allotted for each subsequent child as an incentive to give birth to more children, resulting in *bahato-ditni simji*, multi-child families.

The rhetoric on birth rates is echoed in Romani child-centered rhetoric in development discourse. Romani children, pictured barefoot, dirty, hungry, and seemingly unhappy in development reports, are the target focus of grants and intervention programs to alleviate poverty. Romani children, allegedly forced by their families to beg on the streets of larger cities, are used as the reason for their Romani poverty. They are the unnamed on whose behalf development functions.

Health and Housing

Soviet interventions in housing were motivated by the state's concerns with health and disease. The Soviet laborer, healthy and robust, was meant to help rebuild the USSR after the destruction from World War II. Lack of funding, foresight, and care contributed to a recreation of unbearable living conditions among specific segments of the Romani population. For those who had not been assimilated at the time of the Soviet Union, Soviet housing policies inherently reinforced the health situations that settlement was purported to eradicate. Such situations did not adequately integrate Roms into local economies once nomadism was deemed illegal.

As a result, Roms who live in impoverished settlements have limited access to clean water, electricity, and infrastructure. They live in close quarters and share living space with extended family members and children. Houses, made either from cement or *saman*, are built by Roms themselves. They are typically found at the edges of villages and vary in number from a handful to up to 100 in the larger settlements. Roms built these houses following decrees that outlawed nomadism in the Soviet Union after World War II when Transcarpathia was annexed. The government allotted plots of land, though few efforts were made to extend electricity and water lines into the settlements. With few houses having access to well water, many rely on water from neighboring rivers or other water sources for bathing, washing clothes, and cooking. Through the long, harsh, cold, and damp Transcarpathian winters and the dry, hot summers, Roms cook, bathe, and sleep in close quarters that create physical circumstances, *umovy*, for disease. In such contexts, coughing is one of the primary indicators of *nezdorovlia*, unhealth.

Tuberculosis, Then and Now

Ukraine declared a tuberculosis epidemic in 1995. Traditional sanatoriums had, by then, fallen into disrepair, and people relied on assistance from NGOs for treatment. While much of this treatment was free, it was difficult for rural, economically strapped, and socially marginalized populations to access it. Additionally, the stigma attached to tuberculosis prevented people from reaching out for medical attention, which perpetuated the spread of the disease. Tuberculosis among Roms was exacerbated by living conditions and lack of access to healthcare. Non-Romani NGOs focusing on combating tuberculosis concentrated their efforts on upending the disease among the majority population. Romani NGOs, as discussed in earlier chapters, focused at this time mainly on cultural initiatives. The extreme spikes in racist attitudes regarding Roms following the fall of the Soviet Union, coupled with the corruption of a medical community that did not treat patients who were unable to pay bribes, prevented Roms from accessing adequate medical assistance. Many died because they did not get the needed assistance and treatment they needed.

Smoking augments the tuberculosis epidemic, though it is not the only factor in its spread. Nevertheless, a high rate of smoking among Roms, especially among Romani musicians, is an essential part of the story concerning Romani health. Smoking is a highly performative aspect of musicianship, and by extension, also of fieldwork. Therefore, an analysis of smoking among Romani musicians frames this chapter's analyses of health and disease within broader histories of performance and aesthetics. Musicians smoke between sets, audiences smoke while listening to others perform music, and it seems as though most of my interlocutors smoked before, during, and after interviews. Smoking is such a pervasive part of local culture that not doing it draws attention in ways one might not expect. Not smoking might indicate that a person is sick; not smoking might also indicate that one cannot afford to purchase cigarettes. Thus, a social status symbol, inscribed in a deadly habit, contributes to a cycle through which poverty itself contributes to actions that actively deteriorate health connected to activities, like making music, that alleviate poverty through money-making activities like musical performance.

Intervention programs promoted by Romani NGOs have worked toward trying to decrease smoking levels among Roms. Romani-focused foreign missionary programs have also actively promoted smoking and drinking cessation programs. These churches, however, also discourage engagement in secular music and dance activities, a tough thing to do among communities in which music-making is central to group socializing and to the economic state of the members of the communities. Such intervention programs are also gendered in nature, aimed at the health of men whose average lifespan is significantly shorter than that of women among Roms in particular and in Ukraine. Women sign up their husbands for such cessation programs, and the Ukrainian ministry of health has also begun to include smoking cessation in their health campaigns. Nevertheless, the levels of illness from various ailments are very high among Roms, and physical realities play an

136 RESOUNDING POVERTY

essential role in shaping how sound is produced, listened to, and understood among Roms.

With access to healthcare so limited, Roms rely on their ears, listening to how a family member breathes, speaks, and coughs to identify audible markers of disease. In cases of tuberculosis, for instance, coughing is the primary symptom of the disease. Coughing is also the predominant way *M. tuberculosis* is aerosolized from the lung and released into the environment. In other words, coughing allows others to conclude about a person's health. It is the most audible way in which disease is spread.[11]

Smoking and the Singing Voice

Cigarettes produced in the United States have played a central role in shaping global smoking habits. They played a central role in the marketing of American popular music in the twentieth century (Cooper and Schurk 1999). Such music, consumed globally, incorporates many lyrics that mention cigarettes and smoking (Cooper and Schurk 1999). Some musicians smoke that last cigarette before they go on stage and, in some venues, smoke on stage if it is still allowed. Audience members smoke before, during, and after performances, and bands take smoke breaks. The cigarette is an iconic prop, associated with crooners and lounge musicians and musicians where anti-smoking campaigns have not been as vocal or effective as in the United States. Smoking, as the abject sublime, plays an essential role within this discourse (Fox 2004). Smoking carries status, or at least did so historically. It was a masculine activity that shaped the public sphere and was associated with a performance of personhood and place. Smoking was a habit, as well as an addiction. It was also divorced from the contemporary rhetoric of quitting smoking.

In the Soviet Union, *papirosy*, cigarettes, were aligned with masculinity and grit when in the United States cigarettes were touted as a form of personal luxury, class, and style. Soviet *papirosy* were made with harsher, lower-quality tobacco. Especially those with no filter were often referred to as *smola*, tar, visually describing the texture of one's lungs after smoking. Lung disease and heart disease, endemic among older male smokers who grew up in the Soviet Union, point to habit-related health issues that Romani musicians face.

Among Roms, the famous *manouche* jazz player Django Reinhardt (1910–1953) embodies the figure of the smoking musician. Django, a guitar player, is smartly dressed in pictures, and his best-known photo features a cigarette in his mouth (Figure 7.1). While scholars have focused on the physical state of Django's left hand, burned during a fire that engulfed his covered wagon in a Romani caravan near Paris in 1928 and leaving him with only two fingers with which to play, Django's cigarette smoking is rarely noted.[12] These aspects of his personhood offer a range of possibilities for analysis in terms of disability studies and its intersection with class studies. The fire that affected Django's left hand took place in a wooden caravan in a traveling Romani community, and the community's displacement prevented firefighters from finding the scene, let alone putting out the blaze. The resulting deformity

Figure 7.1 Django Reinhardt (1910–1953) playing his guitar backstage in New York in 1946.
Photo by William Gottlieb/Redferns/Getty Images.

138 RESOUNDING POVERTY

in the left hand led Django to develop a style of playing that was decidedly unique. His left hand, so significantly altered from its state before the accident, pushed Django into a literature that exoticizes people for their musicianship despite or because of their disability.

Django smoked three packs of Gauloise unfiltered cigarettes a day. Unfiltered cigarettes, the cheapest on the market, burn the throat upon inhaling. They are made of strong tobacco and have a very powerful smell that permeates the person's clothes and skin. After a smoker finishes a cigarette, their lungs retain a measure of smoke, which emanates from the mouth as "smoker's breath." Yellowed teeth and fingers are also visible signs of smoking. Thus, all aspects of Django's presentation and physical well-being are connected to and influenced by the fact that he smoked. Smoking was a social outlet. It was part of his mystique and allure and also something that drew other smokers to him. His smoking affected his lungs and his vocal cords. Presumably, his habit also shaped (or was shaped by) his emotional state, influencing his interpretations of the music and, perhaps, his compositional tendencies.[13] While these last two statements are not quantifiable since, at the time of Django's life, nobody would have thought to make the connection between smoking, emotions, and music, yet it is such an obvious connection that it is still overlooked in contemporary analyses of musicians who battle substance addictions.

Smoking and Fieldwork

Smoking continues to pervade social interactions among Roms. During my fieldwork, I smoked to what amounted to two packs of cigarettes daily. I had been a smoker through college, having picked up the habit during my study-abroad year in Vienna, where most Romani musicians with whom I interacted smoked. What began as a social habit associated with music continued as a social habit associated with fieldwork. During my time in the field, it took a tremendous amount of energy to tune my ears to the various languages spoken in the Transcarpathian region. At a Romani gathering, it was common to hear Hungarian, Slovak, Ukrainian, Russian, and Romani in one conversation, with words borrowed from different languages in one sentence. It was months before I could identify the languages and years before I could understand the conversations. Social interactions were often exhausting for me since I could not express what I wished to ask. Since my formal interviews with interlocutors were conducted in Ukrainian and Russian, the switches between the other languages often left me silent at the table, trying to find a way to pass the time until my ears picked up familiar words. Smoking offered an outlet for these pauses.

I noticed many patterns of smoking behavior. At times, it was acceptable to smoke at the table. At other times, smokers left the room and smoked outside in groups. Cigarettes, especially filtered cigarettes that hurt less at the inhale, were relatively expensive. It was common for cigarettes to be sold individually, with a Romani woman sitting on a chair at the crossroads in the settlement, selling cigarettes and sunflower seeds. Cigarettes were something that I could offer to the social exchange. As an American, it was expected that I had the means to offer cigarettes when asked. Unable to smoke the unfiltered cigarettes the locals smoked (at least not without choking), I purchased more expensive cigarettes with recessed filters. These were relatively rare among Roms and were quickly identified as the brand that *I* smoked. Thus, that type of cigarette in one's hand identified the smoker as socially connected with me.

After twenty years in the field, neither the interlocutors with whom I once smoked nor I have continued the habit for various reasons. While I faced my health battles, perhaps due to smoking, many of my male interlocutors and musician friends had been pressured by their wives over the years to participate in NGO-sponsored and church-related smoking cessation programs. Moreover, husbands, fathers, and brothers continued to control the smoking habits of Romani women, many of whom have cut down on the habit significantly, especially during pregnancy thanks to prenatal care programs set up by NGOs that actively promote women's health programs in Romani communities. Poorer Roms, including men, women, and children, continue to smoke, and the cigarette continues to be a primary form of social exchange during fieldwork situations in rural settings.

When we speak of tangible networks and exchanges, objects as simple— or as culturally loaded—as cigarettes take on significant meaning. Cigarettes had carried historical weight since the Soviet era when black market cigarettes from the United States were used as currency, as were jeans and cultural objects from the West. Packs of Marlboro cigarettes were given as tips by Americans traveling in the Soviet Union. The exchange of *goods* (as opposed to currency) for services carried over into the post-Soviet economy, which was, by the mid-1990s in the depths of the recession that followed the Soviet collapse.

140 RESOUNDING POVERTY

Today, locals buy Ukrainian-made cigarettes and sell them in outdoor marketplaces across the borders. Often, I provide the capital, usually in the amount of twenty USD, to purchase the cigarettes, and am repaid when people return from a long day in Hungary or Slovakia, having earned a few dollars from selling the goods at a higher value. Women roll cigarettes stuffed into pantyhose to wrap around their waists and cross the border with the contraband. They cross the border early in the morning, sell their cigarettes, and then return in the evening. This gendered cigarette smuggling mirrors the scrap metal economy that contributes to much of the missing pothole covers in town, collected by poor Romani men and sold on the black market. These economies are not limited to Roms, but play a large part in shaping the financial exchanges of the poorer in the region.

Cigarettes and Gender: The Case of *Carmen*

Smoking allowed me entrance into the world of Romani women who walked off into the darkness to smoke at social gatherings or bought individual cigarettes from the lady at the village crossroads, which they smoked behind fences where the men in their family did not see them. Since so much control was placed on women's movements, smoking as a form of rebellion allowed women to create gendered spaces. Too often, Romani women, when presented as having agency, are analyzed in terms of sexuality without offering more nuanced understandings of how such agency is actually garnered. In the section that follows, I focus on Carmen, the most famous Romani woman in classical music. My interest in Carmen is primarily that of a laborer in a cigarette factory and her role within the gendered history of women's labor in the tobacco industry. Such an analysis helps broaden our understandings of cigarettes as commodities that women once made. In keeping with the economic focus of the book, this chapter also analyzes the 1933 staging of *Carmen* by Moscow's Teatr Romen, the intentions of which were to use the opera to highlight the theme of Romani women's labor and their potential economic contributions to the new Soviet state.[14]

In French composer Georges Bizet's 1874 opera *Carmen* based on the eponymous 1845 novella by Prosper Mérimée, the female protagonist, Carmen, is cast as free-spirited, strong, defiant, demanding, sexually arousing, alluring, and dismissive. This ideological construct of the Romani woman stands in direct opposition to the proper, controlled, chaste, submissive woman held as the Victorian European ideal. This ideal with which the stereotype of the Romani woman is contrasted is, ironically, the ideal of womanhood within many Romani communities. However, the hyper-sexualization and oriental fascination with the forbidden and taboo world of the Romani Other in music is projected onto Carmen. The character of Carmen overtly woos and seduces the captain of the guard, Don José, after being arrested for fighting with other female workers at the cigarette factory. Don José, who has fallen captive to Carmen's charm, complies with her wishes and allows her to escape her imprisonment. Foolishly believing in her promises of love, he is punished for his actions by his superiors and loses his job, honor, dignity, and pride. In the end, Don José, a broken man, pitifully pleads for Carmen's love, which she has since promised to a rich bullfighter. In his despair and anger, Don José murders Carmen. While Don José commits a heinous crime, the audience continues to sympathize with him and identifies him as a victim of alleged Romani female shrewdness.

The exotic and mysterious Carmen is juxtaposed with the code of proper female behavior and morality prevalent across nineteenth-century Europe (Baumann 1996). Carmen is strong and confident; she unleashes her sexuality in order to gain favors and attain impunity. She craves status and recognition and attains them at the cost of Don José, a man she to whom she has promised her love. Don José, unable to control his sexual urges toward Carmen, is punished for his weakness. He loses everything he has worked for, and through him, one is to learn that no good can come from reveling in sexual pleasure. He is a broken man because he gave in to temptation; he sacrificed his purity and masculine pride through his involvement with a Romani woman, portrayed as unfaithful, as a conniving prostitute. Don José's transformation and Carmen's murder embody a message to the nineteenth-century middle-class audience: Carmen's deviant, immoral actions would not be tolerated; any contact with her would ultimately lead to pain and eventual social, spiritual, and moral ruin.

In 1933, non-Romani administrators interpreted Mérimée's novella *Carmen* for the stage at Moscow's Teatr Romen. The Soviet reviewing committee, Glavrepertkom, was highly critical of the proposal, stating that "although it was clear that Romen was attempting an interpretation of *Carmen* that reflected the social inequalities of *petit-bourgeois* liberalism, it had nonetheless failed to make a compelling ideological justification for the play's inclusion in the theatre's repertoire" (O'Keeffe 2013, 225). The theater's first director, Jewish activist Moishe Goldblat, defended his choice of production, which premiered in April 1934, stating that in this retelling, "Carmen offered an ethnographic portrait of an era in which 'the Spanish merchant *bourgeoisie* exploited (*ispol'zovala*) the backwardness and ignorance (*temnoty*) of the Gypsy masses'" (O'Keeffe 2013, 226). Teatr Romen's interpretation would shed light on the everyday life of nineteenth-century Roms and provide an analysis of class divisions among Roms themselves. A theater critic at *Vecherniaia Moskva* praised the production for correcting Mérimée's mistaken *bourgeois* assumption that the presumed predilection for banditry and deceit among Roms was a biological affliction instead of a socioeconomic one. A modern-day *Carmen*, Goldblat argued, "under the dictatorship of the proletariat" would have been "inconceivable" considering affirmative action programs and the social networks that were being put in place for minorities in the early Soviet Union (O'Keeffe 2013, 228).

Susan McClary has analyzed Carmen's role as a laborer as well, positioning the story in terms of the struggles between an exploited urban labor force and the growing middle class whose increasingly bourgeoisie lifestyle depended on it (McClary 1992, 35–36). It is not by coincidence that we meet Carmen in the context of a cigarette factory where she refuses to work for a miserly wage. *Carmen* is as much a statement about women's empowerment in the workforce as it is about her transgressive relationship with Don José, both as a *Gadje*, non-Rom, and as a man in a different social position. While soldiers had the lowest social status in European society at the time of the premier, in this opera, they represent the state and the rule of law; they are simulacra of loyalty, of duty, of steadfastness. Carmen breaks laws by joining a band of thieves, but she also breaks the social rules of conduct, not only through her relationship with a non-Rom but also through her ability to provide for herself prior to this relationship. When we meet Carmen, she is employed; she earns a living working in a cigarette factory. A *flamenco* version of the opera was performed in London in 2002 by the Andalusian dance troupe La Cuadra de Sevilla. The troupe was set up in 1971 by Salvador Tavora, who based his reworked version of Carmen on stories of his great-great-grandmother, a cigar seller from Andalusia. "The cigar sellers' way of life was revolutionary. These were women who were able to fend for themselves. They did not need a man—as a cigar seller, Carmen was a symbol of liberation in a very conservative society."[15]

Tobacco production and consumption were closely monitored by the Spanish imperial government, which monopolized the industry in 1637, soon after tobacco was introduced to Europe via colonial trade from the

Americas. From the beginning of the seventeenth century, all Spanish production of tobacco products was concentrated in Seville under a centralized manufacturing system (Muñoz 2006, 2). In 1887, the state leased the management of the tobacco monopoly to a private company, Compañía Arrendataria de Tabacos (or CAT), which introduced machinery to the cigarette-making process. With the introduction of the Bonsack machine in 1881 and cigar-making machines in the 1920s, the mechanization of production brought with it an important change in the division of labor inside the tobacco industry. In those countries in which tobacco products were manufactured mainly by men, mechanization came with the substitution of a male labor force with female workers, except in the production of high-quality handmade cigars, which continued to be manufactured by men (Muñoz 2006, 2). Though female labor was cheaper than male labor, that 95 percent of the cigarette-making force in Spain was female cannot be overlooked. That a Romani woman was hired in this context, even if in a fictional representation, attests that lower-class women laborers played an integral, albeit, unacknowledged role in the imperial tobacco economy. Furthermore, an emphasis on nineteenth-century campaigns to curb addictions (Muñoz 2005) added a secondary layer to Carmen's allure of the forbidden.

While Bizet's opera was deemed scandalous for its portrayal of sexuality, today, *Carmen* continues to face scrutiny from health-conscious opera producers. The chorus of the cigarette girls vividly describes the smoking women, "*Mine coquette! Fumant toutes. Du bout des dents, la cigarette* [Flirtatious looks! All smoking. At the end of their teeth, a cigarette]."[16] The vivid smoking imagery, as well as the portrayal of smokers on stage, led the Western Australian Opera Company to postpone their planned 2015 production of Carmen over fears that the opera glamorizes smoking. The opera company acted in response to pressure from Healthway, a state-based agency that had promised 400,000 AUD in funding support for two years.[17]

Music and Health

A growing number of studies in ethnomusicology now focus on the relationship between music and health (Koen and Lloyd 2008). Scholars analyze disabilities as aspects of being, whether deafness or blindness, that shape performance practices (Howe and Jensen-Moulton 2016). Others have looked

144 RESOUNDING POVERTY

at how autism and depression shape sensory aesthetics. More obscure in this growing scholarly literature is the intersection between health and musical labor.

The relationship between health and economic precarity is such that musicians who are ill cannot control their schedule or predict whether they will work. While in cases where access to healthcare is feasible, there is a sense of how long a person may need to not work in order to feel better, among the poor, who have little to no access to medicine, an illness might continue for a much more extended period, morphing into another, often more severe *neduha*, illness. Illness is very often associated with time, often with no clear delineation of when or whether the illness might pass—time, again, marches on, the ill musician waiting for the passing of the illness, the ability to perform again; waiting for the inevitable time at which they will *not* be able to perform again. This fatalistic approach to being unable to retain a status of health plays intensely into Romani realities, with an illness often serving as a delineating mark between a musician performing and not being able to perform either publicly or in the home. In other words, illness often serves as the liminal space between having made music with one's body and not being able to do so because of the long-term effects of illness, or not wishing to do so because of the psychological ramifications of physical illness, once a relative state of physical health has returned.

Among Roms, especially those who have limited access to healthcare, a person might not even know to which illness they have succumbed. There is general talk of *neduha* but few details are ever shared or revealed, if only because they are unknown. During my fieldwork, it was, unfortunately, all too common, for my interlocutors to ask that I take X rays to be read by a doctor in the United States and bring back medicine on a return trip. Handwritten analyses from local clinics or hospitals in neighboring towns or even the capital (travel to which involved, at the time, close to a twenty-four-hour train ride) told of the gravity of health situations. Some of these X rays were outdated by more than a few years, and by the time I saw them they reinforced the stark realities of health issues faced by the Roms. They say this had not been the case in the Soviet era when access to socialized medicine had brought awareness of modern medical practices into Romani communities. However, the growing corruption in medicine following the Soviet collapse rendered access to healthcare impossible because of racist attitudes toward Roms and the inabilities of Roms to afford the necessary bribes. Death was a looming reality.

What the Cough Makes Audible

The cough emotes an instrumentality of voice that disrupts other instrumentalities. Sometimes it is forced and voluntary. Its purpose is to clear the throat, force out blockage, phlegm, and offer respite. Other times, it is involuntary, tightening the throat, hurting the part of our body that connects our torso to our head. Through its encompassing sensations, it draws our listening attention to the sounds emanating from our mouths that are neither speech nor music, sounds that engage our vocal cords nevertheless. As David Applebaum astutely notes, the cough is, indeed, a return to voice (Applebaum 1990, 10–11).

Romani realities of living in close quarters and harsh conditions reflect on their bodies in visible and invisible ways. The audible, particularly coughing, is the most significant sign of changes in health. In Romani houses, coughing is discussed with great seriousness; people react quickly to persons who cough, offering herbs or tea. Coughing places limits on social interactions and often frames where and with whom one can interact in the house. Children are kept away from older family members who cough, and the coughing adult tends to be sequestered to only part of the house. Even in a smaller house, the coughing adult, depending on degree of illness, is quarantined in a corner at the back. When I was invited to conduct interviews with Romani families in their homes, conversations took place in the front room of the house, no matter how well I knew the family. Since my focus had been on gathering the histories of musicians, I admit that I took no notice of some of the extraneous sounds in the house at the time of recording. However, during the writing of this book, I fell ill for a year, and in my re-listenings to recorded conversations and fieldwork sessions, I began to take note of a sound I recognized but had at the time relegated to an unmarked noise in the background.

Once identified as such, the cough was an unmistakable and constant sound in the majority of my recordings. It evoked the presence of the unseen person, made audible through their deviation from a typical standard of health. This person was unidentified, or identified only through kinship. Whether they were the father, mother, uncle, or other relative, their audible identity offered context to the workings of the family. Their presence implied duty, time, and effort to reinforce kinship ties and responsibilities. The care of a relative took great effort in Ukraine, where corruption guided access to medicine and medical attention (Polese 2014). In a time and place where a doctor will not see patients without up-front payment for services, access to medical attention is out of reach for many in remote villages which must travel to larger towns with clinics. Patients must bring their materials, including gauze and even syringes, and purchase all medicines and supplies used in any checkup or surgery. In the 1990s, medical goods sent to Ukraine by Western countries were readily available on the black market. Today, even with a crackdown on corruption in the health system, doctors are still unconvinced that Roms might have access to funds via development aid organizations through grants explicitly intended to address this situation. Sickness is often viewed as a hopeless experience, and once a person has been taken to a hospital, general sentiments are that they will not return.

The Cough in Music

Music studies that engage with disability studies have, to date, primarily focused on physical difference as a characteristic of the performer. Sounded ailments like coughing are hardly discussed in musicological studies, yet they shape the music produced and create sensitivities of listening that influence the way people relate to each other and the sounds around them. Coughing is perhaps the single-most audible expression of unhealth, rendering it one of the most significant indicators of physical dis/ability.[18] In still graphic art, the cough is inaudible, and thus paintings and photographs cannot fully capture the physical convulsions, the muscular spasms, the pain and exhaustion of a prolonged cough, the attendant and indicative sounds, and the ultimate destruction wrought to the vocal cords.

Considered culturally in the West as a disturbance during classical music concerts, the cough is expected to be suppressed or silenced while listening to or performing music. Audience members arriving at the University of Pittsburgh's annual holiday concert are met by a student greeter holding a tray of cough drops at the entrance to Heinz Chapel. Signaling the etiquette of silence while listening to classical music, when questioned, the explanation rests in the concert being recorded live for radio, the cough drops meant to suppress audience sounds. The cough soundtrack is, of course, a very recognizable aspect of live concert recording, amplified to various degrees based on microphone placement, performance space, and the music being performed. Some audience members try to time their coughs or suppress them until a more boisterous part of the music or breaks between pieces. Recent research suggests that people cough twice as much during performances as they do in everyday life and even use coughing to critique the performance (Burland and Pitts 2014, 2).

Singers have canceled performances when throat ailments do not allow them to produce the desired pitches or do so at the desired volume. Opera singers, in particular, have rituals before their performance that they believe will create optimal conditions for producing sounds. Some do not speak, the idea being that they are resting their throats or their vocal cords. They do not drink milk to produce additional phlegm; they drink water with lemon to clear it. The idea of removing unwanted blockage and additional work clearing the throat presents the way we think about the throat as an otherwise clean passage that produces sound. Such throat-clearings are to be done *before* a singer produces sound, and certainly not *during* the performance. These are not rendered audibly in music unless a cough punctuates a performance or is rendered purposefully, either by a listener, speaker, or singer.[19]

Dismissed as an annoying disturbance, coughing functions as an audible marker of physical well-being (or lack thereof). One does not cough without reason. Whether a cough is conscious or uncontrolled, suppressed or vocalized, and the volume at which it is produced, sends messages that are both socially coded and, often, universally understood. Coughs, especially prolonged coughs, leave their mark in direct and indirect ways. They weaken the body; they disrupt the sleep—of those ill with the cough and those around them; they complicate breathing and impact eating patterns. Perhaps most significant, coughs hurt the vocal cords. They make speech difficult, especially prolonged speech, because of the disruptions to saliva production and breath intake processes. The association between coughing and difficulty breathing indicates the relationship between the throat and the lungs. The lungs, considered a person's lifeline and listened to since the nineteenth century for sounds that demonstrate whether they are clear (of fluid, of phlegm, or disease), are the audible indicator of un/health (Sterne 2003). Such discourse extends to the ubiquitous "death rattle" resulting from respiratory secretions that signal a person's transition to the final stage of the dying process.

Researchers have amassed a collection of cough sounds related to tuberculosis (Botha et al. 2018). According to Botha et al., cough audio analysis can contain information indicative of the disease in detection and classification. Cough detection deals with identifying and localizing coughing sounds in general audio (Woolf and Rosenberg 1964; Birring et al. 2008; Larson et al.

148 RESOUNDING POVERTY

2012; Proano et al. 2016). After coughs have been detected, their frequency can be calculated and correlated to disease diagnosis or treatment. Cough classification aims to diagnose specific illnesses or conditions through analysis of cough sounds. Spectral analysis has revealed differences in the timbre and tonal quality of different types of cough, which can assist a diagnosis (Martinek et al. 2013).

Tuberculosis and the Arts

Nina Eidsheim points out that a musician's body is always inscribed in the timbre of the voice (Eidsheim 2018).[20] Such arguments, for the most part, assume that a healthy body is producing music. However, performances are riddled with depictions of ailing bodies, bodies in various stages of disability, especially in the portrayal of mental states, and, of course, death, as the ultimate salvation from pain and suffering. Coughing as related to tuberculosis, in particular, is depicted in European operas of the nineteenth century, when the disease was at its most prevalent. Attitudes regarding the moral and social implications of the disease were captured in three notable operas in which leading women succumb to the disease, namely *Les contes d'Hoffmann* (1881) by Jacques Offenbach (1819–1890), *La traviata* (1853) by Giuseppe Verdi (1813–1901), and *La Bohème* (1896) by Giacomo Puccini (1858–1924). In these operas, the heroines, Antonia, Violetta, and Mimi, battle the untreatable disease (Hutcheon and Hutcheon 1996). The representation of female characters as "diseased" reinforces the narratives of the time that marked female bodies as weak, as not good enough, as unable to live up to the ideal of the able-bodied man. The three women also neither give birth nor are represented as mothers in the operas. On the contrary, they are defined through their sexuality, either as virgins or sexual deviants. The three women embody attitudes toward the incurable, or not worthy of being cured, the female body whose inability to reproduce renders it useless. The prostitute Violetta succumbs to the illness through the prism of a classic trope of punishment for her sexual promiscuity. Mimi dies unmarried. Antonia dies a sufferer, maddened by disease.[21]

In the Romantic formulation, consumption was aestheticized positively as a sign of passion, spirituality, and genius (Lawlor 2007). The Victorian feminine ideal was emaciated and consumptive and influenced the construction of the nineteenth-century social body through its pathologizing of the

SOUND HEALTH 149

gender, class, and economic and aesthetic status (Byrne 2011). In *Illness as Metaphor*, Susan Sontag shows us how diseases are culturally constructed and how literally and aesthetic representations of disease help people experience illness through proceedings through the arts (Sontag 1978).[22] As David Morens states, "To grasp the human suffering perpetrated by tuberculosis, we may need to recall the past when incurable and incomprehensible, the disease had to be deciphered by metaphors—metaphors that changed as societal views of the disease changed over time. We may need to recall the lives of dying artists and the work they created and let art paint their faces, sculpt their shapes and contours, and compose leitmotivs. Perhaps such *past* images will help fix the gazes of *today's* victims, whose faces we do not seem to be able to see" (Morens 2002).[23]

Artists depicted the disease as a way to process fears of an incurable disease. Alice Neel (1900–1984), an American visual artist who worked for the Works Progress Administration (WPA), painted portraits of people around her. In the 1930s, she moved to Spanish Harlem where she first encountered tuberculosis. Neel thought of herself as a realist painter who worked to capture the emotions of the subjects she painted. In "T.B. Harlem," Neel captures the drama of poverty and illness. Her subject is Carlos Negrón, the brother of her then-lover, José Santiago. The bandage on Negrón's chest covers the wound from his thoracoplasty, a procedure to collapse and "rest" the tuberculosis-infected lung by removing ribs.

The association of disease with hygiene and the substandard living conditions in Harlem's impoverished, crowded areas led to the mounting of active campaigns by nurses and doctors to help curb the disease. Harlem was the site of a bitter conflict between physicians about whether to accept philanthropy in order to establish a Black-controlled hospital (Calhoon 2001). In Black neighborhoods, there is still great distrust of government health interventions, and tuberculosis has remained relatively high at 37 percent when considering its perceived eradication by the 1950s (CDCP 2017). Economically disadvantaged, predominantly African American towns like Marion, Alabama, where 33 percent of the population lives below the poverty line, have seen a resurgence of the disease in the last decade.[24] In the case of Alabama, local African Americans express fears about interactions with state institutions due to experiments done on African Americans in neighboring Tuskegee where men were injected with diseases without their knowledge or consent as part of a health study. Thus, a combination of malicious intent toward minorities on the part of the state (similar to the forced sterilizations

150 RESOUNDING POVERTY

of Romani women in Slovakia described earlier), alongside poorer living conditions and a general lack of financial means to access healthcare, has contributed to the spread of disease in disenfranchised communities.

(Not) Making Music with Tuberculosis

Audience engagements with tuberculosis are based on historical representations of musicians most visibly afflicted with the disease. Until the twentieth century, tuberculosis in Western Europe was most prominently associated with genius and creativity, and people with the disease were perceived to have a "special and creative energy" (Abbott 1982, 126). Polish composer Frédéric Chopin's (1810–1849) tuberculosis was believed to have offered him the *spes phthisica*, "a physiological condition where the unwillingness of the victim to accept the gravity of their circumstances led to uncharacteristic optimism" (Lauer 2017, 63). Bouts of creativity were credited to s*pes phthisica* and tuberculosis was seen as a necessity to becoming an artist (Lauer 2017, 63–64). Such narratives circulate as regards upper- and middle-class creatives of the nineteenth century. In musicological literature, tuberculosis as a disease is analyzed in relation to artists acknowledged for their contributions to the arts. The disease is rarely mentioned as a positive attribute for creativity among the unnamed poor who continue to suffer from epidemic proportions. It is rarely mentioned at all in contexts where it is not perceived to enhance the performative or creative aspect of musical experience.

Romani musicians, ill with tuberculosis, did not attribute their performance skills to the disease. Their bodies weakened from the lack of access to medicine, their spirits weary from the stress of disease, they rarely allowed me to come into a house where they or someone in their family was ill. For people with whom I had closer ties, I brought gifts of food or offered money for medicine. After my first fieldwork trip in 1999, I bought a stethoscope for Dr. Fedir Andrash, a Romani pulmonologist based in Sambir, to allow him to visit patients at home. I was tested for tuberculosis upon every return to the United States. The disease serves as an actor in this drama, one that controls all action. It is audible through coughing and the cries of pain, frustration, fear, and sorrow. It silences the musicians who create musical sounds by rendering their bodies weak, unable to hold instruments, unable to sing. It removes people from their loved ones, cutting short their exchanges with younger family members who are kept away from the transmitter of the disease. The disease also divides the living space, with sheets or closed doors (in larger homes) behind which the *tuberkuloznyk*, a person with tuberculosis, catches his breath. Loved ones sit, listening intently, to the sounds of the coughs that punctuate the heavy air and thick silence that blankets the houses of those who suffer.

8

Release

Traumas, my own and those of my interlocutors, have made it difficult to publish these stories within a chronology of experience. In contexts of chaos, precise documentation becomes a luxury, a sought-after ideal that always seems out of reach. Thus, many of the accounts within these pages have been called up from memory, rather than from tidily documented notes. The memories are fragmented and disjointed, at times even a bit irrational. They are triggered by sounds: of music, of language, and of the landscape. Much like the stories that we tell and retell, sometimes with vivid details that have been forgotten until we tell tales, this book settles upon truths as they are felt and remembered. It draws from that liminal space between fact and feeling, between what people say and what we hear, between the facts and what they *mean*. It sits with the uncomfortable and the awkward and articulates what may seem without focus but is essential nonetheless. In so doing, it serves, much like the sounds it contextualizes, as an emotional outlet and release.

Recent discussions of time in trauma research have begun to analyze time as an uneven, meaningful, and overt force that influences trajectories of adaptation in the context of traumatic loss (Saltzman 2019). Saltzman describes how markers in time push our current representations of time forward and, in doing so, alter the narrative around pathological grief by removing the time limitation on grief and mourning. This framework recognizes grief as a cyclical process that unfolds in the context of meaningful, rather than chronological, time. This cyclical process, evident in my own life and the lives of my interlocutors, frames the very nature of this book and guides the re-listening process, a return to memories glossed over, denied, too painful to engage.

Music and (Traumatic) Memory

The lack of access to mental health programs in post-Soviet spaces reinforces a Soviet-era separation of physical needs from psychological and emotional needs. Mental and physical states inform each other, and it is through such

ReSounding Poverty. Adriana N. Helbig, Oxford University Press. © Oxford University Press 2023.
DOI: 10.1093/oso/9780197631768.003.0009

154 RESOUNDING POVERTY

alignments that we learn more about the complexities of the bodies into we are born, in which we live, and through which we engage with the world and the other bodies therein. As the psychological and the physical complement and strengthen each other, they subsequently weaken each other. This chapter draws attention to how traumas are vocalized in interviews. It also gives space to the silenced, unarticulated traumas unable to be heard except by those who have lived through it. Such traumas go through various phases of partial silencings and fragmented articulations.

Recognizing psychological and emotional states is paramount if we understand how people produce, engage with, or remove themselves from sound. The retreat from sound must be understood as a companion mode of depression. If ethnomusicology is to engage seriously with and contribute to the study of disabilities, it must, as a discipline, be comfortable with writing about and engaging with degrees of silence (Ochoa Gautier 2015). In other words, as scholars of music, we must learn to be comfortable in situations where sound is not the primary mode of interaction.[1] As described in earlier chapters, this silence might exist because people might not have access to instruments or have broken instruments. It might mean that people are in mourning and, by tradition, do not listen to music or dance during these times. It might be because people are in physical or mental states that prevent them from producing music or that sound creates physical pain. It might be that people in the depths of depression simply do not want to listen to or engage with music-making, perhaps because it reminds them of times past, of people who are no longer in their lives, either through death, separation, as in migration or imprisonment, or maybe because they simply *cannot*. In the case of those who are ill, it is believed that music, and more accurately, sound in general, may cause more harm than good. It may irritate emotions and disturb sleep, which is considered to be crucial to healing. However, I noted how people struggling with illness expressed increased sensitivity to loud, harsh, or especially high-pitched sounds. Children were shooed away, and the emphasis on silence in the house was paramount. Our sensitivities to such situations allow us to see value beyond that at which we are looking. The body remembers past traumas and holds on to pain from generations before.[2] Thus, to think about Romani health, a holistic approach, to which sound can significantly contribute, can help us better understand the challenges that lie ahead.

While initially, I came to this region guided by an interest in its musical traditions, various ethnographic practices brought forth the most painful memories among my interlocutors. For instance, the generally accepted fieldwork practice of asking for signed written permission to use ethnographic material served as an emotional trigger for Romani interlocutors. This document became the source of great stress for my interlocutors, many of whom could not sign their names due to illiteracy in the rural areas. They also feared any formal paperwork since it usually signaled a dynamic of power and one associated with the state. In the Soviet Union, the *propyska*, the document that assigned a place of living, restricted traditional Romani nomadic movements. In independent Ukraine, with regime changes and new passports, Romani settlements were often subjected to wild schemes by local politicians intending to steal their votes. Police were also particularly cruel, assigning crimes to members of the Romani community: crimes that they did not commit. Often arrested on fake charges or blamed for local crimes, Romani men were arrested on Fridays, only to be released on Mondays with no legal representation. They signed papers written in languages they could not read or understand, admitting to crimes they did not commit. Thus the prospect of the interview and ethnography, in general, was contentious among Roms from the start. It caused great stress for local Romani communities to have a non-Romani person living in their midst. I heard of this only after years of my visits and learned that Romani interlocutors shared my activities with the police so as not to be held responsible for my safety should something happen to me. They were afraid that I would blame them should my equipment be stolen or should I be harmed or harassed in any way.

Fieldwork as Emotional Labor

Musicological literature has focused greatly on the *expression* of emotion, but the focus centering on the emotions expressed focuses only on the ones we see and hear. Trauma, however, walls off certain aspects of ourselves and renders them private, inaccessible to others or indeed to ourselves (Casper and Wertheimer 2016). In *Cruel Optimism*, Lauren Berlant pushes against conventional trauma theory that focuses on exceptional shock and data loss in the memory and experience of catastrophe. She argues that "crisis is not exceptional to history or consciousness but a process embedded in the ordinary that unfolds in stories about navigating what is overwhelming" (Berlant 2011, 231). What Berlant does not articulate as such in her theorizations of "performative silence" are the privileges inherent in the type of silence necessary for healing. When we speak of trauma, we also speak of the entitlement of healing, letting go, of moving on, disassociating, forgiving, and forgetting. Such opportunities, however, are not open to everyone, and it is only in rare moments that people living in a constant state of stress might let down their guard. Those who experience post-traumatic stress (PTS) cannot consciously or subconsciously access certain feelings or cannot control them when they come. Fear, anxiety, uncertainty, and stress are accompanied by genuine emotional, psychological, and physical reactions. The fight-or-flight feeling is stored in the body and leads to ailments, disease, and pain.

It is in this state of pain that I have attempted to write my book many times, wondering over the years how to frame it, which elements to tease out, which to leave in. Moreover, it was only recently that in a conversation with my colleague and department chair, Mathew Rosenblum, I recognized a way back. Rosenblum, a composer, had taken on the monumental task of incorporating a recording of his Jewish grandmother retelling the westward escape across the border from the collapsing Russian Empire, a story that had been ritualized and retold at every gathering when he was a child. As the border in question now constitutes the western border of Ukraine, Rosenblum incorporated a traditional lament from the region into his composition *Lament/Witches' Sabbath* (2018) that fuses his family history with the region. He asked me to help find the source file for the lament and offer a translation. It was through the re-listenings to Rosenblum's composition that I recognized the similarity between his grandmother's retelling of the story of escape, my own family's (not sharing) of histories of displacement and loss, and conversation patterns among Romani women, the segment of the population that I spent the most time with in the field. Family stories that had been wrapped in pain and silence were given a voice through fieldwork experiences that, in turn, stirred disparate strands of memory from their hidden spaces.

The Interview as Lament

The emotional labor of fieldwork and collective healing came forth in the interviews during which I held space for the stories of Roms who shared their pain. The recounting of such experiences to my family members gave space for their stories to emerge *in relation* to the stories I told of others.

This collective trauma and pain, which I recognized as a shared experience through memories of (state) violence, allowed me to process such narratives through the pain of listening. I cast such interviews as laments because they serve as a genre through which the performer and listener might share bonds, reckoning, understanding, and potential release.

Laments, commonly referred to in Ukraine as *holosinniya* or *ladkannia*, vocalizations, share characteristics of repetition, identifiable sonic and textual tropes, and melodic lines that rise and fall. Laments are characterized by a repetitive structure that alters slightly with each repetition. Each repetition gradually moves the listener into a new emotional state. Similarly, the interview, as a source of memory, provides contexts for ritualized repetition. The constant return to stories from our past offers a ritualized release. However, each revisit meets us at the same point as our last return. We are often "stuck," and it is on us to "work through it."

The study of laments is widespread in the study of ethnomusicology. Much of the writing about laments focuses on their roles in ritual, on their structure and aesthetic elements (Mazo 1994), on their cognitive impact (Tolbert 1990; Vaughn 1990), and the genre's association with women (Holst-Warhaft 1992). Recording technology and Internet access have broadened how we engage with laments (Goluboff 2008): they allow us to displace and relive the moment of death through time and place, to rewind sonically through the five stages of grief—denial, anger, bargaining, depression, and acceptance (Kübler-Ross 1969). On the one hand, this allows us to process death on our terms; on the other, sonic recycling prevents closure and hinders the recovery of grief.

Interview responses, viewed as laments, offer potent moments of release. Laments are characterized by a repetitive structure that alters slightly with each repetition. Each repetition gradually moves the listener into a new emotional state. Similarly, the interview, as a source of memory, provides contexts for ritualized repetition. The constant return to stories from the past offers a ritualized release. However, each revisit meets at the same point from last return. It accesses the same sights and sounds, though in altered emotional states of engagement, especially when framed by anticipation. Humans look for patterns to foresee outcomes; laments provide such patterns.

To create a sense of safe space for the interview, I never set up the microphone initially. Instead, I sat informally and allowed the person to share with me the details of their day. This small-talk rapport-building exercise can sometimes last an hour or more. When I slowly begin to set up

158 RESOUNDING POVERTY

the recorder, conversations tend to focus on the everyday, with the person being interviewed sharing details about their family, where they are now, where they work, when they might be back, or not. These details are telling because it is infrequent that a family is complete. Often a son or a daughter is away, doing seasonal work abroad. Romani women make regular trips to other parts of Ukraine together, in groups of sisters, cousins, and neighbors, to purchase clothes to resell at local *bazaars*. Such trips are dangerous, taking into account anti-Romani sentiments and the precarious nature of moving goods from place to place. Those left behind during such trips mention the travelers often and express anxieties over whether they will have a successful trip. The mentioning of those who are absent brings great pain to those who stay at home.

The term *zarobitky*, earnings, from the word *zarobyty*, to earn money, is a typical reality of post-Soviet economies. These stories of personal separation involving travel across large distances (often abroad) for work constitute a large part of the conversation, leading into perhaps the more official part of the interview where, for instance, I steer the conversation toward music. In the field, with my limited supply of batteries, tape, film, and, in recent years, digital storage space, I have often not recorded these moments, considering them to be, perhaps, not directly relevant to the interview. They were, however, a significant emotional part of the buildup. Intimate sharing reminded me that what constituted the actual start of the interview was very blurry; the stories that precede the recorded part of the interview are crucial, though seemingly tangential, to the interview itself.

The interviews tended to take place in the interlocutor's home, and I always brought a big box of chocolates and a box of either tea or coffee. These were luxury items for Roms. A box of chocolates, costing approximately five USD, or fruit and nut-filled sweets, was a gift one might bring for someone celebrating a jubilee or festive occasion. Thus the chocolates themselves signaled my respect for the person and allowed me to show my honor to them without offering money per se. While in some instances I did offer money upon leaving the house, offering money for an interview or recording upfront would have been considered rude and inappropriate. However, the chocolates were not opened so that the host could regift them, a common thing people did with such boxes of chocolates at the time. Even when the host insisted on opening them, I asked them not to, citing my tree nut allergy as the reason for it. In this way, I allowed the host to save the chocolates to regift or, more important, to use as a bribe when dealing with administrative bureaucracies, as was the custom in the early years of post-Soviet transition, a reality held over from the former system. On rare occasions, I accepted a cup of tea from the tea box I would bring. Coffee, much like the chocolates, served as a cash commodity, and very often, I knew that the persons to whom I brought such gifts would sell them at the market later. However, if the interview was going well, I would, perhaps halfway through, reach into my backpack and pull out a bottle of local brandy, which in some cases cost less than the box of chocolates. It was at this time in the interview that other members of the family were called into the room, some bringing in instruments, and the mood would become festive. At times, an interview with one person could turn into an event with close to twenty people. I learned to bring more than one bottle of brandy.

It was in the course of these interviews that different stories would emerge. The majority of tales would deal with the past. People would tell me about the musicians who played at their wedding, or they would reminisce about a beautiful singer in their community. The majority of people I interviewed were older women because they constituted the most significant percentage of the older population. It was, unfortunately, not common to find men over the age of sixty with whom to speak. The life expectancy for Roms is approximately fifteen years less than for non-Roms (Parekh and Rose 2011, 140). Second, these interviews were usually set up through networks of women that I had established through fieldwork in other areas. They tended to be with family members of those I had already met. Neighbors would come by as well, but women did these introductions in a relatively gender-segregated social group, so this became the norm for my fieldwork. Exceptions were made for male musicians, though these interviews tended to be conducted with *groups* of musicians rather than with individual musicians one on one because it was not deemed acceptable for me to be alone in a room with a Romani man. Romani men associated with NGOs treated me differently, mainly because I am an American, though the longer I stayed in the field, the more I lost this autonomous footing.

During the interview process, in the home, I strengthened my connections, again and again, among women. Women, often widows, would sing the song of their deceased husbands for me. In some Romani communities, a person has "their" song, one that they either composed or always sang at special events, one song associated with them. These intimate singings would bring up the emotions of grief and loss. The interview, thus, became a context for witnessing (Oliver 2001). It served as a space for people to share and

160 RESOUNDING POVERTY

to be heard. An intimate one-on-one pushed boundaries of interactions in ways that were not typical between Roms and non-Roms. Eventually, I became known as *svoja*, "ours," connected through familiar mannerisms, vocal expressions, ways of speaking, asking, empathizing. I was also connected to Roms through the kinship network of a Romani leader who had been greatly respected in Romani communities throughout Transcarpathia. As his granddaughter's godmother, I was accepted as kin and referred to by family members as *kuma*, denoting my closeness to the family through a religious ritual that carried great social significance. In my many returns, I have retained this status in the community, moving now into the role of elder, as the generation with whom I worked most closely has progressed, as have I, into middle age.

Trauma and Silence

Ethnography among those who have experienced trauma takes a long time. A form of deep listening, it also involves the entire body. One engages with the sounds and the intonations in ways that reflect a deep sense of compassion and empathy. Words shared hold deep emotions that are often reserved for the most sacred moments, those told in the evening, in the quiet, when the mind and heart are at relative peace and the worries of the day set aside. Such exchanges brought the interview beyond the present into the realm of the subconscious. Locked eyes, the rise and fall of the voice, the use of hand gestures, and the proximity of leaned-in bodies communicated trust and a sense of unburdening and relief. Such conversations were sometimes interrupted by a middle-aged son coming in to check on his mother, jolting the narrative out of its surreal realm. Stark reactions to such interruptions revealed how our minds use feelings, sounds, and language to hide and reveal simultaneously what we secretly think and feel. In this safety of sharing, in allowing ourselves to articulate the depths of our thoughts and feelings, the processing and release of trauma occurs. Not allowing oneself to say out loud, or, in the case of the ethnographer, to write about, to sound, to give credence to, means that we are not yet finished working through our feelings about things.

Silence is not necessarily absence. Instead, pitched against the vocalized, it offers new dimensions for experiencing. Sitting together in silence with someone is beyond measure. A form of witnessing, of burden sharing, of connection, silence allows for connection through body and breath.[3] While at first, I mistook silence as (my) waiting for someone to share, I came to realize that silence was indicative of a fathomless bond. Being able to trust enough to sit in silence was to be able to be, feel, to mourn, and heal. Silence, itself, is not the opposite of sound. It can be the active withholding of articulation as a *way* of articulating that which goes unsaid. Silence makes obvious that which goes without saying.

On Ethnographic Forgiveness

Fieldwork is hard work; it is often difficult to muster the desire to engage with people altogether. Depending on the level of training, the context in which the work is done, and myriad personal factors, fieldwork can often have detrimental effects for the ethnographer. Moreover, it can be a debilitating experience for the scholar. I share the details of one instance to elucidate a memory of an interview that has crippled me for years.

I remember the dark, musty one-room house. I could barely see the face of the older woman I was interviewing. The sun was setting, and I was in the village later than I had anticipated. I usually arrived in the morning to catch the men before fishing or selling at the market. I would introduce myself to the men and then follow them to their homes, to ask their wives to welcome me. Such were the hierarchies of fieldwork, and I played into those dynamics as a young American woman. The woman sitting across from me had asked me to interview her. She was neither a musician nor a relative of the people I had come to see. She was elderly and ill and had heard that an American was in the village; she wanted to share her story. I generally felt overwhelmed by this kind of request because such stories were too much to listen to, too challenging to comprehend. I felt helpless, unclear of what my role in this exchange could be. I set up my SONY tape recorder on the table between us.

My shoes were wet, muddy from walking from house to house in the spring mountain mud, a reminder that I was not from these parts. I lacked the big rubber boots to the knee that I saw people in town wear. I noticed that she was barefoot, her gnarled feet aching with arthritis in the dampness of the evening. My heart broke. Again. As it had so many times before this. I pressed "record," wondering what stories she wished to share. She talked about her son who had died, about her daughter-in-law who had gone to Russia searching for work, about her sadness and heartache. She cried.

I pressed "stop" on the recording. She did not notice. But I did not want to hear anymore, and I could not bear the thought of hearing it again through re-listenings of fieldwork recordings.

This moment comes back to haunt me years after it happened. In fact, it has been almost twenty years since this moment. I have often wondered why I stopped recording. I have wondered how I would hear this story today, in my mid-forties: what reactions and insights might I have, was there anything I could have done, or if listening was meant to be the extent of my doing? Do age and maturity play a role in ethnographic encounters? Do we have any control over what we understand at the time? Are there ways to reconcile the mistakes of our youth?

I think of the energy I had back then, biking from village to village, recording musicians, translating the Romani newspaper, traveling across the border numerous times, often recklessly, too ignorant of the dangers of traveling alone. I do not have the same energy today as I write this story. However, I have a different energy, a new outlook, and forgiveness for my younger fieldworker-self. I have empathy for this woman I interviewed, to whom I acted respectfully but whose story I did not record because I wanted to save batteries and blank cassettes for music. How do I reconcile the blankness, the emptiness of that session? It is a missing story, a missing link, yet my sorrow over it consumes my heart. Her story feeds my shame over my actions. How many more stories did I ignore or deem unimportant because they were tangential to the music? These are the traps of fieldwork that we know well, the navel-gazing moments to which we return in the solitude of the mind's eye, or sometimes choose to ignore again, to push to the side because they are still too complicated. These are the moments that do not often make it into books. These are the laments, the testaments, the witnessings, and the healings that augment our interactions, informing our later work, the undergird future engagements.

It often came at a brutal cost to me, holding the feelings of these people close to my heart. While they, in their telling, were not necessarily sharing with me, but rather allowing themselves to express feelings in the context provided, it has, nevertheless, been an essential aspect of repatriation when I return to the field with my digitized recordings and recall specific details to the children of the people who have passed. Thus, I now participate in yet another link in the remembrance chain. I show the videos and play the audio of those moments and bring back the memories of people and events either to those whom I interviewed or to their children and those who, perhaps, were not yet old enough to know them (Figure 8.1). In this sense, my witnessing takes on an additional temporal frame in that I experience it multiple times, colored by the generational aspect of those experiencing it alongside me.

Figure 8.1 Roms in Bilky, Transcarpathia, crowd around the author's laptop in May 2016 to watch footage of family musicians from the early 2000s who have since passed.
Photo by author.

Phenomenologies of Suffering

What does it mean to ask what it feels like to be poor, verbally assaulted, spit on, pushed away, made fun of, silenced, spoken on behalf of, infantilized, and forgotten? This question returns us to the picture that frames the book's cover with the two Romani children on the street who, like so many, sing to beg. It asks us to consider how such experiences shape their futures. It also addresses themes of imprisonment that shape Romani realities and fieldwork experiences. The number of my interlocutors who find themselves in and out of prison continues to rise, reinforcing once again the parallels between systemic racism, economic marginalization and disparity, and life choices. In the form of the prison system, the state draws parallels with what Angela Davis terms the "prison industrial complex" (Davis 1999). Davis plays an important role in these stories because of her notoriety in the Soviet Union for her outspokenness as a communist fighting for African American rights. Relationships between the Soviet Union and African Americans have been addressed in numerous writings, and I analyzed engagements with such histories among

164   RESOUNDING POVERTY

English-speaking African musicians living on the territories of Ukraine in my previous book, *Hip-Hop Ukraine: Music, Race, and African Migration* (2014). However, the research for that book was conducted during the 2004 Orange Revolution and its aftermath. The political situation had become so tense in Transcarpathia that I began to travel instead to eastern Ukraine while engaging with Romani communities, but following emerging stories of African migrants that were beginning to reshape minority discourse in Ukraine. Thus, the title of this chapter—"Release"—is as much about my *own* letting go as it is about the processes through which interlocutors engage with difficult experiences. As a witness to their stories, I have held on to their words years after they have let go, using the interview exchange to vocalize and exorcize their feelings. Much like a therapist, the ethnographer listens, witnesses, and acknowledges, prodding, inquiring, pushing for depth. However, unlike therapists, ethnographers are not trained to deal with situations when the interview brings people to tears of mourning, sadness, or release.

This situation, all too common during my work among Roms, has pushed me to wonder about my own research project's effects on me as a person. As a young scholar, I could not have anticipated such difficulties, nor could my advisors. Who in the late 1990s, at an Ivy League school in the United States, could have foreseen the degrees of trauma Roms in the former Soviet Union experienced? English-language ethnomusicological literature at the time focused on village repertoires, written by US-based ethnographers focusing primarily on music-making in social context. After all, as Katherine Verdery's diaries reveal, scholarship in Eastern Europe and the Balkans during the Soviet era was guided by monitored interactions of Americans in rural areas (Verdery 2018). Local ethnographers took different approaches; they omitted most discussions of social contexts altogether. The books published on rural repertoires in the Soviet Union were predominantly on organology and song structures. Extensive volumes of song lyrics were also published. These books offered no guidance for work on Romani music. Thus, I had no blueprint for much of what I learned in the field and I felt that I had not received adequate training. This feeling hindered me from feeling I had something to say until I began to bring my students into the field. Wishing to create experiences for them that somehow gave them the knowledge and protected them somewhat from experiencing trauma in the field, I tapped into my family's experiences as travel agents to create experiences during which I could anticipate how my students might feel. Predicting feelings, however, is not possible and people process emotions based on their abilities, disabilities, past experiences, preconceived notions, and perceptions of what is happening as it happens. Nevertheless, the need to protect is still very strong with me and taps into ongoing discussions in ethnomusicology as regards safety. Conference themes, panel discussions, and numerous publications now address how to choose projects in which safety for the ethnographer is a high priority; this provides a sense of relief for me, knowing at least, that the ethnographer's experiences, concerns, and traumas can be acknowledged (Appert 2017).[4]

I was harmed and harassed many times, especially on trains. In one of my most horrific memories of such things, I had been assigned to a train compartment with three men. They were becoming increasingly drunk and, to my horror, I soon realized that the door to the compartment had been locked from the outside by the accomplice train conductor whom they had paid to do so. While I was saved by the persons in the compartment next to me who heard my poundings, I am forever reminded of such events and feel that such experiences made me more attuned to the everyday harassment that Roms face. The sharing of such events, however, was simply not done. It seemed that people, especially women, did not speak of such difficulties. Instead, they internalized them. There was a culture of not speaking the obvious, simply being expected to move on because there was little anyone could do to help. In the context of people celebrated for their music on stage, I learned very quickly that Roms were, in fact, not only unheard but silenced in all other spheres in life. They were also self-editing, never sharing too much about their present or past hardships. One could feel it, though, in the way they walked or in the heaviness with which they went about their daily chores. One could see it in their eyes and in their often depressed states.

Making Suffering Matter

The recent spike in nationalist-motivated attacks against Roms in Ukraine amid broader violence in the country has drawn an unprecedented number of journalists into Romani communities. Media visits are conspicuous and, often, unannounced. The journalist(s), accompanied by a cameraperson and media crew, set up camera tripods and equipment at a distance to a Romani house, usually the home of the *birov*, elder, or a male Romani representative who serves as the community spokesperson. By now, such a representative exists within most communities to engage with Romani NGOs in neighboring towns if the community does not have an organization of some sort. The *birov* speaks to the media on behalf of the community, his family, and neighbors standing by. The interviews are almost always conducted outside the home. Rarely do media representatives enter the home. In part, they are not invited to do so. However, they also express little interest in doing so. When the interview is outside, the camera can pan out and zoom in onto the faces of onlookers. It can also capture the surrounding environment, including broken windows in *saman* houses, a stray dog, a barefoot child, or a mountain of garbage that collects at the edge of a settlement. Few Transcarpathian villages have trash-collecting services, and most rural dwellers recycle/burn/compost their refuse. In the poorest Romani communities, neighbors throw trash onto a large collective pile, walking distance to the majority of the homes. Such images, taken out of context, and without much explanation for the reasons behind them, result in what journalists refer to as *kolorytnyi siuzhet*, a colorful performance. Such media *siuzhety* appear with regular frequency now on national and local television stations in Ukraine. They are also streamlined on corresponding online links and digitally archived, accessible to viewers around the world (Figure 8.2).

The concluding analysis of this volume focuses on the aural elements of these *siuzhety* and positions them within a broader context of Romani-related

Figure 8.2 A Romani house in Transcarpathia made of *saman* and scrap metal.
Photo by Volodymyr Baleha/Shutterstock.

media representations regarding poverty. In the 1990s, the earliest development reports and human rights reports on Roms incorporated black-and-white pictures that offered snapshots into poverty. Romani families were pictured seated in front of their homes; their children huddled around them with a large group of people. If Roms were photographed alone, the picture was intended to highlight (in most cases) the individual's suffering from police brutality. Many pictures of bruised Romani bodies fill the (predominantly) English-language publications from this time.

It seems that the plethora of information regarding Romani human rights abuses has not made journalists more informed. The poverty accented in media reports is not cast within broader understandings of the reasons behind it. After gaining information on whatever brought the journalists into the community, whether an unprovoked physical attack by ultranationalists or an altercation between an individual non-Rom and a Rom that results in physical harm, journalists couch the video into broader rhetoric of Romani unemployment, lack of education, and unhealthy living conditions. They then turn the cameras toward the women, who, until now, have been silent. In such cases, Romani women turn the conversation from police brutality toward economic issues that impact the lives of their children and family.

The nature of these *siuzhety* highlights Romani women's voices. I cast the sing-song styles of women's talk in media reports as laments, akin to the emotional sharing I have documented in conversations and interviews. Soundbites regarding the lack of running water, electricity, the lack of adequate school supplies, are the most common. The timbre of the voice is strained, raspy, and has a high pitch. Romani women tend to rise to a shout in such recordings, visibly agitated and expressing heightened emotion over the complex factors that put a strain on their everyday experiences. Their litany offers up suffering for broader consumption by those who look on and those who watch the segments on the evening television or YouTube.

I have been present during media "visits" to Romani communities. The feelings of stress linger long after the journalists have gone. Their questions stir people into emotional states filled with anger, disappointment, grief, and pain. Their traumas are put on display. Their labor of suffering and their performativity of pain are offered, much as in the staged vocal performances, for non-Romani consumption. The feelings, however, are real, and they take a tremendous physical and mental toll. People are exhausted. Some continue to talk; others shut down. Coping mechanisms, modeled on those of family members, are often not enough to process the gravity of the realities most Roms face.

The effects of such constant abuse and disruption call to mind Jasbir Puer's theory of debility that describes how the Israeli state uses physical harm and social exclusion to control (and maim) the Palestinian population. Puer distinguishes debility from disability as a form of the slow wearing-out of the poor and disenfranchised in capitalist contexts and draws our attention to the process of becoming disabled in war and under colonial occupation (Puer 2017). Asma Abbas pushes us to rethink the subjectivity of the sufferer critically. She proposes a move away from the labor of suffering to the politics of suffering (Abbas 2010, 144). She pushes us to think in ways that "make suffering matter to constitute a richer sense of justice instead of being in an external, apologetic, instrumental, vulnerable, even embarrassed, relation to it" (Abbas 2010, 144). Such demonstrations are not yet possible among the poor, many of whom suffer from acute depression and post-traumatic stress (PTS) (Van der Merwe 2006). Mental and physical states inform each other. Through such alignments, we learn more about the complexities of the bodies into which we are born, in which we live, and through which we engage with the world and the other bodies therein.

A recent film, funded by the International Renaissance Foundation, titled *Seven Histories of Successful Romani women in Ukraine*,[5] has become instrumental in forging support networks among more affluent and impoverished Romani women. It features the lives of seven urban women, four of whom are musicians and one of whom is a poet: Julia Kondur, president of the Romani women's fund Chirikli; poetess Rani Romani; Mila Krykunova, actress of the Kyiv-based Teatr Romance directed by husband Ihor Krykunov; community activist Maryna Kasanska; and singers and activists Zhuzhuna Duduchava, Liudmyla Karafetova, and Liubov Vlasova. These Romani women were interviewed about their life stories, and the film premiered in Kyiv in 2017. Subsequently, the film was shown in various towns and villages throughout Ukraine as part of an effort to introduce rural Roms to the history and culture of elite Roms in Ukraine. Such visits, however, did much more than that in that, for the first time, relatively affluent, educated, older Romani women came to speak to other Romani women and connected, as women.

The older female musician-activists (among the exceptions to this group is Julia Kondur, who is not a musician herself but was married to Romani musician Anatoliy Kondur and took over his activist work after his passing in 2002) have representative agency from the Soviet stage. Romani women singers express emotions through lyrics and the quality of their voice. Their musical contributions differ from those of Romani men on numerous levels, precisely because they perform using their voice. Historically, Romani women did not play instruments. To date, it is extremely rare for a Romani woman to perform on an instrument on stage, particularly in a performance group that includes both men and women. Such has been the characteristic of the *Ruska Roma* performance aesthetic embraced among Roms in eastern, central, and southern Ukraine. This aesthetic differs from Romani male musical traditions associated with urban restaurant music in Transcarpathia, more akin to Hungarian Romani traditions that feature instrumental virtuosity on violin and *cimbalom*. *Ruska Roma* emote particular vocal qualities, and women form the center of the performance ensemble. Romani women incorporate embellishments, ornamentations, melismas, and dramatic cry-breaks to portray their vocal virtuosity, maturity, and agency. Their music is punctuated by cry-breaks and a timbral quality akin to crying or weeping. Their vocal performance style is emotional.

Romani female singers draw on specific cultural agencies that help performers to harness authority. Age is a crucial element for garnering respect, and an older Romani woman beyond her childbearing years claims a community status that empowers her in a traditionally patriarchal society. When a person of such stature cries on stage, it opens the door for others to process feelings and emotions. Listening, then, is not a passive activity. With music serving as an emotional trigger, the feelings rise together with the sounds that bring them up. Such vocal aesthetics are rooted in pauses and breaks, improvisatory silences that allow a particularly long, emotive embellishment to rest, to take up space, and to allow for feelings, the singer's and among those who listen, to rise and fall.

The presence of these Kyiv-based Romani musicians in impoverished Transcarpathian Romani communities cannot be understated. The conversations turn to family, women's health, and emotions. The rhetoric shifts from large-scale, top-down solutions to what Kathleen Stewart calls "ordinary affects," or on-the-ground realities that offer reprieve, one woman to another (Stewart 2007). Much like the bonding moments I was privy to during intimate interviews with Romani women, the presence of Romani women from Kyiv, albeit members of different Romani groups with different languages, traditions, and musical aesthetics, points to shifts within Romani rights advocacy that now make room for new voices and a broader spectrum of perspectives.[6] In writing this book, the hope is that by holding space for more diverse Romani voice, those who have been silenced, metaphorically, symbolically, and in reality, get the opportunity to have their say.

Reflection

From my office at the University of Pittsburgh, I opened and closed my Internet browser hundreds and thousands of times, opening numerous windows in various languages, following the 2014 Revolution of Dignity events as they unfolded in real time. I watched cell phone footage from bases in Crimea that had once been shared by Russian and Ukrainian navy personnel, once friends, now enemies. I read Twitter feeds about the proclamations of two autonomous republics in eastern Ukraine (Donetsk and Luhansk), and about the downing of ML-17, the Malaysia Airlines flight carrying 298 passengers in rebel-held eastern Ukraine in May 2014—and in response to which, on July 21, 2014, I began my week-long hunger strike and documented it with a picture I uploaded to my Facebook and Twitter accounts. The hunger strike had made me into a digitized symbol of revolution in my own right: a picture circulated online of me standing in front of the University of Pittsburgh's Cathedral of Learning, an iconic building on campus, wearing a white scarf on my forehead that read *Ya holoduju* ("I am on a hunger strike" in Ukrainian). The scarf resembled those worn by student hunger strikers in Kyiv on the eve of Ukraine's declaration of independence, which indexed the scarves worn by student protesters in Tiananmen Square (Figure 9.1).

The post went viral across English-, Russian-, and Ukrainian-language social media. The immediacy of the response in terms of support and criticism from cyber-users around the world shaped much of my thinking on how cyber time and space shape people's emotional engagements with politics and protest on the Internet.

During this time of violence, tweeting about the killings of protestors became synonymous with on-the-ground activism, physical fighting, and personal sacrifice. I embodied this stress through my attempts to process events that directly affected my personal and professional life. I put aside my first attempts to write this book, unable to concentrate. The situation seemed doubly ironic, considering that my dissertation research on this very topic had been upended by the 2004 Orange Revolution a decade before.

ReSounding Poverty. Adriana N. Helbig, Oxford University Press. © Oxford University Press 2023.
DOI: 10.1093/oso/9780197631768.003.0010

Figure 9.1 The author's viral picture announcing a week-long hunger strike to protest Russia's aggression in eastern Ukraine. The University of Pittsburgh's iconic Cathedral of Learning forms the backdrop. 2014.
Photo: Nancy Murrell.

While I had been involved on the ground during the protests during that brutal winter in Kyiv ten years prior, in 2014 I made a conscious decision to stay in the West, helping mobilize much-needed funds and materials for family members and friends who were being drafted without training and

REFLECTION 173

equipment to fight in eastern Ukraine. The number of requests for help proved overwhelming. I turned to the Internet to process my anxiety.

Online activism requires a genuine form of labor. Moving it offline requires a different set of skills and demands unforeseen physical, emotional, and psychological challenges. Moreover, when the Internet is introduced halfway through a research project, fieldwork methods require constant retooling in an ever-shifting context. Such was the nature of the very unique and unforeseeable fieldwork that shaped this book. Following Manuel Castells, I have given much thought to "timeless time," where new technologies, including communication networks, are breaking down the biological sense of time as well as logical sequences of time (Castells 1996–1998). Such concepts are increasingly important in Ukraine, which fought one of the world's first "real-time" Internet-based anti-government revolutions, the documentation of which circulates in painful details online. The digital age has compressed concepts of time and space, offering new ways of experiencing and conceptualizing feelings, thoughts, and actions. Technologies like the Internet facilitate real-time connection and communication, reshaping understandings of distance and reconstituting relationships between the past and present (Gotved 2006; Schäfer, Fachner, and Smukalla 2013). Such plasticities continuously reformulate our positions within cyber realities. Our abilities to negotiate digital and physical worlds engage our capacities to draw lines between them. The Internet serves as a space of both action and stasis, a source of new and archived information that brings back the past through engagements with the present. This collapsing of time and space is central to the Internet's effectiveness in mobilizing political thought, action, and emotion. This cyber-driven mobilization is evident in the ten years separating Ukraine's 2004 Orange Revolution from the 2014 Revolution of Dignity.

Between 2004 and 2014, Internet usage in Ukraine grew from 0.4 percent to 49 percent of the population.[1] Among these were Romani colleagues, friends, musicians, and activists from my fieldwork and with whom I began to interact through social media for the first time since meeting them in the late 1990s. During the 2014 Revolution of Dignity, the Internet became a space for sharing information and a space for real-time engagement with and knowledge of political activities. Mobile access to the Internet offered real-time knowledge of violence and simultaneously created spaces for the processing of political upheaval (Tufekci 2017). People turned to the Internet to express anger, fear, anxiety, and sadness. Social media also offered a space for mourning and grieving. From gunfire to protest chants and laments, the Internet became a source of live-streamed sounds that moved across time and space, compressing, conflating, altering, and reinforcing relationships between the real and the cyber real. It also brought my field site into my home, allowing me to engage, for the first time, with my Romani friends and colleagues in ways that did not require my physical presence in Ukraine.

During this time, my Romani friends and colleagues and I found each other on different sides of the political spectrum. The central role of the past, especially the brief period of independence in 1937 before Transcarpathia was incorporated into Interwar Czechoslovakia, guides what Paul Magosci refers to as "the heritage of autonomy" regarding the region where I did my fieldwork (Magosci 2015), and Romani leaders were pushing back against the nationalizing discourses of the pro-Western candidates who had garnered strong support in other parts of western Ukraine, including Halychyna, Galicia, from where my family hails. My hunger strike was interpreted as support for pro-Western ideologies. On my (English-language) protest sign, I described my actions as a "hunger strike against Putin's aggression in Ukraine."

I returned to Transcarpathia in 2016 once the fighting had ceased. It was the first time I allowed myself to share my family's stories of trauma and loss with my interlocutors. These stories had emerged from the depths of memory, clicked into being through the endless hours I spent in front of the computer attempting to make sense of the dramatic violence on the streets of cities I knew well.

There is, what one might call, a loss of (a sense) of time among those dealing with trauma. Whether primary or compounded through generational trauma, their experiences keep them in a parallel state of past and present.[2] In the present global culture of immediacy, where experiences are shared instantaneously on social media and are often lost amid gigabytes of data, there is something to be said for keeping experiences for ourselves, for sitting long enough with an experience until it becomes a memory. There is a risk in this, especially for ethnographers, for not publishing and, perhaps, even waiting too long to publish. Nevertheless, this book has been just that—a testament to waiting. It offers an ethnographic argument for sitting with a story until the researcher has taken the time they have needed to tell the story.

Notes

Acknowledgments

1. CET Academic Programs is a study abroad organization that partners with universities to develop and deliver innovative educational programs abroad.

Awareness

1. "Auschwitz-Birkenau—Sources of the Memorial's Financing," http://70.auschwitz. org/index.php?option=com_content&view=article&id=80&Itemid=173&lang=en. Accessed May 20, 2021.
2. Since 2008, I have served as an expert witness for Romani asylum seekers in the United States. Expert witness testimonies require written and oral documentation of statistics and ethnographic data that strengthen the applicant's case for asylum.
3. In July 2017, a group of Romani asylum seekers from Romania who had moved to a small college town near Pittsburgh drew national media attention that stemmed from a funeral they held for one of their own. Commemorating the deceased young man in a public park, hundreds of Roms arrived in California, Pennsylvania, a town with a population of just over 6,000. A child's urge to defecate beneath a bush drew the town's ire, resulting in weeks of negative national media coverage on the "Gypsy threat" headed by the conservative pundit Tucker Carlson.
4. Gogol Bordello and Via Romen collaborate with Vadim Kolpakov, a renowned seven-string guitarist from Teatr Romen. In addition to the groups mentioned above, Kolpakov performs with the Kolpakov Trio and Gypsy Soul, VS Guitar Duo, and Zingaresca Duo. He was also involved in the Gogol Bordello collaboration with Madonna on her "Sticky & Sweet" world tour in 2008 throughout North and South America, Mexico, and Europe. During the group's performance in Bucharest, Madonna was booed by fans when she condemned the discrimination of Roms in Romania.
5. Through his observations of musical tourism at Bulgaria's Koprivshtitsa Festival, Ian MacMillen concludes that such musical encounters foster "reciprocal forms of witnessing" (MacMillen 2015, 231).
6. Jan Yoor's *The Gypsies* (1967), Isabel Fonseca's *Bury Me Standing: The Gypsies and Their Journey* (1995), and Mattijs van de Port's *Gypsies, Wars & Other Instances of the Wild: Civilisation and Its Discontents in a Serbian Town* (1998) are among the first books I read on Romani topics. The authors capture the chaos, disorder, violence, and

176 NOTES

unpredictability that shaped their research, aspects of my experience in the field that I have become more comfortable with as a senior scholar. Unlike Garth Cartwright's repertoire-focused ethnographic experiences among Romani musicians in *Princes Amongst Men: Journeys with Gypsy Musicians* (2005), I focus on music's role in the Romani rights movement, as this has been the primary frame through which I have engaged with Romani Studies.

7. Tzigania Tours, a US-based nonprofit organization that introduced tourism into Romania's Romani settlements, is an example of one of many emerging Romani tourism-oriented projects throughout Europe. The organization, run by Chuck Todaro, an American journalist who has lived in Romanian Romani settlements since 2005, is working on a book manuscript entitled *Do Not Ask Me of Living or Dying—I'd Rather Sing*. He describes his organization's intentions on its website in the following way: "TzT promotes real life. We invite people into the community to see the Roms as they really are. You won't find 'performance art' in our Tzigania plans, only strong doses of reality overflowing with the Gypsies indulging in their natural bohemian lifestyle." Yet, the "performance art," which widely refers to public Romani musical culture popularized on stage, at festivals, and in films, is precisely the image of the alluring Romani woman that is capitalized upon in the marketing campaign for this company. The "naturalness" of the tourist-Rom interaction draws on Romani musical culture as exoticized allure.

8. Within the real world of Romani music, places like Clejani, Romania, the village home of the famous Romani band Taraf de Haïdouks, have been compounded with narratives of musical and Romani authenticity. The band's popularity has resulted in an increase in travel to Clejani by journalists, scholars, musicians, tourists, and music fans. In the case of Clejani, the place itself is equally as significant as the band. The story of Clejani has been mythologized through the narrative of Stephane Karo, the Belgian who spent weeks attempting to find the musical place where Speranta Radulescu had taken Swiss colleague Lauren Aubert to record the sounds that would bring Karo to Romania. Karo "discovered" Clejani after two weeks of travel, moving from village to village searching for the musicians who had produced the music that brought him to Romania. The trope of discovery and movement is also exploited in Tony Gatlif's 1998 film *Gadjo Dilo* (Crazy stranger). The film features the story of a young Frenchman who inherits an old cassette tape that features a traditional Romani singer recorded by his anthropologist father. Seeing her voice as a link to his dead father and a channel for his grief, the young man travels to Romania in search of the songstress. The process through which consumers of Romani music search for the so-called musical source is tied with a physical place, emotional release, and musical reward, ideas that are transmitted and marketed to potential niche tourists.

9. Living in Romani villages in the Carpathian region throughout the late 1990s and 2000s opened my eyes to the dramatic realities of the silenced poor. They were the street cleaners, the beggars, the sick, the ones left behind by family members searching for work across borders, and those upon whom family members incarcerated for petty crimes depended. I documented the tremendous loss of musical repertoire, a situation that resulted from the lack of economic opportunities among older musicians to

NOTES 177

pass on musical traditions to younger generations. In the dire poverty of socialist collapse, older musicians were forced to sell their violins, accordions, and guitars to help make ends meet.

Chapter 1

1. Faith Hillis analyzes how, starting in the nineteenth century, this region of contemporary Ukraine, once the periphery of the Russian Empire, became the hotbed of Russian nationalism. She explains that nineteenth-century provincial intellectuals came to see local folk customs as the common unifying factor of an ancient nation that united all Orthodox East Slavs (Hillis 2013). This region lies at the heart of the violent conflict between the Russian Federation and Ukraine.
2. "Ukraine Refugee Crisis." *UNHRC: The UN Refugee Agency*, https://www.unrefugees. org/emergencies/ukraine/. Accessed January 15, 2020.
3. "Ukraine Population 2020" *World Population Review*, http://worldpopulationreview. com/countries/ukraine-population/. Accessed January 15, 2020.
4. For songs from the Chornobyl region, see *Chornobyl Songs Project: Living Culture from a Lost World* (Smithsonian Folkways, 2011), a project initiated by Evhen Yefremov, Maria Sonevytsky, and Ensemble Hilka in New York.
5. "A Twelve Year Old Boy Called the Child of the Maidan, Exchanged his Childhood for War," http://euromaidanpress.com/2014/05/14/a-12-year-old-boy-called-the-child-of-maidan-exchanged-his-childhood-for-war/. Accessed March 22, 2019.
6. Iuliia Mendel, "Attacks on Roma Force Ukraine to Confront an Old Ethnic Enmity," *New York Times*, July 21, 2018, https://www.nytimes.com/2018/07/21/world/europe/ ukraine-roma-attacks.html. Accessed March 22, 2019.
7. Human Rights Watch. "Ukraine: Investigate, Punish Hate Crimes: Violent Attacks by Radical Groups Increasing," June 14, 2018, https://www.hrw.org/news/2018/06/14/ ukraine-investigate-punish-hate-crimes. Accessed April 16, 2019.
8. The appellation Slovākika Roma (Slovak Roms) is partly synonymous with Čexika Roma (Czechoslovak Roms), referring to Roms from the territories of post–World War II Czechoslovakia. It is often encountered in exonymic reference to Roms from Slovakia who have remained in Transcarpathia through marriage or political circumstances.
9. Romani activists in Uzhhorod use the designation Kalederash for Roms in Pidvynohradiv and Korolevo. However, their language is close to Transylvanian Romani dialects. Katalin Kovalcsik, who did research in the community of Korolevo-Pidvinohradiv Roms in the late 1980s, claims that they call themselves Cerhari (Kovalcsik 2000).
10. Lovara are present in Transcarpathia's Khust region though some Roms in Uzhhorod claim Lovara ancestry.
11. Rumungri is a name by which Vlax (more specifically the Lovara) in East Central Europe call other Roms whom they view as (culturally or linguistically or both) assimilated. It comes from Rom Ungro "Rom [who is] Hungarian" and was first used

178 NOTES

in Hungarian-speaking regions for Hungarian-speaking Roms. The term is now used in other countries in Central Europe. The word is an exo-ethnonym used by Lovara and their related communities for other Roms.

12. I encountered references to Roms as Egyptians during my fieldwork in Bessarabia in 2003. For more on "Egyptians" as a census category in post-communist Eastern Europe, see Friedman 2007.

13. Johann Christian Christoph Rüdiger, a German cameralist, linguist, and professor at the University of Halle, discovered a strong affinity between Romani and Hindustani languages (Rüdiger 1782). Looking toward India, German scholar and ethnographer Heinrich Moritz Gottlieb Grellman further supported this claim of Romani heritage from popular travelers' journals that informed about the existence of a caste of Pariahs, whose color, build, character, morals, and customs showed many similarities with the image he had of Roms and their way of life. Grellman assigned a common basis and common roots to all Roms (Grellman 1787 [2000]).

14. The *Tsyhanska doroha*, Gypsy road, trope is evident in non-Romani cultural artifacts like the *pysanka*, the Ukrainian Easter egg. *Tsyhanska doroha* is a meandering design, a continuous route between two colored fields. The two colors, red and black, accent the difference between good and evil. The design is drawn so that evil cannot find its way off the "Gypsy road" and harm the recipient of the *pysanka*. http://eggs-files.tri pod.com/pysanky_4.html. Accessed January 15, 2020.

15. The Romani neighborhood in Lviv, located in a section of town called Briukhovychi, is referred to by non-Roms as "India," and its inhabitants as *Indiïtsi*, Indians. The use of the signifier "India" in this context, however, has racial undertones. Non-Roms often point to the alleged cultural and physical similarities between dark-skinned *Tsyhany* and *Indiïtsi*. Numerous contemporary Ukrainian newspaper articles have compared *Tsyhany* to India's so-called Untouchables. Thus, depending on context, "India" functions as either a marker of inclusion in terms of shared history and a marker of exclusion as a marker of nomadism.

16. Prior to the collapse of the Russian Empire, most Roms on the territories of today's eastern Ukraine lived as nomads or led a semi-nomadic lifestyle. During the winter months, they sought permanent dwellings with peasants or camped at the edge of villages. During the summer months, they traveled from village to village as entertainers, metalworkers, and horse traders. To this day, both longer and more recently settled Romani groups in Lviv who migrated from eastern regions like Zaporizhzhia, Luhansk, and Dnipropetrovsk during World War II mark the beginning of the historical migration season in early May. Traditionally, men and women celebrated this day separately—men repaired wagons, cleaned rifles, and cooked *kasha*, a celebratory meal of buckwheat and chicken; women sewed tent flaps, mended clothes, and prepared items necessary for the road.

17. The Bollywood influence on Romani music occurred throughout Eastern Europe and the Balkans. Esma Redžepova's album cover from 1969 depicts her wearing a sari.

18. Olena Yurchenko, personal communication, May 2, 2002, Lviv.

NOTES 179

Chapter 2

1. The economic spiral, a consequence of the collapsing socialist system, brought unprecedented corruption in all sectors of society (Holmes 2006). Deep-rooted corruption gripped even the nonprofit sector, funded by monies from the West to help improve the dire economic situation for Romani communities. While many grants were received, few projects were realized because the money filled the pockets of persons within development aid, further weakening the representative power of those in greatest need within society. Such pervasive postsocialist corruption continues to destabilize the precarious realities of impoverished Roms. Certain development persons have trustworthy reputations, while others are known to have their hands in dirty money, business, and politics. That such corruption is not monitored per se by the grant-giving agencies is yet another way that international programs function as alternate economies in the postsocialist sphere.

2. Diane Chandler's novel *The Road to Donetsk*, winner of the People's Book Prize for Fiction in 2016, has brought the extensive aid network in Ukraine into the genre of romance through the characters of Vanessa, an idealistic development aid worker, and a jaded USAID worker named Dan (Chandler 2015).

3. Samuel Araújo and Vincenzo Cambria, in their study of music-making in Rio de Janeiro's *favelas*, slums, note that NGOs with music programs flock to impoverished communities to offer assistance through music-related activities that can generate income by appealing to audiences outside the *favelas* (Araújo and Cambria 2013, 33–34). Local musical practices are often overlooked in favor of music with a higher-class appeal.

4. In her study of the popular music genre *manele* among Roms in Romania, Margaret Beissinger shows how the music serves as a platform among Roms to express fantasies associated with oligarch (male) privilege, including money, possessions, women, and prestige (Beissinger 2016, 128).

5. An Uzhhorod newspaper dated July 18, 2002, featured an article written by a Ukrainian journalist about the three Uzhhorod Romani camps under the heading "Black Elite with a Street Cleaner's Broom," which reflects the general attitude in Uzhhorod that "*Tsyhan je Tsyhan*/a Gypsy is a Gypsy" (*Zakarpatska Pravda*, July 18–24, 2002). A social media campaign in 2016 pushed back against the denigration of street cleaners and featured upwardly mobile Roms posing with brooms in Facebook posts.

6. Ada Engebrigtsen, in her ethnographic study of Roms in a Transylvanian village, notes that the *bulibaşă*, Romani elder, acts as an intermediary between the Romani community, politicians, and non-Romani NGOs (Engebrigtsen 2007, 117–24).

7. A 1999 report by the European Center for Minority Issues notes that individuals belonging to the lower castes respect the musicians and accept their authority. However, the report states that alleged conflicts have emerged in cases where donors and regional authorities have cooperated and worked directly with representatives of the lower castes, contributing to "social confusion" within the traditional structure of Romani society (Trier 1999, 40).

180 NOTES

8. Interview with a worker (identity withheld) at the National Minorities Council in Uzhhorod, Transcarpathia, October 17, 2002.

9. During the presidential elections of 1991 and 1994, Romani NGOs were relatively less active, and the network of Romani NGOs had not yet been established. The presidential election of 1999 was the first in which Romani NGOs began to actively engage in politics, engaging with local politicians and beginning to exert pressures on them to consider the needs of local Romani populations. Due to widespread corruption in Ukrainian elections that have led to the 2004 Orange Revolution and the 2013/2014 Revolution of Dignity, it is difficult to assess how Romani votes were allegedly stolen and miscast vis-à-vis other segments of the population. The 2019 elections saw a record number of Romani political representatives running for local office.

10. Russell Reed, "One-for-None: Aid Dependency and the 'Toms Model,'" *Harvard Political Review*, March 22, 2017. .

11. Notable exceptions include Margaret Beissinger, whose work among rural Romani musicians in Romania documents the epic singing traditions of *lăutar*, professional musicians, in the 1980s, at the time of Nicolae Ceaușescu (Beissinger 1991, 2001; see also Engebrigtsen 2007).

12. The Universal Declaration of Human Rights adopted by the United Nations in 1948 introduced a discourse regarding human dignity and a concept of equal and inalienable rights of all members of the human race. Every person, it was declared, had the right to life, liberty, and security. Every person is entitled to equal protection against discrimination, violence, degrading treatment, and cruel punishment. In 2006, the Human Rights Council replaced the United Nations Commission on Human Rights as the intergovernmental body responsible for human rights. The Human Rights Council now reviews human rights records in 192 UN member states once every four years. Romani rights continue to be a top priority in such reviews, holding UN member states accountable for securing the safety and well-being of their Roma citizens.

13. Committee on Elimination of Racial Discrimination Concludes Fifty-Ninth Session. https://www.un.org/press/en/2001/rd917.doc.htm. Accessed June 12, 2019.

14. Commission on Security & Cooperation in Europe: US Helsinki Commission. "Attacks on Roma in Ukraine." Senate Visitor Center, Washington, DC, July 25, 2018. https://www.csce.gov/international-impact/events/attacks-roma-ukraine. Accessed June 6, 2019.

15. Interview with Volodymyra Kravchenko, Kyiv, August 24, 2006.

16. Ioana Szeman argues that while NGOs in Romania often contribute to the status quo of monotonic performativity, they offer possibilities of critique and redefinition of ethnic-based definitions of citizenship (Szeman 2018).

17. Aladar Adam's father was *birov* of the Shakhta settlement in Uzhhorod.

18. For further reading on the growing field of medical or donor tourism, see Speier 2016.

19. In Slovakia, anti-Romani sentiments reached all-time highs in the 2000s with elections of right-wing nationalist governments. Nationalist sentiments are captured in billboards along highways with headlines like "How long must we support this filth?" with pictures of Romani settlements. Poverty tourism into Slovak Romani

NOTES 181

settlements reinforces the rhetoric of Romani and non-Romani separation to protect the health of the state and nation.

20. Kevin Karnes identifies eighteenth-century travel writings that mention of village music-making as integral to the "invention" of the concept of Eastern Europe in the eighteenth century (Karnes 2018). Musical niche tourism augments such historically codified discourses of difference that hold the promise of authentic experience.

Chapter 3

1. The use of the arts to draw attention to political agendas is common in developing countries throughout Latin America and the African continent. This approach has been critiqued by scholars like George Yúdice (2003), and Chérie Rivers Ndaliko and Samuel Anderson (2020), and echoed by scholars in the Balkans where arts initiatives are used to strengthen inter-ethnic relations in the aftermath of war.

2. Mark Katz, a founding director of Next Level, a US Department of State–funded program that sends US hip-hop artists abroad to foster cultural exchange, conflict transformation, and entrepreneurship, has placed himself and the university he works in at the center of a transglobal network that emphasizes shared social and cultural values. Organizing events in thirty countries on six continents, Katz has aligned his research interests with the US government's historical uses of music as soft-power diplomacy to internationalize discourses of democracy and equal rights through hip-hop, a genre once censored on US airwaves and scrutinized closely by the FBI for its anti-establishment rhetoric (Katz 2019). As Katz suggests, "Hip-hop . . . can facilitate these kinds of relationships and outcomes for three reasons: its popularity, its accessibility, and its appealing mythos. Hip-hop is known and practiced all over the world, which means that wherever Next Level goes, hip-hop already exists, or is at least known. We thus use it as a bridge, a means to connect people who would have little reason to interact otherwise" (Katz 2017). Katz has effectively used his position as a musicologist and professor to foster relationships among hip-hop musicians and disenfranchised youth worldwide to push forward messages of hope, equality, and human rights.

3. For an analysis of ideological clashes that surround NGO-sponsored arts projects in conflict zones across the African continent, see also Ndaliko and Anderson 2020.

4. Recent ethnomusicological publications point to the interpolation between music and human rights advocacy as an increasing norm rather than an exception. Angela Impey's work in western Maputaland, a region that shares borders with South Africa, Mozambique, and Swaziland, shows how people resist political borders through song. Impey analyzes how *amaculo manihamba*, women's walking songs, helped reshape imaginaries of place in the context of internationally driven transboundary environmental land conservation efforts (Impey 2018). Her work brings forth stories of people whose voices are silenced in the region where they live. Similarly, Alex Chavez, in his analysis of *huapango arribeño*, a musical genre originating in north-central Mexico, draws on multi-cited ethnographic fieldwork to show how Mexicans living on both sides of the US-Mexico border use music to form meaningful communities

182 NOTES

amid harsh US immigration policies (Chavez 2017). His work stands as a critique of anti-immigration rhetoric and serves as a call to awareness of the dangerous frameworks within which such musical traditions are forced to persevere.

5. Rebecca Dirksen brings our attention to the interpolation of applied ethnomusicology and development. However, she points to the difficulty in researching music-related programs initiated by large-scale and small-scale organizations because such programs are often short-lived due to limited funding (Dirksen 2012). Dirksen has charted new paths for applied ethnomusicologists by laying the foundational groundwork of an Indiana University-based project titled the Ethnomusicology Advocacy Toolkit. The Ethnomusicology Advocacy Toolkit includes (1) information pertaining to advocacy organizations that work in music and the arts; (2) guidance on interfacing with local and national institutions and elected representatives; (3) a list of potential funders and tips to manage support; (4) an overview of multicultural music education and leading proponents; (5) a review of monitoring and evaluation (M&E) as a means to develop quantitative and qualitative data collection models; (6) an introduction to copyright law including case studies; and (7) general resources including a glossary and extended bibliography. One notable feature of the toolkit is (8) a set of filmed interview profiles with scholars who describe their work as applied, activist, engaged, or advocacy. This set of resources reinforces the increasingly central role of applied work within a discipline that views itself steeped in critical consciousness and connected with musical traditions that serve as catalysts for positive change.

6. Through his research among Palestinian musicians, David McDonald urges us to come forward, and to stand on the barricades, so to speak, alongside the people with whom we work (McDonald 2013).

7. Eva Brems, Laurens Lavrysen, and Lieselot Verdonck argue that universities must bear responsibility for human rights (Brems et al. 2019).

8. The Homestead Strike of 1892 was a violent labor dispute between union workers and the Carnegie Steel Company near Pittsburgh.

9. Arriving to teach at the University of Pittsburgh in 2008, less than a mile away from Duquesne University, I felt quite at home, having met many of the Duquesne University Tamburitzan dancers over the years while working as a rehearsal accompanist between 1993–2003 for the Ukrainian folk dance camps in upstate New York run by dancer and choreographer Roma Pryma-Bohachevsky (1927–2004). These experiences formed the basis of my master's thesis at Columbia University titled "Negotiating Authenticity in an Invented Tradition" (2001, unpublished).

10. The University of Pittsburgh Nationality Rooms are on the first and third floors of the Cathedral of Learning, a forty-two-story Late Gothic Revival building commissioned in 1921 and formally dedicated in 1937. A part of the funding for the building came from the "Buy a Brick for Pitt" campaign. Each schoolchild was encouraged to send a dime as part of the fundraiser along with a letter explaining how they had earned the dime. 97,000 certificates were issued to children for dime (brick) donations. The first and third floors of the Cathedral of Learning house the Nationality Rooms were built through donations from ethnic communities that had settled in Allegheny

County. The first rooms were completed in 1938, and new rooms have been added as recently as 2019. The Nationality Rooms are steered by committees that sponsor events and offer scholarships to their affiliated countries. This structure, unfortunately, marginalizes Roms, a minority in every nation-state.

11. Death looms large among impoverished Roms, and Romani cosmologies are such that the dead are not mentioned for a year after they are buried. They are released from their earthly responsibilities, and their favorite belongings are often buried along with them. Large funerals among Roms have been documented by scholars including Carol Miller (2010), Péter Szuhay and Edit Kőszegi (2005), Steve Piskor (2012), Ioanida Costache, and others.

12. I attended many funerals for those who lost their lives to suicide, alcohol, and smoking. I also mourned the man who accidentally electrocuted himself on the city telephone pole he had climbed to cut a live wire with scissors, hoping to sell the wire at the *bazaar* to feed his family.

13. This sentiment is similar to the Romani proverb from which Isabel Fonseca draws the title of her book: "Bury me standing because I have lived on my knees" (Fonseca 1995).

14. For a multidimensional analysis of the role of world music ensembles in university settings, see Solis 2004.

15. Performance groups like Gogol Bordello have been a staple on college campuses for almost two decades. The soundtracks of Emir Kusturica films have become increasingly popular on college radio shows. Moreover, concerts of "Gypsy"/Balkan fusion-inspired groups that draw on a hipster aesthetic, odd meters, brass harmonies, and often-nonsensical English-language lyrics, were both accessible to a university crowd and common enough in the 2000s that a big percentage of students had engaged with this type of sound long before they had entered my classroom.

16. Zuzana Jurková's interview with Khamoro festival organizers Jelena Silajdžić and her husband, music director Džemil Silajdžić, highlights how so-called expressive specialists create the context in which there certain musical (and cultural) manifestations are understood as Romani and how such festival settings help determine what is perceived as Romani music (Jurková 2019).

17. There is a certain irony in Romani involvement in the Tánchaz movement because, as Mary Taylor points out, folk revivals in Hungary were associated with an exclusionary form of Hungarianness and closely tied with determinations of citizenship and relationships to the state (Taylor 2008). Roms do not enjoy equal rights and privileges in Hungary. Their participation in the Tánchaz movement was an attempt at inclusion that contributed to their further exclusion due to the movement's fostering of Hungarian nationalism.

18. "Overall numbers by ethnicity or category of deportee," Memorial and Museum Auschwitz-Birkenau: Former German Nazi Concentration and Extermination Camp, http://auschwitz.org/en/history/the-number-of-victims/overall-numbers-by-ethnicity-or-category-of-deportee. Accessed April 15, 2021.

19. For an example of undergraduate research that emerged from these experiences, see Zajdel 2013.

184   NOTES

Chapter 4

1. The interactive website JewishGen KehilaLinks offers information on Jewish families in Uzhhorod. Tabs include links to the following categories: Town, Town Views, Religious, Cemetery, Holocaust, and Family. https://kehilalinks.jewishgen.org/uzhhorod. Accessed June 13, 2019.
2. Changing conceptions of Europe have resulted in various claims to the geographical center of Europe, the first being in 1775 by the Polish royal astronomer and cartographer Szymon Antoni Sobiekrajski, who calculated it to be in the town of Suchowola in modern northeastern Poland. The method used was calculating equal distances from the extreme points of Europe: the westernmost point in Portugal, the easternmost point in the Central Urals, the northernmost point in Norway, and the southernmost point in Greece. In 1815, a second Austro-Hungarian declaration allegedly named the mining town of Kremnica in modern-day Slovakia as the geographical center of Europe. However, the method used for calculating is unknown.
3. Ivan Franko's short story *Tsyhany* (Gypsies) (1882) was translated from Ukrainian by Adriana Helbig and Oksana Kruhliy.
4. According to the most recent census in 2001, there are 47,587 *Tsyhany* in Ukraine. Unofficial estimates place the number of Roms in Ukraine between 120,000 and 400,000. The statistics used in this book follow those presented by Romani politicians and Romani NGO leaders in Transcarpathia, where recent work has shown that Roms were omitted from the 2001 census and inscribed as Ukrainian or Hungarian to secure greater government funding for those groups. For more information regarding census figures on "Gypsies" under Communist and on "Roms" and "Egyptians" in post-Communist Eastern Europe, see Friedman 2007.
5. The root of this endonym stems from the Greek word *Atsigani*, the name of a heathen sect in the Byzantine Empire, and means "untouchable." Like the word Gypsy, a term applied to Roma groups by outsiders who had erroneously thought they had come from Egypt, *Tsyhan* carries the racial implications of an outsider, one who comes from someplace else and does not belong "here." Hence, the dark-skinned nomad, whose wanderings position him beyond the control of the state, is vilified in contrast to the morally good, law-abiding citizen.
6. Oksana Sapeliak, *Ethnohrafichni studiï v Naukovomu Tovarystvi im. Shevchenka* [Ethnographic studies in the Shevchenko Scientific Society] (Lviv: Shevchenko Scientific Society Press, 2002).
7. Volodymyr Hnatiuk, *Etnohrafichni materialy z uhorskoï Rusi* [Ethnographic materials from Hungarian Rus] (Lviv, 1909).
8. Jurij Zhatkovych, "Zamitky etnohrafichni z uhorskoï Rusi [Ethnographic notes from Hungarian Rus]," in *Etnohrafichnyĭ zbirnyk tom 2* [Ethnographic collection Vol. 2], (Lviv, 1896).
9. Fedir Vovk, *Antropolohichni doslidy ukrajinskoho naselennia halychyny, bukovyny ï uhorshchyny—Materialy do Ukraïnsko-Ruskoï Etnolohiï tom 10* [Anthropological studies of the Ukrainian population in Galicia, Bukovyna, and Hungary—Materials for Ukrainian-Rus Ethnology Vol. 10] (Lviv, 1908).

NOTES 185

10. Filarett Kolessa, "Narodni pisni z pidkarpatsk'koï Rusi' [Folk Songs from Sub-Carpathian Rus]," *Naukovyï zbirnik tovarystva "Prosvita" v Uzhhorodi* [Scholarly collection of the "Prosvita" organization in Uzhhorod] (Uzhhorod, 1938), xiii–xiv.

11. Audra Simpson argues that anthropological knowledge was in imperial contexts to gather knowledge about the colonized. Such knowledge facilitated governance (Simpson 2007).

12. A loose translation from the Ruthenian-language song "Eĭ, zahud my, hudachku" (Play for me, musician), transcribed by Filarett Kolessa in Radvanka, Transcarpathia, is as follows: "Play for me, musician / I'll kill a (female) cat for you / If it's not enough, / I'll skin the fat off a (female) cat. // Play for me, musician / on thin strings / If it's not enough / I'll skin the fat off a (male) cat. //" The non-Rom offers the Romani violinist a dead cat if he plays a song of the listener's choosing. The non-Romani listener seeks pleasure in the Romani violinist's music but disrespects him by not offering monetary compensation.

13. Mykola Dmytrenko, *Ukraïnska folklorystyka druhoï polovyny XIX stolittia: Shkoly, postati, problemy* [Ukrainian folkloristics of the second half of the nineteenth century: Schools, figures, problems] (Kyiv: Stal, 2004).

14. ibid., 174.

15. ibid., 207.

16. ibid., 179.

17. The book *Kalo Rom* [Black Gypsy] written by Volodymyr Fedynyshynets describes the history of interactions among Romani groups in Uzhhorod. It was published with grants from the Open Society Institute and the International Renaissance Foundation. The project was proposed by Villie Pap, leader of the Lautary (Musicians) Romani organization in Uzhhorod and director of the Uzhhorod National Romani Theater. See Volodymyr Fedynyshynets, *Kalo Rom/Chornyĭ Tsyhan* [Black Gypsy] (Uzhhorod: V. Padiak Press, 2001).

18. In contrast, Russian scholars published numerous volumes on *Tsygan* folklore. Efim Druts and Aleksei Gessler, *Skazki i pesni rozhdennyje na doroge* [Stories and songs born on the road] (Moscow: Nauka, 1985); Efim Druts and Aleksei Gessler, *Narodnyje pesni russkikh tsygan* [Folk Songs of Russian Gypsies] (Moscow: Sovetskii Kompozitor, 1988); R. S. Demeter and P. S. Demeter, *Obraztsy folklora tsygan-kelderarei* [Folklore of Kelderari Gypsies] (Moscow: Eastern Literatures, 1981).

19. Victor Chovka from the Uzhhorod Roma television program *Romano lav* (Romani voice) hosted a feature segment with Kandra Horvath Jozsef Dzanesz titled "The Three Hundred Year History of a Musical Dynasty." It was posted to Facebook in May 2019 by the interviewer.

20. Kandra Horvath's style emanates the now popular postsocialist aesthetic among more affluent Romani men who don crisp white shirts, skinny black ties with smartly tailored black suits, black shoes with slightly rounded-up front tips, and black sunglasses.

21. For more information on Hungarian Romani musical styles, see Hooker 2013; Irén Kertesz Wilkinson 1990, 1995, 1997, 2002; and Barbara Rose Lange 2003.

22. In Uzhhorod, discothèques organized by Romani leaders for Romani youths are often run at two Rom-only schools in proximity to the main Romani settlement in

186 NOTES

Radvanka and the smaller Romani settlement in Shakhta on the opposite end of Uzhhorod. The school near the Shakhta settlement was built in the 1920s as a school for Roms and has remained segregated. The school near the Radvanka settlement evolved into a segregated school for Roma when non-Romani parents pulled their children out of the school in the 1970s as more and more Roms from the local vicinity began to attend. Socializing and dancing at discos take place under strict adult supervision. However, it is interesting to note that teens only visit the disco in their particular camp, whether Radvanka or Shakhta due to the historical, cultural, and economic differences among the city's Romani groups.

23. Eleanor Kelly, "Roma Hip-Hop and Rap Emerges onto the World Stage," Open Society Foundations, 2012, https://www.opensocietyfoundations.org/voices/roma-hip-hop-and-rap-emerges-world-stage. Accessed June 20, 2019.

24. For an in-depth study of *lăutari* in Romania and the role of male Romani musicians in political and ethnic identity construction, see Beissinger 1991, 2001.

25. Dirt, poverty, and disease were perceived as the greatest threats to the socialist state. The countryside was described as *hlykhyi*, deaf (i.e., disabled) and in need of reform (Starks 2008, 14).

26. Volodymyr Fedynyshynets, *Kalo Rom/Chornyĭ Tsyhan* (Uzhhorod: V. Padiak Press, 2001), 55–60.

Chapter 5

1. Such narratives are documented by human rights organizations like the European Roma Rights Center that report police harassment of Roms in Ukraine (Cahn 1997).

2. North Korean communist leaders deny the existence of poverty and hunger in their country for similar reasons.

3. Svetlana Alexievich, originally from Ivano-Frankivsk, Ukraine, poignantly captures the dramas of this time in her 2017 award-winning novel *Secondhand Time: The Last of the Soviets: An Oral History*, trans. Béla Shayevich (New York: Penguin Random House).

4. Svanibor Pettan, in his musical ethnography of Kosovo Roms, notes that Kosovo Albanians for whom Roms performed for feasts expressed solidarity for Albanian protestors killed by Serbian armed forces in 1990 by omitting music from their feasts (Pettan 2002, 246). Pettan illustrates how Kosovo Romani musicians who had historically performed for Albanian celebrations, including circumcisions and weddings, suffered an economic blow to their livelihood because of the violence in the region.

5. Huub van Baar offers an extensive critique of neoliberal governmentality concerning European Romani groups following the fall of communism. Van Baar argues that the programs that set out to improve the lives of Roms have inadvertently laid the foundations of problems that the programs intended to solve (van Baar 2011). Angéla Kóczé and Márton Rövid point to a politics of "double discourse" that frame a neoliberal approach toward Romani integration. These contradictory discourses speak to different audiences and create anti-Romani approaches that maintain critical

NOTES 187

difference and subordination through the racialization of Romani populations (Kóczé and Rövid 2017). See also Van Baar and Angéla Kóczé 2020.

6. In his dissertation, Eben Friedman compares policies in Slovakia against the "Romani Problematic" that commission projects to address specific issues. He compares this piecemeal approach to Rom-focused politics in Macedonia, where Roms are included as a nationality in the 1991 Constitution and are not subject to targeted policies. Friedman notes the low level of violence against Roms in Macedonia in comparison to Slovakia. He illustrates how states take different approaches to ethnic heterogeneity by attempting to eliminate ethnic heterogeneity in some cases while adopting measures that contribute to more peaceful coexistence in others. He makes a case for integration as a method for managing rather than eliminating differences (Friedman 2002). The special issue "Talking about Roma: Implications for Social Inclusion," *Social Inclusion* 3, no. 5 (2015), guest-edited by Friedman, explores various approaches to Romani integration from various scholarly, temporal, and geographic perspectives.

7. Every group is judged and perceived differently in every context as to the reasons for their poverty. In the United States, the idiom "pull yourself up by your bootstraps" means to help yourself through your own merits. The phrase, embodying a social as well as a political ideology, reflects a strong emphasis on self-actualization. This rhetoric implies that those who cannot pull themselves out of poverty do not succeed because they do not work hard enough or lack specific skills, or are perhaps held back because of a character flaw. Unsurprisingly, those who have (consciously or unwittingly) used their white privilege to get ahead deny that opportunities for self-actualization are determined, at least in part, by skin color (Rothenberg 2015).

8. Commission on Security and Cooperation in Europe. "Attacks on Roma in Ukraine." July 25, 2018. https://www.csce.gov/international-impact/events/attacks-roma-ukra ine. Accessed March 20, 2023.

9. Tom O'Neill, "Home of the Roma Kings," *National Geographic* (2012), https://www. nationalgeographic.com/magazine/2012/09/wealthy-roma/. Accessed March 26, 2019. See also Peter Godwin, "Gypsies: The Outsiders," *National Geographic* (April 2001). Scholars Elena Marushiakova and Veselin Popov's self-ascribed "photo book" titled *Gypsies/Roma: In Times Past and Present* (2000) offers a wide range of photographs of Romani houses, including a large number of affluent homes built by Roms in Bulgaria in the 1990s.

10. Historically, economic exchanges between Roms and non-Roms are fraught with anxiety, distrust, and allegations of deceit to such a degree that the concept has spawned words for cheating: like unto its English counterpart is the Ukrainian word *vytsyhanyty,* meaning "to gyp" (to fleece, swindle, or hoodwink, especially out of money), itself derived from the derogatory connotations of the term "Gypsy." The English etymology of "to gyp" is derived from "Gypsy" as well.

11. Throughout my fieldwork, I served as a photographer for weddings, funerals, and other community occasions. Physical photographs were highly requested because they the most tangible and long-lasting document. Photographs taken by me continue to appear in newspaper articles published by the *Romani Yag* newspaper, in

188   NOTES

museum exhibitions, and increasingly, as repositories of community histories as requested by local libraries and archives in Transcarpathia responding to Romani calls for inclusion.

12. Migrant labor among Roms follows paths similar to those of non-Roms in Ukraine. Family members travel for months at a time, abroad to Russia, or, for those with Hungarian passports, to Hungary and then throughout the European Union, in search of work. The critical difference in migration is that unlike non-Roms, among whom migration is gendered, with non-Romani women traveling to Italy to work as domestic laborers and non-Romani men traveling to Portugal as construction workers, Roms travel as families. It is common for married couples to travel together and to bring young children on the journey. This movement follows historical patterns of migrant labor in which whole families traveled together from village to village, entertaining, selling goods, and providing labor in the countryside.

13. The equipment I have used throughout two decades of fieldwork has changed dramatically over the years, leading to a specific set of problems akin to projects that originated long before the advent of the iPhone, Facebook, YouTube, and the like. Generous university grants have allowed me to digitize materials first recorded on DAT, Sony MiniDisc, and even a SONY cassette recorder, eventually settling on a SONY WAV recorder. The myriad technologies through which I have accumulated data have posed as much of a barrier for repatriating the materials in a format accessible to my interlocutors today as they did at various points during my fieldwork. For the most part, my interlocutors have not had any playback equipment, whether cassette recorders or VHS players (for which I had to reformat from my HSTC to the SECAM system used in the former Soviet Union). The majority do not have laptops, though younger Romani professionals now own smartphones (Apple products are not sold in Ukraine; Nokia is the most common brand). The sharing of ethnographic recordings with the community is a public event, usually in a local schoolhouse or Soviet-era community center (a former House of Culture, Dom Kultury).

Chapter 6

1. It is faster to access these Romani houses by cutting across the sunflower field on foot than attempting to access the Romani section of the village via the unpaved road. Roms prefer to take this path than walk through the non-Romani part of the village to get home. Romani sections of villages are not considered to be part of the village itself. Romani houses, often only a few feet away from the last non-Romani house in the village, stand on the edges of villages, on lands where Romani travelers once set up winter camps.

2. Instruments have traditionally been made from surrounding wood and materials available to them (Dirksen 2019). Taking such instruments out of their natural environments often wreaks havoc on their make-up and hinders their ability to produce sound.

NOTES 189

3. Today, *bazaars*, once held on public land and open for trade by all during the Soviet era, are controlled by *oligarchs*, economically strong men who own the once-public land and privatized the petty trade. Roms can no longer afford to trade at the larger inter-ethnic *bazaars* in towns and engage with informal trade with other Roms. Many *bazaars*, institutionalized with standard booths, have grown to function as malls (with larger modern malls built nearby). The former bazaar stalls are set-up haphazardly and are reminiscent of the step-by-step buildup of economic complexes that marked the beginnings of the transition postsocialist market economy.

4. Had I based my research in Kyiv, this book would have focused on the theatrical productions of Teatr Romance and the performances of Kyiv-based Romani elites who had been affiliated with Soviet-era Romani stage performance culture and were recreating such scenes in the capital of independent Ukraine. My travels throughout Transcarpathia were only possible through connections from my mother, a travel agent whose business Scope Travel Inc. had focused on bringing US tourists to the Soviet Union. Scope Travel Inc. emphasized the Ukrainian SSR and later independent Ukraine. I relied on my mother's professional and personal networks from the Soviet-era travel agency called InTourist to help facilitate my in-country travel during my first years in the field. It was not until the infrastructure improved, especially after the 2004 Orange Revolution, that I could begin to travel independently.

5. After World War II, many ethnic Russian military personnel were transferred to Transcarpathia to protect the newly constituted western border of the Soviet Union. They were allotted prime city center housing that many remodeled and sold following the fall of communism. An unbalanced access to capital by certain groups contributed to ethnicity playing a significant role in Transcarpathia's postsocialist economics.

6. Lani Seelinger, "These Putin Piano Playing Theories Insinuate There's More to It than Music," https://www.bustle.com/p/these-putin-piano-playing-theories-insinuate-theres-more-to-it-than-music-57997.

7. Leonid Bershidsky, "Russian Rappers Are Giving Up on Putin," December 14, 2018, *Moscow Times*, https://www.themoscowtimes.com/2018/12/14/russian-rappers-are-giving-up-on-putin-op-ed-a63832. Accessed December 1, 2019.

8. "Anger in Moscow, Joy in Kiev, after Ukraine's Eurovision Triumph," May 15, 2016, https://www.theguardian.com/tv-and-radio/2016/may/15/moscow-kiev-ukraine-eurovision-russia-boycott-jamala-1944. Accessed December 1, 2019.

9. Matt Rahaim shows that at the time when Indians were working to liberate themselves from British rule, British and Indian music enthusiasts found common ground in declaring the harmonium unfit for Indian music. There were three principal objections to the harmonium. First, it cannot glide smoothly between discrete notes; second, that its tuning is wrong; and third, that it is un-Indian (Rahaim 2011, 658).

10. Lev Sergeyevich Termen, known in the West as Leon Theremin, invented the instrument that bears his name while working at the Physical-Technical Institute in St. Petersburg. Working on a high-frequency oscillator as a device for measuring the electrical insulating properties of gases, Theremin added an audio tone in an attempt to improve the device. He discovered that pitch would change when he moved his hand near it. That was in 1922. The CIA would dub one of Theremin's future inventions "the

190 NOTES

Thing"—the wireless "bug" of the Cold War era that could be activated and energized by directing high-frequency energy at it from a distance. This energy transformed the device into a broadcasting microphone that could be monitored by a radio receiver (Glinsky 2000).

11. The English-language documentary *Elektro Moskva* (2014) offers insights into the worlds of synthesizer builder-musicians and how they shaped the punk and rock music scenes in the USSR, a part played by the electric guitar in concurrent popular music scenes in the West.

12. Damascus Kafumbe, in his discussion of musical analysis of the Kawuugulu Clan-Royal Musical Ensemble of the Kingdom of Buganda (among the traditional subkingdoms of modern-day Uganda), argues that the ensemble sustains a complex sociopolitical hierarchy. It interweaves and maintains a delicate balance between kin and clan ties and royal prerogatives through musical performance and storytelling that integrates human and nonhuman stories. Kafumbe describes this phenomenon as "tuning the kingdom" and compares it to the process of tensioning or stretching Kiganda drums, which are constantly moving in and out of tune (Kafumbe 2018).

13. Shaun Williams, "Cimbalom Tuning, Soviet Style," September 6, 2010. http://beyond karpaty.mutiny.net/2010/09/cimbalom-tuning-soviet-style/.

14. Ibid.

15. Among the most popular instruments is the *bayan*, a chromatic button accordion developed in the early twentieth century and named after the eleventh-century bard Boyan. The professionalization of the *bayan* allowed for the performance of melodies that relied on chromaticism and merged the performance of folk music, newly composed folk music, and classical music repertoires. To date, the halls of postsocialist conservatories are flooded with sounds of Bach fugues and Beethoven sonatas performed on the *bayan*. Long past the socialist experiment of making the music of the bourgeoisie available for the proletariat through the modification of folk instruments that can produce the necessary sounds, this class-based fusion of musical styles and repertoires is now guided by aesthetic choice than a political mandate. That said, such performances are becoming much more an attribute of post-Soviet musicianship tied to a class project. Today, the most commonly played instruments are, in fact, foreign-made pianos that carry with them not only markers of class but, more important, cosmopolitanism and a new, post-Soviet understanding of modernity.

16. Thomas Porcello identifies the phenomenon known as print-through, an audible pre- and post-echo of the signal transferred through adjacent layers of magnetic (analog) audiotape when the tape is wound on a reel. Porcello argues that print-through broadens our experiences of recorded music that, in practice, "do not begin with the first note and end with the last" (Porcello 2003, 265).

17. For a discussion on sounds that emanate from the degeneration of musical recordings, see Bates 2004.

18. When specific repertoires call for period instruments of the Baroque, for instance, we expect them to produce the desired pitch. While modern instruments tune to A = 440 Hz, historically accurate performances tune to A = 415 Hz. This darker tuning shapes an agreed-upon aesthetic among musicologists as to a more accurate rendition of the

music of this time based on the physical capabilities of period instruments. Claudio Monteverdi (1567–1643), whose music marks a transition from Renaissance to Baroque aesthetics, makes a note of the so-called Venetian tuning of A = 460 Hz for some of his works (Cyr 2011, Frosch 2003). Numerous exceptions throughout history exist as regards tunings. Moreover, within Western contemporary repertoires over the last century or more, composers have called upon instruments to produce sounds in untraditional ways. While I am not aware of works that call for performances on old or broken instruments, such instruments are often used in ethnomusicological discourse in war contexts. Vedran Smailović, the so-called cellist of Sarajevo, performed Albinoni's Adagio in G minor in ruined buildings during the siege of Sarajevo (1992–1996). Antuanetta Mishchenko, a protest pianist in Kyiv, joined hundreds of protest pianists in the winter of 2013/2014 during the EuroMaidan, playing on pianos painted blue and yellow, the colors of the Ukrainian flag. The upright pianos were rolled out on flatbeds and onto the streets where most of the violence was taking place. Moreover, Aeham Ahmad, a refugee pianist, played his out-of-tune upright piano in June 2014 on a street that had been bombed in Damascus, Syria.

19. As Regula Qureshi, in her studies on the Indian *sarangi*, reminds us, "Instruments mean. They have meaning through cultural knowledge permeated with physicality and affect: embodied knowledge" (Qureshi 2000, 810). Qureshi observes that a musical instrument offers a special kind of material memory in its dual capacity as both a physical body and its embodied acoustic identity. Doubly meaningful as a cultural product and as a tool to articulate cultural meaning through sound, an instrument can become a privileged site for retaining cultural and social memory in the face of newly hegemonic resignifications (Qureshi 2000, 811).

20. The music played for the German officer in the film comprises parts of Chopin's Ballade No. 1 in G Minor (Op. 23, No. 1). In real life, Szpilman played Chopin's Nocturne No. 1 in C♯ Minor (Op. 27, No. 1).

21. Soviet and post-Soviet policies of *propyska*, official address registrations, played an essential part in forcefully settling any Roms still leading a nomadic lifestyle in after World War II. Moved into block housing on the outskirts of towns and villages, nomadic Roms were forced to abandon kinship ties and traditional occupations and crafts such as horse-trading, blacksmithing, carpentry, and metalworking. In some cases, nomadic Roms, having never lived in apartments, built campfires in living rooms and brought their horses (animals central to Romani cultural identity, business interests, and nomadic way of life) inside their homes, much to the horror—and amusement—of their non-Romani neighbors. Michael Stewart describes similar accounts in socialist Hungary (Stewart 1997).

Chapter 7

1. My mother's visit to my fieldwork site in May 1999 elucidated how older Romani men and women interacted with her. She was not only their age at the time (the same age that I am now, writing this book), but she bonded over shared pain and loss with my

192 NOTES

interlocutors. It was she, not I, who, like my Romani interlocutors, had lost siblings and extended family during the war. Furthermore, it was she, not I, who, like my Romani interlocutors, had lived with survivor guilt. She had survived cancer in the 1960s at a time when few did. They connected with the scars on her body from the surgeries and the difficulties she had breathing. They spoke of her raspy voice with concern and offered herbal remedies for her chronic cough. It is very much in the re-listenings and reconceptualizings of histories of mishearing (Ochoa Gautier 2014, 81) that I recognized, more so now than at the time, which sounds produced by the body served as the most critical aural frames of fieldwork.

2. As a member of the Romani Yag team, I often accompanied interviewers on visits to Romani communities. However, the information put forth in this chapter is recalled from memory because during such trips, my goal was to take pictures for publications and documents. We did not record the conversations but instead wrote the information we needed to submit reports or incorporate into newspaper stories. While my colleagues knew that I had an interest in music, it was generally assumed that it was inappropriate to incorporate music-related questions into the conversations. In later years, I often traveled to such villages by myself with the specific goal of recording music. However, many of my attempts proved unsuccessful. I came to accept that the ability to produce music was inextricably linked to the physical health of the musician. In *saman* houses, interviews were often cut short and conversations were conducted in spurts, interrupted by a request for water or a break to rest the vocal cords. Such realities also contributed to the lack of desire some musicians had toward singing. However, some would push through, not wishing to disappoint their ethnographer-guest who had traveled to record their music.

3. Anthropology was among the disciplines politicized by the Nazis.

4. The rhetoric of eugenics serves as a trigger for Roms familiar with Romani Holocaust history. Moreover, interactions with state-controlled medical establishments continue to evoke fears among those aware of the consequences of historical interactions with the state.

5. Polish historian Piotr Warweniuk writes that Roms fleeing from Transcarpathia to Lviv were not as persecuted in the German-occupied city as in the rural countryside and had a greater chance of surviving World War II (Warweniuk 2017).

6. The late Ukrainian Romani poet and activist Mikhail Kozymyrenko (1938–2005) lost thirty-seven members during the Soviet perpetrated Terror-Famine of 1932–1933, *Holodomor* (literally, Death by Hunger). While statistics place the number of Ukrainian deaths at close to 4 million, it is not clear how many of these victims are Romani. To date, Romani politicians and intellectuals have invested their limited resources into documenting Romani Holocaust histories in Ukraine. Significant assistance is needed to help research the devastating toll of the *Holodomor* on Romani populations.

7. In 1920, the Russian Soviet Republic became the first country in the world to allow abortion in all circumstances, but throughout the twentieth century, the legality of abortion changed more than once, with a ban being enacted again from 1936 to 1955.

NOTES   193

8. Anne Sutherland explains how *marime*, pollution taboos regarding Romani (women's) bodies, contribute to ongoing distrust of medical establishments and personnel among Roms in the United States (Sutherland 2017).

9. Involuntary sterilizations of Romani women have continued well after the socialist period. For a review of domestic and international activism for Romani and other women harmed by coercive, forced, and involuntary sterilization in former Czechoslovakia and the Czech Republic, see Albert and Szilvasi 2017.

10. Patrick Strickland, "Life in Slovakia's Slums: Poverty and Segregation," *Aljazeera*, May 10, 2017, https://www.aljazeera.com/indepth/features/2017/04/life-slovakia-roma-slums-poverty-segregation-170425090756677.html. Accessed January 8, 2020.

11. This chapter focuses primarily on tuberculosis and smoking. However, it acknowledges the extensive range of other throat and lung-related ailments, including goiters and thyroid issues in the aftermath of the Chernobyl disaster that wreaked ecological havoc and had a profound impact on health. It also acknowledges death as a result of pneumonia and the weakening of the body through AIDS, a disease not talked about among Roma, but one that continues to spread, especially through the reuse of contaminated needles in Ukraine.

12. Siv Brun Lie notes that the scarring from the fire altered Django's playing technique. With his third and fourth fingers virtually unusable, he had to rely on his index finger, middle finger, and thumb (Lie 2019, 675–76).

13. For in-depth discussions of Django Reinhardt's musical contributions to *manouche* jazz, see Lie 2020, 2019, 2017, 2013.

14. For a detailed history of tobacco use and production in the Russia Empire and the Soviet Union, see Starks 2018.

15. Anna Valeta, "Carmen: The Icon who Rolled Cigars on Her Thighs," *Independent*, February 17, 2002, https://www.independent.co.uk/arts-entertainment/music/featu res/carmen-the-icon-who-rolled-cigars-on-her-thighs-9271572.html.   Accessed December 17, 2018.

16. For an analysis of *Carmen* and smoking from the perspective of an art historian, see Mitchell 1987.

17. Daniel Emerson, "WA Opera to Stage Comeback of Carmen Three Years after It Was Pulled Following Smoking Row," *The West Australian*, November 28, 2017, https:// thewest.com.au/news/wa/wa-opera-to-stage-comeback-of-carmen-three-years-after-it-was-pulled-following-smoking-row-ng-b88673821z.   Accessed   January 15, 2020.

18. Throughout his book *Making Noise: From Babel to the Big Bang & Beyond* (2011), Hillel Schwartz analyzes the role of the larynx, throat, tongue, teeth, and lips in the making of and masking of sound through coughing and other bodily noises.

19. Loudon and Roberts note that singing can spread tuberculosis, citing instances where people were infected at choir practice. They concluded that coughing produces the same amount of droplet nuclei as singing (Loudon and Roberts 1968, 48–49). They also reported on singing-related outbreaks, including a boarding school outbreak where rates of infection were higher among students in the choir (50).

194 NOTES

20. This section draws on well-known examples from classical music to illustrate points about tuberculosis and the arts. While I did not come across Romani songs about tuberculosis, there are certainly musical pieces that reference the disease. For instance, the famous Turkish Romani clarinetist Mustafa Kandıralı has an instrumental piece in which prolonged rhythmic coughing (in 9/8 time) can be understood as referencing tuberculosis.

21. In popular music, Van Morisson brought back the nineteenth-century trope of the bedside vigil in his blues-infused song "T.B. Sheets" recorded in 1967 on the same album that opened with the now-infamous "Brown Eyed Girl." "T.B. Sheets" stands in stark contrast in terms of theme and deals with a disease whose spread had, by the 1960s, been somewhat curbed in the West and had begun to fall away in popular consciousness. The song is sung from the point of view of a male lover who watches as his loved one lies dying from an incurable disease. The protagonist in Morrison's song is unable to cope with his lover's illness and approaching death and ultimately abandons her. Morrison punctuates the song with haunting vocal interjections that embody the dying woman's gasps for breath. He is vocalizing the internal dialogue of a man tormented by his inability to cope, a man who, in the end, abandons his lover. Morrison, who grew up among Belfast's working class, sings as one who has experienced the disease and the torments of not only the sufferers but of those who love them. Poverty, substandard living conditions, and lack of access to medical care, exacerbated by prejudice, left the Irish especially vulnerable. John Lee Hooker covered "T.B. Sheets" on his 1971 studio album, *Never Get Out of These Blues Alive*. In 1927, Okeh Records released "T.B. Blues" by Victoria Spivey, the first of several songs the blueswoman wrote and recorded about tuberculosis. The song speaks of a woman going to visit her ailing mother in Denver, Colorado, home to numerous sanatoriums that, through its dry climate at high elevations, helped to relieve symptoms. Spivey's song was widely covered, rewritten, and imitated by various artists including Josh White, Leadbelly, and Champion Jack Dupree. As tuberculosis was common among African Americans, various aspects of tuberculosis are explored in songs of the time. Themes of abandonment by friends are evident in songs by Buddy Moss ("T.B. Is Killing Me" [1931]) and Sonny Boy Williamson, and in "T.B. Blues" (1939).

22. Focusing on tuberculosis, cancer, and expanding her narrative to include AIDS (Sontag 1989), Susan Sontag pushes against rhetoric that blames the patient for contracting a life-threatening disease, particularly ones that, at the height of their stigmas, were culturally misunderstood and driven by fear because they had no cure. Such is the case of the musical *Rent*, based loosely on the narrative frame of Puccini's tubercular heroine Mimi in *La Bohème*. *Rent* destigmatizes AIDS through the portrayal of the disease in ways that allow audiences to connect, sympathize, and rally for the character rather than stigmatize him, as was the case at the time (Tift 2007).

23. David Morens, "At the Deathbed of Consumptive Art," 2002, https://www.ncbi.nlm.nih.gov/pmc/articles/PMC2738548/.

24. Erica Hersh, "Tuberculosis in Rural America: What Tuberculosis in Marion, LA Tells Us," https://www.hsph.harvard.edu/ecpe/tuberculosis-in-rural-america-what-tuberculosis-in-marion-al-tells-us/.

Chapter 8

1. In *Listening to War: Sound, Music, Trauma, and Survival in Wartime Iraq* (2015), J. Martin Daughtry addresses how post-traumatic stress (PTS) and experiences of military violence shape perspectives on silence, sound, and listening.
2. Studies point to the silent presence of the Holocaust among families, whose tacit knowledge of the past shapes everyday experiences (Kidron 2003, 2009).
3. In her analysis of the Turkish *ney*, a reed instrument, Denise Gill offers a new approach to the study of pain through an instrument's anthropomorphization. Gill traces *ney* making from its cutting in the reed bed to its production of sound. Gill states that the *ney* wails, cries, and laments as an expression of separation. The instrument's sounds embody its sadness and give voice to melancholy (Gill 2017, 64–67).
4. Lillie Gordon presented a paper at the 2018 Society for Ethnomusicology conference in Albuquerque, New Mexico, based on interviews with female ethnomusicologists, recounting their stories of harassment and violence in the field. My stories constituted some of the data she presented.
5. The film was created by Kyiv-based scholar-activist Nataliya Zinevych.
6. LGBTQ issues are not as prominent among Romani activists in Ukraine where discrimination continues to escalate amid rising nationalism. For more on Romani gender politics in Central, Eastern, and South-Eastern Europe, see Kóczé et al. 2018.

Reflection

1. Internet World Stats, Usage and Population Statistics, "Ukraine Internet Usage and Marketing Report," www.internetworldstats.com/euro/ua.htm. Accessed September 25, 2017.
2. Marci Shore, in a synopsis of her ethnography of the EuroMaidan, describes the 2014 Revolution of Dignity as "an existential transformation: the blurring of night and day, the loss of a sense of time, the sudden disappearance of fear, the imperative to make choices" (Shore 2018, back matter).

References

Abbas, Asma. (2010). *Liberalism and Human Suffering: Materialist Reflections on Politics, Ethics, and Aesthetics*. New York: Palgrave Macmillan.

Abbott, E. C. (1982). "Composers and Tuberculosis: The Effects on Creativity." *Canadian Medical Association Journal* 126(5): 534, 536–38, 543–44.

Acton, Thomas. (1974).*Gypsy Politics and Social Change*. London: Routledge.

Ahmed, Sara. (2010). *The Promise of Happiness*. Durham, NC: Duke University Press.

Albert, Gwendolyn, and Marek Szilvasi. (2017). "Intersectional Discrimination of Romani Forcibly Sterilized in the Former Czechoslovakia and Czech Republic." *Health and Human Rights Journal* 17(2): 23–34.

Alexievich, Svetlana. (2017). *Secondhand Time: The Last of the Soviets: An Oral History*. Translated by Béla Shayevich. New York: Penguin Random House.

Allina-Pisano, Jessica. (2007). *The Post-Soviet Potemkin Village: Politics and Property Rights in the Black Earth*. Cambridge: Cambridge University Press.

Allison, Roy. (2014). "Russian 'Deniable' Intervention in Ukraine: How and Why Russia Broke the Rules." *International Affairs* 90(6): 1255–97.

Alvarez, Sonia, Evelina Dagnino, and Arturo Escobar, eds. (1998). *Cultures of Politics, Politics of Cultures: Re-visioning Latin American Social Movements*. Boulder, CO: Westview Press.

Appert, Catherine. (2017). "Engendering Musical Ethnography." *Ethnomusicology* 61(3): 446–67.

Applebaum, David. (1990). *Voice*. Albany: State University of New York Press.

Araújo, Samuel, and Vincezo Cambria. (2013). "Sound Praxis, Poverty, and Social Participation: Perspectives from a Collaborative Study in Rio de Janeiro." *Yearbook for Traditional Music* 45: 28–42.

Bakhtin, Mikhail. 1982. *The Dialogic Imagination: Four Essays* (Trans. Caryl Emerson and Michael Holquist). Austin, TX: University of Texas Press.

Barannikov, Aleksei. (1931). *Ukrain'ski tsyhany*. [Ukrainian Gypsies], Kyiv.

Barannikov, Aleksei. (1933a). *Ukrain'ski ta pivdenno rosijski tsyhanski dialekty*. [Ukrainian and South Russian Gypsy dialects]. Leningrad.

Barannikov, Aleksei. (1933b). *Tsygany SSSR. Kratkii istoriko-etnograficheskii ocherk.* [Gypsies of the USSR: A brief historical ethnographic study]. Moscow 1931.

Barany, Zoltan. (2002). *The East European Gypsies: Regime Change, Marginality, and Ethnopolitics*. Cambridge: Cambridge University Press.

Bardasi, Elena, and Wodon, Quentin. (2006). "Measuring Time Poverty and Analyzing Its Determinants: Concepts and Application to Guinea." MPRA Paper 11082, University Library of Munich, Germany. https://ideas.repec.org/p/pra/mprapa/11082.html. Accessed March 1, 2019.

Bates, Eliot. (2004). "Glitches, Bugs, and Hisses: The Degeneration of Musical Recordings and the Contemporary Musical Work." In *Bad Music: The Music We Love to Hate*, edited by Christopher Washburn and Maiken Derno, 275–93. New York: Routledge.

198 REFERENCES

Baumann, Max Peter. (1996). "The Reflection of the Roma in European Art Music." *The World of Music* 38(1): 95–138.

Beckerman, Michael. (2015). "Oh, the Stories We Tell!: Performer-Audience-Disability." In *The Oxford Handbook of Music and Disability Studies*, edited by Blake Howe, Stephanie Jensen-Mouton, Neil William Lerner, and Joseph Nathan Straus, 293–304. New York: Oxford University Press.

Beissinger, Margaret. (1991). *The Art of the Lăutar: The Epic Tradition of Romania.* New York: Garland Publishing.

Beissinger, Margaret. (2001). "Occupation and Ethnicity: Constructing Identity among Professional Romani (Gypsy) Musicians in Romania." *Slavic Review* 60(1): 24–49.

Beissinger, Margaret. (2016). "Romanian *Manele* and Regional Parallels: 'Oriental' Ethnopop in the Balkans." In *Manele in Romania: Cultural Expression and Social Meaning in Balkan Popular Music*, edited by Margaret Beissinger, Speranta Radulescu, and Anna Giurchescu, 95–138. Lanham, MD: Rowman & Littlefield.

Beissinger, Margaret, Speranta Radulescu, and Anna Giurchescu, eds. (2016). *Manele in Romania: Cultural Expression and Social Meaning in Balkan Popular Music.* Lanham, MD: Rowman & Littlefield.

Beníšek, Michael. (2013). "Serednye Romani: A North Central Romani Variety of Transcarpathian Ukraine." In *Romani V. Papers from the Annual Meeting of the Gypsy Lore Society*, edited by B. Schrammel-Leber and B. Tiefenbacher, 42–60. Graz, University of Graz.

Beníšek, Michael. (2017). *Eastern Uzh Varieties of North Central Romani.* PhD diss., Charles University, Prague.

Berlant, Lauren. (2011). *Cruel Optimism.* Durham: Duke University Press.

Berner, Margit. (2010). "Large-Scale Anthropological Surveys in Austria-Hungary, 1871–1918." In *Doing Anthropology in Wartime and War Zones: World War I and the Cultural Sciences in Europe*, edited by Reinhard Johler, Christian Marchetti, and Monique Scheer, 233–54. London: Transcript Publishing.

Bhabha, Hommi. (1990). *Nation and Narration.* New York: Routledge.

Bhavnani, Kum-Kum, John Fora, and Priya Kurian, eds. (2016). *Feminist Futures: Reimagining Women, Culture, and Development.* London: Zed Books.

Birring, S. S., T. Fleming, S. Matos, A. A. Raj, D. H. Evans, and I. D. Pavord. (2008). "The Leicester Cough Monitor: Preliminary Validation of an Automated Cough Detection System in Chronic Cough." *European Respiratory Journal* 31: 1013–18.

Bobri, Vladimir. (1961). "Gypsies and Gypsy Choruses of Old Russia." *Journal of the Gypsy Lore Society* 40: 112–19.

Booth, Eric, and Tricia Tunstall. (2016). *Playing for Their Lives: The Global El Sistema Movement for Social Change Through Music.* New York: W. W. Norton.

Botha G. H. R., G. Theron, R. M. Warren, M. Klopper, K. Dheda, P. D. van Helden, and T. R. Niesler. 2018. "Detection of tuberculosis by automatic cough sound analysis." *Physiological Measurement* 39(4): 045005.

Brems, Eva, Laurens Lavrysen, and Lieselot Verdonck. (2019). "Universities as Human Rights Actors." *Journal of Human Rights Practice* 11(1): 229–38.

Brown, Kate. (2019). *Manual for Survival: A Chernobyl Guide for the Future.* New York: W. W. Norton.

Brüggemann, Christian, and Eben Friedman. (2017). "The Decade of Roma Inclusion: Origins, Actors, and Legacies." *European Education* 49(1): 1–9.

REFERENCES 199

Burland, Karen, and Stephanie Pitts, eds. (2014). *Coughing and Clapping: Investigating Audience Experience*. Farnham: Ashgate.

Byrne, Katherine. (2011). *Tuberculosis and the Victorian Literary Imagination* Cambridge: Cambridge University Press.

Cahn, Claude. (1997). *The Misery of Law—The Rights of Roma in the Transcarpathian Region of Ukraine*. Budapest: European Roma Rights Center.

Calhoon, Claudia. (2001). "Tuberculosis, Race, and the Delivery of Health Care in Harlem, 1922–1939." *Radical History Review* 80: 101–19.

Cartwright, Garth. (2005). *Princes amongst Men: Journeys with Gypsy Musicians*. London: Serpent's Tale.

Casper, Monica, and Eric Wertheimer. (2016). *Critical Trauma Studies: Understanding Violence, Conflict, and Memory in Everyday Life*. New York: New York University Press.

Castells, Manuel. (1996–1998). *The Information Age. Economy, Society and Culture, Vol. 1, 2, 3*. Oxford: Blackwell Publishers.

Cavandoli, Sofia. (2016). "The Unresolved Dilemma of Self-Determination: Crimea, Donetsk and Luhansk." *International Journal of Human Rights* 20(7): 875–92.

Centers for Disease Control and Prevention (CDCP) (2017). *Tuberculosis: African American Community*. https://www.cdc.gov/tb/topic/populations/tbinafricanameric ans/default.htm. Accessed June 18, 2019.

Chandler, Diane. (2015). *The Road to Donetsk*. London: Blackbird Digital Books.

Chavez, Alex. (2017). *Sounds of Crossing: Music, Migration, and the Aural Poetics of Huapango Arribeño*. Durham, NC: Duke University Press.

Chlebak, Nicolas. (2015). *The "Adaptability" of the Balalaika: An Ethnomusicological Investigation of the Russian Traditional Folk Instrument*. College honors thesis, University of Vermont College of Arts and Sciences.

Cooper, B. Lee, and William Schurk. (1999). "Singing, Smoking, and Sentimentality: Cigarette Imagery in Contemporary Recordings." *Popular Music and Society* 23(3): 79–88.

Crewe, Emma, and Elizabeth Harrison. (1998). *Whose Development?: An Ethnography of Aid*. New York: Zen Books.

Crowe, David. (1994). *A History of the Gypsies of Eastern Europe and Russia*. New York: St. Martin's Press.

Cyr, Mary. (2011). *Performing Baroque Music*. London: Routledge.

Daughtry, J. Martin. (2015). *Listening to War: Sound, Music, Trauma, and Survival in Wartime Iraq*. New York: Oxford University Press.

Dave, Nomi. 2015. "Music and the Myth of Universality: Sounding Human Rights and Capabilities." *Journal of Human Rights Practice* 7(1): 1–17.

Derrett, Ros, Norman Douglas, and Ngaire Douglas. (2001). *Special Interest Tourism: Starting with the Individual*. Milton, Australia: John Wiley and Sons Australia.

Dickinson, Jennifer. (1999). *Life on the Edge: Understanding Social Change through Everyday Conversation in a Ukrainian Border Community*. PhD diss., University of Michigan.

Dirksen, Rebecca. (2012). "Reconsidering Theory and Practice in Ethnomusicology: Applying, Advocating, and Engaging Beyond Academia." *Ethnomusicology Review* 17. https://www.ethnomusicologyreview.ucla.edu/journal/volume/17/piece/602. Accessed November 23, 2019.

200 REFERENCES

Dirksen, Rebecca. (2013). "Surviving Material Poverty by Employing Cultural Wealth: Putting Music in the Service of Community in Haiti." *Yearbook for Traditional Music* 45: 43–57.

Dirksen, Rebecca. (2019). "Haiti's Drums and Trees: Facing Loss of the Sacred." *Ethnomusicology* 63(1): 43–77.

Dudwick, Nora, Elizabeth Gomart, Alexandre Marc, and Kathleen Kuehst, eds. (2003). *When Things Fall Apart: Qualitative Studies of Poverty in the Former Soviet Union*. Washington, DC: The World Bank.

Easterly, William, and Tobias Pfutze. (2008). "Where Does the Money Go? Best and Worst Practices in Foreign Aid." *Journal of Economic Perspectives* 22(2): 29–52.

Edelman, Marc, and Angelique Haugerud. (2005). *The Anthropology of Development and Globalization: From Classical Political Economy to Contemporary Neoliberalism*. Malden, MA: Blackwell.

Eidscheim, Nina Sun. (2019). *The Race of Sound: Listening, Timbre, and Vocality in African American Music*. Durham, NC: Duke University Press.

Elšík, Viktor, and Michael Beníšek. (2020). "Romani Dialectology." In *The Palgrave Handbook of Romani Language and Linguistics*, edited by Yaron Matras and Anton Tenser, 389–427. Cham, Switzerland: Palgrave Macmillan.

Engebrigtsen, Ada. (2007). *Exploring Gypsiness: Power, Exchange, and Interdependence in a Transylvanian Village*. New York: Berghahn Books.

Escobar, Arturo. (1995). *Encountering Development: The Making and Unmaking of the Third World*. Princeton, NJ: Princeton University Press.

European Roma Rights Center (ERRC). (2001). *Roma Rights in Ukraine: Published Materials 1997–2001*. Budapest: ERRC.

European Roma Rights Center (ERRC). (2005). *In Search of Happy Gypsies: Persecution of Pariah Minorities in Russia*. Budapest: ERRC.

European Roma Rights Center (ERRC). (2006). *Proceedings Discontinued: The Inertia of Roma Rights Change in Ukraine*. Budapest: ERRC.

European Roma Rights Center (ERRC). (2011). *Funding Roma Rights: Challenges and Prospects*. Budapest: ERRC.

European Roma Rights Center (ERRC). (2012). *Challenges of Representation: Voices on Roma Politics, Power and Participation*. Budapest: ERRC.

Ferguson, James. (2015). *Give a Man a Fish: Reflections on the New Politics of Distribution*. Durham NC: Duke University Press.

Fiol, Stefan. (2013). "Of Lack and Loss: Assessing Cultural and Musical Poverty in Uttarakhand." *Yearbook for Traditional Music* 45: 83–96.

Fonseca, Isabel. (1995). *Bury Me Standing: The Gypsies and Their Journey*. New York: Vintage.

Fox, Aaron. (2004). "White Trash Alchemies of the Abject Sublime: Country as Bad Music." In *Bad Music: The Music We Love to Hate*, ed. Christopher Washburn and Maiken Derno, 39–61. New York: Routledge.

Fraser, Angus. (1992). *The Gypsies*. Oxford: Blackwell Publishing.

Frenzel, Fabian. (2016). *Slumming It: The Tourist Valorization of Urban Poverty*. London: Zed Books.

Frenzel, Fabian, Ko Koens, and Malte Steinbrink. (2012). *Poverty Tourism: Poverty, Power, and Ethics*. New York: Routledge.

REFERENCES 201

Friedman, Eben. (2002). *Explaining the Political Integration of Minorities: Roms as a Hard Case: Comparing Roms in Slovakia and Macedonia.* PhD diss., University of California, San Diego.

Friedman, Eben. (2007). "The Politics of the Census: Of Gypsies, Roms, and Egyptians." *Anthropology of East Europe Review* 25(2): 67–77.

Frosch, Reinhart. (2003). *Meantone Is Beautiful: Studies on Tunings of Musical Instruments.* New York: Peter Lang Publishing.

Gabrielson, Tatiana Nikolayevna. (2006). *Propaganda of Romani Culture in Post-Soviet Ukraine.* PhD diss., University of Texas at Austin.

Gelbart, Petra. (2010). *Learning Music, Race, and Nation in the Czech Republic.* PhD diss., Harvard University.

Gill, Denise. (2017). *Melancholic Modalities: Affect, Islam, & Turkish Classical Musicians.* New York: Oxford University Press.

Glinsky, Albert. (2000). *Theremin: Ether Music and Espionage.* Urbana: University of Illinois Press.

Goluboff, Sascha. (2008). "Communities of Mourning: Mountain Jewish Laments in Azerbaijan and on the Internet." In *Religion, Morality, and Community in Post-Soviet Societies,* edited by Mark Steinberg and Catherine Wanner, 149–77. Bloomington: Indiana University Press.

Gotved, Stine. (2006). "Time and Space in Cyber Social Reality." *New Media & Society* 8(3): 467–86.

Grimshaw, Anna, and Amanda Ravetz, eds. (2004). *Visualizing Anthropology: Experimenting with Image-Based Anthropology.* Chicago: University of Chicago Press.

Greenburg, Cheryl. (1991). *Or Does It Explode?: Black Harlem in the Great Depression.* New York: Oxford University Press.

Grellman, Heinrich Moritz Gottlieb. (1787 [2000]). *Dissertation on the Gipsies: Being an Historical Enquiry, Concerning the Manner of Life, Economy, Customs and Conditions of These People in Europe, and Their Origin.* Written in German, by Heinrich Moritz Gottlieb Grellman. Translated into English by Matthew Raper. London: G. Bigg.

Grill, Jan. (2011). "From Street Busking in Switzerland to Meat Factories in the UK: A Comparative Study of Two Roma Migration Networks from Slovakia." In *Global Connections and Emerging Inequalities in Europe: Perspectives on Poverty and Transnational Migration,* edited by Deema Kaneff and Frances Pine, 79–102. London: Anthem Press.

Guy, Will. (2002). *Between Past and Future: The Roma of Central and Eastern Europe.* Hertfordshire, UK: University of Hertfordshire Press.

Guy, Will. (2009). "EU Initiatives on Roma: Limitations and Ways Forward." In *Romani Politics in Contemporary Europe: Poverty, Mobilization, and the Neo-Liberal Order,* edited by Nando Sigona and Nidhi Trehan, 23–50. Basingstoke: Palgrave Macmillan.

Habermas, Jürgen. (1984). *Theory of Communicative Action.* Boston: Beacon Press.

Halberstam, Judith. (2011). *The Queer Art of Failure.* Durham, NC: Duke University Press.

Hancock, Ian. (2002). *We Are the Romani People.* Hertfordshire, UK: University of Hertfordshire Press.

Hann, Charles, ed. (2002). *Postsocialism: Ideals, Ideologies, and Practices in Eurasia.* London: Routledge.

Hansen, Arve, Andrei Rogatchevski, Ingvar Steinholt, and David-Emil Wikström. (2019). *A War of Songs: Popular Music and Recent Russia-Ukraine Relations.* Stuttgart: Ibidem Verlag.

202 REFERENCES

Harrison, Klisala. (2013). "The Relationship of Poverty to Music." *Yearbook for Traditional Music* 45: 1–12.

Harrison, Klisala. (2020). *Music Downtown Eastside: Human Rights and Capability Development through Music in Urban Poverty*. New York: Oxford University Press.

Harvey, David. (2007). *A Brief History of Neoliberalism*. Oxford: Oxford University Press.

Haskell, Erica. (2015). "The Role of Applied Ethnomusicology in Post-Conflict and Post-Catastrophe Communities." In *The Oxford Handbook of Applied Ethnomusicology*, edited by Jeff Todd Titon and Svanibor Pettan, 453–80. Oxford: Oxford University Press.

Haskell, Erica. (2017). "Funding Festivals: Bringing the World to the Capital, Sarajevo." *Muzikoloski Zbornik* (Musicology—Institute of Musicology, Serbian Academy of Sciences and Arts) 22: 133–49.

Haskell, Erica, Adriana Helbig, and Nino Tsitsishvilli. (2008). "Managing Musical Diversity within Frameworks of Western Development Aid: Views from Ukraine, Georgia, and Bosnia and Herzegovina." *Yearbook for Traditional Music* 40: 46–59.

Helbig, Adriana. (2005). *Music as Political Resource in the Romani Rights Movement in Ukraine*. PhD diss., Columbia University.

Helbig, Adriana. (2006). "The Cyberpolitics of Music in Ukraine's 2004 Orange Revolution." *Current Musicology* 82: 81–101.

Helbig, Adriana. (2009). "Representation and Intracultural Dynamics: Romani Musicians and Cultural Rights Discourse in Ukraine." In *Music and Cultural Rights*, edited by Andrew Weintraub and Bell Yung, 269–95. Urbana: University of Illinois Press.

Helbig, Adriana. (2014). *Hip Hop Ukraine: Music, Race, and African Migration*. Bloomington: Indiana University Press.

Hillis, Faith. (2013). *Children of Rus': Right Bank Ukraine and the Invention of a Russian Nation*. Ithaca, NY: Cornell University Press.

Holmes, Leslie. (2006). *Rotten States?: Corruption, Post-Communism, and Neoliberalism*. Durham, NC: Duke University Press.

Holst-Warhaft, Gail. (1992). *Dangerous Voices: Women's Laments and Greek Literature*. London; New York: Routledge.

Hooker, Lynn. (2013). *Redefining Hungarian Music from Liszt to Bartók*. Oxford: Oxford University Press.

Howe, Blake, and Stephanie Jensen-Moulton, eds. (2016). *The Oxford Handbook of Music and Disability Studies*. New York: Oxford University Press.

Hrycak, Alexandra. (2007). "From Global to Local Feminisms: Transnationalism, Foreign Aid and the Women's Movement in Ukraine." In *Sustainable Feminisms*, edited by Sonita Sarker, 75–93. Bradford, UK: Emerald Group Publishing.

Hrytsak, Yaroslav. (2018). *Ivan Franko and His Community*. Boston: Academic Studies Press.

Hutcheon, Linda, and Michael Hutcheon. (1996). "Famous Last Breaths: The Tubercular Heroine in Opera." *Parallax* 2(1): 1–22.

Ignățoiu-Sora, Emanuela. (2011). "The Discrimination Discourse in Relation to the Roma: Its Limits and Benefits." *Ethnic and Racial Studies* 34(10): 1697–714.

Impey, Angela. (2018). *Song Walking: Women, Music, and Environmental Justice in an African Borderland*. Chicago: Chicago University Press.

Jurková, Zuzana. (2019). "Backstage People." In *Voicing the Unheard: Music as Windows for Minorities*, edited by Yves Defrance, 139–54. Rennes: L'Harmattan.

Kafumbe, Damascus. (2018). *Tuning the Kingdom: Kawuugulu Musical Performance, Politics, and Story Telling in Buganda*. Rochester: University of Rochester Press.

REFERENCES 203

Kapralski, Slawomir, Maria Martyniak, and Joanna Talewicz-Kwiatkowska. (2011). *Roma in Auschwitz*. Oświęcim, Poland: Auschwitz-Birkenau State Museum.

Karnes, Kevin. (2018). "Inventing Eastern Europe in the Ear of the Enlightenment." *Journal of the American Musicological Society* 71(1): 75–108.

Katz, Mark. (2017). "The Case for Hip-Hop Diplomacy." *American Music Review* 46(2): 1–5.

Katz, Mark. (2019). *Build: The Power of Hip Hop Diplomacy in a Divided World*. Oxford: Oxford University Press.

Kertész Wilkinson, Irén. (1990). "Lokes Phen!: An Investigation into the Musical Tempo of Feeling of a Hungarian Gypsy Community Based On Their Own Evaluation." In *100 Years of Gypsy Studies*, edited by Matt Salo, 193–201. Cheverly, MD: Gypsy Lore Society.

Kertész Wilkinson, Irén. (1995). "Therapeutic Aspect of Vlach Gypsy Singing." In *Voice and Ritual: Folklore Commission of the Russian Union of Composers*, edited by K. Dorothova, 107–23. Moscow: Institute of State Art.

Kertész Wilkinson, Irén. (1997). *The Fair Is Ahead of Me: Individual Creativity and Social Contexts in the Performances of a Southern Hungarian Vlach Gypsy Slow Song*. Budapest: Institute for Musicology of the Hungarian Academy for Sciences.

Kertész Wilkinson, Irén. (2002). "Between Life and Death: Mourning and Funerary Rites among the Hungarian Roma." In *Music, Sensation, and Sensuality*, edited by Linda P. Austern, 181–99. London: Routledge,

Kidron, Carol. (2003). "Surviving a Distant Past: A Case Study of the Cultural Construction of Trauma Descendant Identity." *Ethos* 31(4): 513–44.

Kidron, Carol. (2009). "Toward an Ethnography of Silence: The Lived Presence of the Past in the Everyday Life of Holocaust Trauma Survivors and Their Descendants in Israel." *Current Anthropology* 50(1): 5–27.

Kind-Kovács, Friederike, and Jessie Labov, eds. (2013). *Samizdat, Tamizdat, and Beyond: Transnational Media during and after Socialism*. New York: Berghahn Books.

Kirschenblatt-Gimblett, Barbara. (1998). *Destination Culture: Tourism, Museums, and Heritage*. Berkeley: University of California Press.

Knight, Nathaniel. (2000). "'Salvage Biography' and Usable Pasts: Russian Ethnographers Confront the Legacy of Terror." *Kritika: Explorations in Russian and Eurasian History* 1(2): 365–75.

Kóczé, Angéla and Márton Rövid. "Roma and the Politics of Double Discourse in Contemporary Europe." *Identities* 24(6): 684–700.

Kóczé, Angéla Violetta Zentai, Jelena Jovanović, and Enikő Vincze, eds. (2018). *The Romani Women's Movement: Struggles and Debates in Central and Eastern Europe*. New York: Routledge.

Koen, Benjamin, and Jacqueline Lloyd, eds. (2008). *The Oxford Handbook of Medical Ethnomusicology*. New York: Oxford University Press.

Kolar, Walter. (1986). *Duquesne University Tamburitzans: The First Fifty Years Remembered*. Pittsburgh: Tamburitza Press.

Kononenko, Natalie. (1998). *Ukrainian Minstrels: And the Blind Shall Sing*. New York: M. E. Sharpe.

Kononenko, Natalie. (2019). *Ukrainian Epic and Historical Song: Folklore in Context*. Toronto, ON: Toronto University Press.

Kostka, Joanna. (2018). *Financing Roma Inclusion with European Structural Funds*. London: Routledge.

204 REFERENCES

Kotljarchuk, Andrej. (2016a). "Invisible Victims: The Cold War and Representation of the Roma Genocide in Soviet Feature Films, Teleplays and Theater Performances." In *Russische und Sowjetische Geschichte im Film: Von Väterchen Zar, tragischen Helden, russischen Revolutionären und "kalten Krieger,"* edited by Alexander Friedman and Frank Jacob, 129–50. New York: ALTIJA.

Kotljarchuk, Andrej. (2016b). "The Memory of the Roma Holocaust in Ukraine: Mass Graves, Memory Work and the Politics of Commemoration." In *Disputed Memory: Emotions and Memory Politics in Central, Eastern, and South-Eastern Europe,* edited by Tea Sindbæk Andersen and Barbara Törnquist-Plewa, 149–76. Berlin: Walter de Greyter.

Kovalcsik, Katalin. (2000). "Teasing as a Sung Speech Genre of Vlach Gypsy Couples in the Sub-Carpathian Region." *Narodna umjetnost: Croatian Journal of Ethnology and Folklore Research* 37(1): 67–94.

Kovalcsik, Katalin. (2010). "The Romani Musicians on the Stage of Pluri-Culturalism: The Case of the *Kalyi Jag* Group in Hungary." In *Multi-Disciplinary Approaches to Romany Studies,* edited by Michael Stewart and Márton Rövid, 55–70. Budapest: Central European University Press.

Kraus, Richard. (1989). *Pianos and Politics in China: Middle-Class Ambitions and the Struggle over Western Music.* Oxford: Oxford University Press.

Kübler-Ross, Elisabeth. (1969). *On Death and Dying.* New York: Macmillan.

Kucharczyk, Jacek, and Grigorij Mesežnikov, eds. (2015). *Diverging Voices, Converging Policies: The Visegrad States' Reactions to the Russia-Ukraine Conflict.* Warsaw: Heinrich-Böll-Stiftung.

Kuemmerle, Tobias, Oleh Chaskovskyy, Jan Knorn, Volker Radeloff, Ivan Kruhlov, William Keeton, and Patrick Hostert. (2009). "Forest Cover Change and Illegal Logging in the Ukrainian Carpathians in the Transition Period from 1988 to 2007." *Remote Sensing of Environment* 113(6): 1194–207.

Ladányi, János, and Iván Szelényi. (2006). *Patterns of Exclusion: Constructing Gypsy Ethnicity and the Making of an Underclass in Transitional Societies of Europe.* New York: Columbia University Press.

Lange, Barbara Rose. (1997). "Hungarian Rom (Gypsy) Political Activism and the Development of Folklór Ensemble Music." *The World of Music* 39(3): 5–30.

Lange, Barbara Rose. (2003). *Holy Brotherhood: Romani Music in a Hungarian Pentecostal Church.* Oxford: Oxford University Press.

Lange, Barbara Rose. (2018). *Local Fusions: Folk Music Experiments in Central Europe at the Millennium.* New York: Oxford University Press.

Larson, Sandra, Germán Comina, Robert Gilman, Brian Tracey, Marjory Bravard, José W. López. (2012). "Validation of an Automated Cough Detection Algorithm for Tracking Recovery of Pulmonary Tuberculosis." *Plos One.* Accessed April 4, 2023. https://journals.plos.org/plosone/article?id=10.1371/journal.pone.0046229

Lauer, Sarah. (2017). "The Social Impact of the Misconceptions Surrounding Tuberculosis." *Iowa Historical Review* 7(1): 55–78.

Laušević, Mirjana. (2006). *Balkan Fascination: Creating an Alternative Music Culture in America.* Oxford: Oxford University Press.

Lawlor, Clark. (2007). *Consumption and Literature: The Making of the Romantic Disease.* New York: Palgrave.

Lemon, Alaina. (2000). *Between Two Fires: Gypsy Performance and Romani Memory from Pushkin to Post-Socialism.* Durham, NC: Duke University Press.

REFERENCES 205

Lemon, Alaina. (1995). "'What Are They Writing About Us Blacks': Roma and 'Race' in Russia." *Anthropology of East Europe Review* 13(2): 34–40.

Lie, Siv Brun. (2013). "'His Soul Was Wandering and Holy': Employing and Contesting Religious Terminology in Django Fandom." *Popular Music and Society* 36(3): 380–96.

Lie, Siv Brun. (2017). *The Cultural Politics of Jazz Manouche and Romani Representation in France*. PhD diss., New York University.

Lie, Siv Brun. (2019). "Genre, Ethnoracial Alterity, and the Genesis of *Jazz Manouche*." *Journal of the American Musicological Society* 72(3): 665–718.

Lie, Siv Brun. (2020). "Music That Tears You Apart: Jazz Manouche and the Qualia of Ethnorace." *Ethnomusicology* 64(3): 369–93.

Linklater, Andrew. (1998). *The Transformation of Political Community*. Columbia, SC: University of South Carolina Press.

Loudon, Robert, and Rena Marie Roberts. (1968). "Singing and the Dissemination of Tuberculosis." *American Review of Respiratory Disease* 98(2): 297–300.

Mackinlay, Elizabeth, Svanibor Pettan, and Klisala Harrison, eds. (2010). *Applied Ethnomusicology: Historical and Contemporary Approaches*. Newcastle on Tyne, UK: Cambridge Scholars Publishing.

MacMillen, Ian. (2015). "Fascination, Musical Tourism, and the Loss of the Balkan Village (Notes on Bulgaria's Koprivshtitsa Festival)." *Ethnomusicology* 59(2): 227–61.

MacMillen, Ian. (2019). *Playing It Dangerously: Tambura Bands, Race, and Affective Block in Croatia and Its Intimates*. Middletown, CT: Wesleyan University Press.

Magosci, Paul. (2015). "The Heritage of Autonomy in Carpathian Rus' and Ukraine's Transcarpathian Region." *Nationalities Papers* 43(4): 577–94.

Malik, L. P., M. I. Pitiulych, O. S. Peredrii, and V. A. Shynkar. (1991). *Tsyhany zakarpattia: Problemy, shliakhy vyrishennia* [Gypsies of Zakarpattia: Problems, paths to solutions]. Uzhhorod, Ukraine: Zakarpattia Oblast Press.

Malvinni, David. (2004). *The Gypsy Caravan: From Real Roma to Imagined Gypsies in Western Music and Film*. London: Routledge.

March, Richard. (2013). *The Tamburitza Tradition: From the Balkans to the American Midwest*. Madison: University of Wisconsin Press.

Marković, Alexander. (2017). *Gypsy Fingers are Unique!: Identity Politics and Musical Performance among Romani Musicians in Vranje, Serbia*. PhD diss., University of Illinois at Chicago.

Martinek Martin, Sigmund Elisabeth, Lemes Christine, Derndorfer Michael, Aichinger Josef, Winter Siegmund, Jauker Wolfgang, Gschwendtner Manfred, Nesser Hans-Joachim, and Pürerfellner Helmut. (2013). "Asymptomatic Cerebral Lesions During Pulmonary Vein Isolation under Uninterrupted Oral Anticoagulation." *Europace* 15(3): 325–31.

Marushiakova, Elena, and Vesselin Popov. (2000). *Gypsies/Roma in Times Past and Present*. Sofia, Bulgaria: Litavra Publishing House.

Marushiakova, Elena, and Vesselin Popov. (2003). "Ethnic Identities and Economic Strategies of the Gypsies in the Countries of the Former USSR." *Differenz und Integration* 4(1): 289–310.

Marushiakova, Elena, and Vesselin Popov. (2004). "Segmentation vs. Consolidation: The Example of Four Gypsy Groups in CIS." *Romani Studies* 14(2): 145–91.

Matras, Yaron. (2002). *Romani: A Linguistic Introduction*. Cambridge: Cambridge University Press.

206 REFERENCES

Matthews, Mervyn. (1986). *Poverty in the Soviet Union: The Life-Styles of the Underprivileged in Recent Years*. Cambridge: Cambridge University Press.

Mazo, Margarita. (1994). "Lament Made Visible: A Study of Paramusical Elements in Russian Lament." In *Themes and Variations: Writings on Music in Honor of Rulan Chao Pian*, edited by Bell Yung and Joseph Lam, 164–211. Columbus, OH: President and Fellows of Harvard College and the Institute of Chinese Studies of The Chinese University of Hong Kong.

McClary, Susan. (1992). *Georges Bizet, Carmen*. Cambridge: Cambridge University Press.

McDonald, David. (2013). *My Voice Is My Weapon: Music, Nationalism, and the Poetics of Palestinian Resistance*. Durham, NC: Duke University Press.

McGarry, Andrew. (2010). *Who Speaks for Roma?: Political Representation of a Transnational Minority Community*. London: Continuum.

Mishalow, Victor. (2013). *Kharkivska Bandura* [The Kharkiv Bandura]. Kharkiv; Toronto: Savchuk O.O.

Mitchell, Dolores. (1987). "The Iconology of Smoking in Turn-of-the-Century Art." *Source: Notes in the History of Art* 6 (3): 27–33.

Moisala, Pirkko. (2013). "'Nobody Should Be Forced to Make a Living by Begging': Social Exclusion and Cultural Rights of Gāine/Gandharva Musicians of Nepal." *Yearbook for Traditional Music* 45: 13–27.

Ndaliko, Chérie Rivers. (2016). *Necessary Noise: Music, Film, and Charitable Imperialism in the East of Congo*. Oxford: Oxford University Press.

Ndaliko, Chérie Rivers, and Samuel Anderson, eds. (2020). *The Art of Emergency*. Oxford: Oxford University Press.

Manuel, Peter. (1993). *Cassette Culture: Popular Music and Technology in North India*. Chicago: University of Chicago Press.

Miller, Carol. (2010). *The Church of Cheese: Gypsy Ritual in the American Heyday*. Boston: GemmaMedia.

Miller, Frederic, Agnes F. Vandome, and John McBrewster, eds. (2010). *Ghetto Tourism*. Saarbrücken, Germany: VDM Publishing.

Mroz, Lech. (2015). *Roma-Gypsy Presence in the Polish-Lithuanian Commonwealth: 15th–18th Centuries*. Budapest: Central European University Press.

Müller, Tanja. (2013). "The Long Shadow of Band Aid Humanitarianism: Revisiting the Dynamics between Famine and Celebrity." *Third World Quarterly* 34(3): 470–84.

Muñoz, Lina Gálvez. (2005). "Regulating an Addictive Product: The Spanish Government, Brand Advertising and Tobacco Business (1880s to 1930s)." *Business History* 47(3): 401–20.

Muñoz, Lina Gálvez. (2006). "Gender, Cigar, and Cigarettes: Technological Change and National Patterns." *Session 14. Technology, Gender and the Division of Labour XIV International Economic History Congress Helsinki, Finland*. http://www.helsinki.fi/iehc2006/papers1/Galvez.pdf. Accessed June 14, 2019.

Noll, William. (1994). "Cultural Contact through Music Institutions in Ukrainian Lands 1920-1948." In *Music-Cultures in Contact: Convergences and Collisions*, edited by Margaret Kartomi and Stephen Blum, 204–19. New York: Routledge.

Ochoa Gautier, Ana María. (2014). *Aurality: Listening and Knowledge in Nineteenth-Century Colombia*. Durham, NC: Duke University Press.

Ochoa Gautier, Ana María. (2015). "Silence." In *Keywords in Sound*, edited by David Novak and Matt Sakakeeny, 183–92. Durham, NC: Duke University Press.

REFERENCES   207

O'Keefe, Brigid. (2013). *New Soviet Gypsies: National, Performance and Selfhood in the Early Soviet Union.* Toronto: University of Toronto Press.

Oliver, Kelly. (2001). *Witnessing: Beyond Recognition.* Minneapolis: University of Minnesota Press.

Olson, Laura. (2004). *Performing Russia: Folk Revival and Russian Identity.* London: Routledge.

O'Neill, Bruce. (2017). *The Space of Boredom. Homelessness in the Slowing Global Order.* Durham, NC: Duke University Press.

Orenstein, Mitchell. (2008). "Poverty, Inequality, and Democracy: Postcommunist Welfare States." *Journal of Democracy* 19(4): 80–94.

Parekh, Nikesh, and Tamsin Rose. (2011). "Health Inequalities of the Roma in Europe: A Literature Review." *Central European Journal of Public Health* 19(3): 139–42.

Pettan, Svanibor. (2015). *Kosovo through the Eyes of Local Romani (Gypsy) Musicians: Study Guide and DVD.* Ljubljana: University of Ljubljana, Faculty of Arts and the Society for Ethnomusicology.

Pettan, Svanibor. (1996). "Gypsies, Music, and Politics in the Balkans: A Case Study from Kosovo." *The World of Music* 38(1): 33–61.

Pettan, Svanibor. (2001). "Encounter with the 'Others from Within': The Case of Gypsy Musicians in Former Yugoslavia." *The World of Music* 43(2/3): 119–37.

Pettan, Svanibor. (2002). *Rom Musicians in Kosovo: Interaction and Creativity.* Budapest: Institute for Musicology of the Hungarian Academy for Sciences.

Pettan, Svanibor, and Jeff Todd Titon, eds. (2015). *The Oxford Handbook of Applied Ethnomusicology.* New York: Oxford University Press.

Pettan, Svanibor, and Jeff Todd Titon, eds. (2019a). *Theory, Method, Sustainability, and Conflict: An Oxford Handbook of Applied Ethnomusicology, Volume 1.* New York: Oxford University Press.

Pettan, Svanibor, and Jeff Todd Titon, eds. (2019b). *De-Colonization, Heritage, and Advocacy: An Oxford Handbook of Applied Ethnomusicology, Volume 2.* New York: Oxford University Press.

Pettan, Svanibor, and Jeff Todd Titon, eds. (2019c). *Public Ethnomusicology, Education, Archives, & Commerce: An Oxford Handbook of Applied Ethnomusicology, Volume 3.* New York: Oxford University Press.

Phillips, Sarah. (2005a). "Civil Society and Healing: Theorizing Women's Social Activism in Post-Soviet Ukraine." *Ethnos* 70(4): 489–514.

Phillips, Sarah. (2005b). "Will the Market Set Them Free?: Women, NGOs, and Social Enterprise in Ukraine." *Human Organization* 64(3): 251–64.

Phillips, Sarah. (2008). *Women's Social Activism in the New Ukraine: Development and the Politics of Differentiation.* Bloomington: Indiana University Press.

Pishchikova, Elena. (2010). *Promoting Democracy in Post-Communist Ukraine: The Contradictory Outcomes of US Aid to Women's NGOs.* Boulder, CO: Lynne Rienner Publishers.

Piskor, Steve. (2012). *Gypsy Violins: Hungarian-Slovak Gypsies in America.* Cleveland: Saroma.

Plokhy, Serhii. (2018). *Chernobyl: The History of a Nuclear Catastrophe.* New York: Basic Books.

Polese, Abel. (2014). "Informal Payments in Ukrainian Hospitals: On the Boundary between Informal Payments, Gifts, and Bribes." *Anthropological Forum* 24(4): 381–95.

208 REFERENCES

Porcello, Thomas. (2003). "Tails Out: Social Phenomenology and the Ethnographic Representation of Technology in Music Making." In *Music and Technoculture*, edited by René Lysloff and Leslie Gay, 264–89. Middletown, CT: Wesleyan University Press.

Povinelli, Elizabeth. (2002). *The Cunning of Recognition: Indigenous Alterities and the Making of Australian Multiculturalism*. Durham, NC: Duke University Press.

Proaño, Alvaro, Marjory A. Bravard, José W. López, Gwenyth O. Lee, David Bui, Sumona Datta, Germán Comina, Mirko Zimic, Jorge Coronel, Luz Caviedes, José L. Cabrera, Antonio Salas, Eduardo Ticona, Nancy M. Vu, Daniela E. Kirwan, Maria-Cristina I. Loader, Jon S. Friedland, David A. J. Moore, Carlton A. Evans, Brian H. Tracey, Robert H. Gilman, for the Tuberculosis Working Group in Peru. (2017). "Dynamics of Cough Frequency in Adults Undergoing Treatment for Pulmonary Tuberculosis." *Clinical Infectious Diseases* 64(9): 1174–81.

Puar, Jasbir. (2017). *The Right to Maim: Debility, Capacity, Disability*. Durham, NC: Duke University Press.

Qureshi, Regula. 2000. "How Does Music Mean?: Embodied Memories and the Politics of Affect in the Indian *Sarangi*." *American Ethnologist* 27(4): 805–38.

Rahaim, Matthew. (2011). *Musicking Bodies: Gesture and Voice in Hindustani Music*. Middletown, CT: Wesleyan University Press.

Revenga, Ana, Dena Ringold, and William Tracy. (2002). *Poverty and Ethnicity: A Cross-Country Study of Roma Poverty in Central Europe*. Washington DC: World Bank.

Rice, Timothy. (2014). "Ethnomusicology in Times of Trouble." *Yearbook for Traditional Music* 46: 191–209.

Riegler, Alexander. (2003). "Whose Anticipations?" In *Anticipatory Behavior in Adaptive Learning Systems: Foundations, Theories, and Systems*, edited by Martin Butz, Olivier Sigaud, and Pierre Pierre Gérard, 11–22. Dortrecht, Netherlands: Springer Verlag.

Ringold, Dena, Mitchell Orenstein, and Erika Wilkens. (2005). *Roma in an Expanding Europe: Breaking the Poverty Cycle*. Washington, DC: International Bank for Reconstruction and Development.

Rognoni, Rossi. (2019). "Organology and the Others: A Political Perspective." *Journal of the American Musical Instrument Society* 44: 7–17.

Romano, Serena. (2017). *Moralising Poverty: The "Undeserving" Poor in the Public Gaze*. New York: Routledge.

Rothenberg, Paula, ed. (2015). *White Privilege: Essential Readings on the Other Side of Racism*. 5th ed. New York: Worth Publishers.

Round, John, and Emila Kosterina. (2005). "The Construction of 'Poverty' in Post-Soviet Russia." *Perspectives on European Politics and Society* 6(3): 403–34.

Roy, Arundhati. (2016). *The End of Imagination*. Chicago: Haymarket Books.

Rüdiger, Johann Christian Christoph. (1782). "Von der Sprache und Herkunft der Zigeuner aus Indien." In *Neuester Zuwachs der teutschen, fremden und allgemeinen Sprachkunde in eigenen Aufsätzen*, edited by Erstes Stück, 37–84. Leipzig: P. G. Kummer.

Saltzman, Leia. (2019). "It's About Time: Reconceptualizing the Role of Time in Loss and Trauma." *Psychological Trauma: Theory, Research, Practice, and Policy* 11(6): 663–70.

Schäfer, Thomas, Jörg Fachner, and Mario Smukalla. (2013). "Changes in the Representation of Space and Time While Listening to Music." *Frontiers in Psychology* 4(508): 1–15.

Schmelz, Peter. (2009a). "From Scriabin to Pink Floyd: The ANS Synthesizer and the Politics of Soviet Music between Thaw and Stagnation." In *Sound

Commitments: Avant-Garde Music and the Sixties, edited by Robert Adlington, 254–78. New York: Oxford University Press.

Schmelz, Peter. (2009b). *Such Freedom, If Only Musical: Unofficial Soviet Music during the Thaw*. New York: Oxford University Press.

Schwartz, Hillel. (2011). *Making Noise: From Babel to the Big Bang & Beyond*. Cambridge, MA: Zone Books/MIT Press.

Seeman, Sonia. (2019). *Sounding Roman: Representation and Performing Identity in Western Turkey*. New York: Oxford University Press.

Segal, Raz. (2016). *Genocide in the Carpathians: War, Social Breakdown, and Mass Violence 1914–1945*. Stanford, CA: Stanford University Press.

Senders, Stefan, and Allison Truitt, eds. (2007). *Money: Ethnographic Encounters*. New York: Berg.

Shay, Anthony. (2006). *Choreographing Identities: Folk Dance, Ethnicity and Festival in the United States and Canada*. Jefferson, NC: McFarland.

Shore, Marci. (2018). *The Ukrainian Night: An Intimate History of Revolution*. New Haven, CT: Yale University Press.

Silverman, Carol. (2007). "Trafficking in the Exotic with 'Gypsy' Music: Balkan Roma, Cosmopolitanism, and 'World Music' Festivals." In *Balkan Popular Culture and the Ottoman Ecumene: Music, Image, and Regional Political Discourse*, edited by Donna Buchanan, 335–64. Lanham, MD: Scarecrow Press.

Silverman, Carol. (2012). *Romani Routes: Cultural Politics and Balkan Music in Diaspora*. New York: Oxford University Press.

Silverman, Carol. (2018). "From Reflexivity to Collaboration: Changing Roles of a Non-Romani Scholar, Activist, and Performer." *Critical Romani Studies* 1(2): 76–97.

Simpson, Audra. (2007). "On Ethnographic Refusal: Indigeneity, 'Voice' and Colonial Citizenship." *Junctures* 9: 67–80.

Slobin, Mark. (1996). *Retuning Culture: Musical Changes in Central and Eastern Europe*. Durham, NC: Duke University Press.

Sokolová, Vera. (2005). "Planned Parenthood behind the Curtain: Population Policy and Sterilization of Romani Women in Communist Czechoslovakia, 1972–1989." *Anthropology of East Europe Review* 23(1): 79–98.

Solis, Ted, ed. 2004. *Performing Ethnomusicology: Teaching and Representation in World Music Ensembles*. Berkeley and Los Angeles: University of California Press.

Sonevytsky, Maria. (2019). *Wild Music: Sound and Sovereignty in Ukraine*. Middletown, CT: Wesleyan University Press.

Sontag, Susan. (1978). *Illness as Metaphor*. New York: Farrar, Straus & Giroux.

Sontag, Susan. (1989). *AIDS and Its Metaphors*. New York: Farrar, Straus & Giroux.

Soros, George. (1994). "Building an Educational and Cultural Network for Eastern Europe." In *The Arts in the World Economy: Public Policy and Private Philanthropy for a Global Cultural Community*, edited by Olin Robison, Robert Freeman, and Charles Riley, 81–94. Lebanon, NH: University Press of New England.

Speier, Amy. (2016). *Fertility Holidays: IVF Tourism and the Reproduction of Whiteness*. New York: New York University Press.

Spradley, James. (2013). *You Owe Yourself a Drunk: An Ethnography of Urban Nomads*. Long Grove, IL: Waveband Press.

Spur, Endre de. (1959). "Gypsies in the Borough of Braddock, USA." *Journal of the Gypsy Lore Society* 38: 85–94.

210   REFERENCES

Starks, Tricia. (2008). *The Body Soviet: Propaganda, Hygiene, and the Revolutionary State.* Madison: University of Wisconsin Press.

Starks, Tricia. (2018). *Smoking under the Tsars: A History of Tobacco in Imperial Russia.* Ithaca, NY: Cornell University Press.

Starr, S. Frederick. (1983). *Red and Hot: The Fate of Jazz in the Soviet Union, 1917–1980.* Oxford: Oxford University Press.

Sterne, Jonathan. (2003). *The Audible Past: Cultural Origins of Sound Reproduction.* Durham, NC: Duke University Press.

Stewart, Kathleen. (2007). *Ordinary Affects.* Durham, NC: Duke University Press.

Stewart, Michael. (1997). *Time of the Gypsies.* Boulder, CO: West View Press.

Stürmer, Stefan, Anette Rohmann, and Jolanda van der Noll. (2016). "Mobilizing the Global Community to Combat Ebola: Psychological Effects of the Band Aid 30 Campaign." *Journal of Social Psychology*, 156(3): 291–304.

Sutherland, Anne. (2017). *Roma: Modern American Gypsies.* Long Grove, IL: Waveland Press.

Sykes, Jim. (2018). *The Musical Gift: Sonic Generosity in Post-War Sri Lanka.* Oxford: Oxford University Press.

Szeman, Ioana. (2018). *Staging Citizenship: Roma, Performance, and Belonging in EU Romania.* New York: Berghahn Books.

Szuhay, Péter, and Edit Kőszegi. (2005). "Eternal Home: A Vlach Roma Funeral in Kétegyháza, Hungary." *Romani Studies* 15(2): 91–124.

Taylor, Mary. (2008). "Does Folk Dancing Make Hungarians?: Táncház, Folk Dance as Mother Tongue, and Folk National Cultivation." *Hungarian Studies* 22(1–2): 9–29.

Tift, Matthew. (2007). *Musical AIDS: Music, Musicians, and the Cultural Construction of HIV/AIDS in the United States.* PhD diss., University of Wisconsin–Madison.

Titon, Jeff Todd. (2013). "Music and the US War on Poverty: Some Reflections." *Yearbook for Traditional Music* 45: 74–82.

Tolbert, Elizabeth. (1990). "Women Cry with Words: Symbolization of Affect in Karelian Lament." *Yearbook for Traditional Music* 22: 80–105.

Tomoff, Kiril. (2015). *Virtuosi Abroad: Soviet Music and Imperial Competition during the Early Cold War, 1945–1958.* Ithaca, NY: Cornell University Press.

Trehan, Nidhi, and Nando Sigona, eds. (2009). *Romani Politics in Contemporary Europe: Poverty, Ethnic Mobilization, and the Neoliberal Order.* Basingstoke, UK: Palgrave Macmillan.

Trier, Tom. (1999). *Interethnic Relations in Transcarpathian Ukraine (ECMI Report #4).* Flensburg, Germany: European Centre for Minority Issues.

Tsenova, Valeria, ed. (1998). *Underground Music from the Former USSR.* New York: Routledge.

Tufekci, Zeynep. (2017). *Twitter and Tear Gas: The Power and Fragility of Networked Protest.* New Haven, CT: Yale University Press.

United Nations Development Programme (UNDP). (2002). *The Roma in Central and Eastern Europe: Avoiding the Dependency Trap* (UNDP/ILO Regional Human Development Report). Bratislava, Slovakia: UNDP.

Van Baar, Huub. (2011). *The European Roma: Minority Representation, Memory, and the Limits of Transnational Governmentality.* PhD diss., Universiteit van Amsterdam.

Van Baar, Huub, and Angéla Kóczé, eds. (2020). *The Roma and Their Struggle for Identity in Contemporary Europe. Romani Studies Series.* New York: Berghahn Books.

REFERENCES 211

Van de Port, Mattijs. (1998). *Gypsies, Wars & Other Instances of the Wild: Civilization and Its Discontents in a Serbian Town*. Amsterdam: Amsterdam University Press.

Van der Merwe, Karen. (2006). "The Phenomenology of Experiencing Poverty: An Exploration." *Journal for Transdisciplinary Research in Southern Africa* 2(1): 131–44.

Vaughn, Kathryn. (1990). "Exploring Emotion in Sub-Structural Aspects of Karelian Lament: Application of Time Series Analysis to Digitized Melody." *Yearbook for Traditional Music* 22: 106–22.

Verdery, Katherine. (2018). *My Life as a Spy: Investigations in a Secret Police File*. Durham, NC: Duke University Press.

Von Eschen, Penny. (2006). *Stachmo Blows Up the World: Jazz Ambassadors Play the Cold War*. Cambridge, MA: Harvard University Press.

Walker, Julian. (2013). "Time Poverty, Gender and Well-being: Lessons from the Kyrgyz Swiss Swedish Health Programme." *Development in Practice* 23(1): 57–68.

Wawrzeniuk, Piotr. (2018). "'Lwów Saved Us': Roma Survival in Lemberg 1941–44." *Journal of Genocide Research* 20(3): 327–50.

Wedel, Janine. (2001). *Collision and Collusion: The Strange Case of Western Aid in Eastern Europe*. New York: St. Martin's Griffin.

Weeden, Clare. (2014). *Responsible Tourist Behavior*. New York: Routledge.

Williams, Glyn. (2002). "The Hidden Ethnic Cleansing of Muslims in the Soviet Union: The Exile and Repatriation of the Crimean Tatars." *Journal of Contemporary History* 37(3): 323–47.

Wilson, Andrew. (2005). *Ukraine's Orange Revolution*. New Haven, CT: Yale University Press.

Woolf, C. R. and A. Rosenberg. 1964. "Objective Assessment of Cough Suppressants under Clinical Conditions using a Tape Recorded System." *Thorax* 19(2):125–30.

Xiao-Mei, Zhu. (2012 [2007]). *The Secret Piano: From Mao's Labor Camps to Bach's Goldberg Variations*. Translated into English by Ellen Hinsey. Las Vegas, NV: AmazonCrossing.

Yoors, Jan. (1967). *The Gypsies*. Long Grove, IL: Waveland.

Young, Ross. (2019). *Tie Up the Lion: An Insight Into Voluntourism*. Pennsauken, NJ: Book Baby.

Yúdice, George. (2003). *Expediency of Culture: Uses of Culture in the Global Era*. Durham, NC: Duke University Press.

Zajdel, Evan. (2013). *Narrative Threads: Ethnographic Tourism, Romani Tourist Tales, and Fiber Art*. Undergraduate BPhil thesis, University of Pittsburgh.

Index

For the benefit of digital users, indexed terms that span two pages (e.g., 52–53) may, on occasion, appear on only one of those pages.

Figures are indicated by *f* following the page number

abortion, 132, 192n.7
academic freedom, 59
   See also education
accordion, 92, 101, 107, 108, 110, 111,
   176–77n.9, 190n.15
acoustic(s), 126, 191n.19
   degeneration of, 120–21
activism, 2, 25–26, 171
   online, 173
Adam, Aladar, 24, 26, 27, 39, 48–49, 50,
   84*f*, 180n.17
advocacy, 5–6, 11–12, 16, 55–56, 58, 104–
   5, 169, 195nn.4–5
aesthetic(s), 55–56, 64–65, 135, 143–44,
   148–49, 157, 185n.18, 190n.15,
   190–91n.18
   hipster, 183n.15
   musical, 85–86, 87, 117–18
   performance, 2, 7–8, 9, 15, 17, 109, 124–
   26, 127, 168–69
   pop, 92
   postsocialist, 185n.20
   Romani, 24, 28–29, 32, 65, 75, 84–
   85, 127–28
   rural, 124–25
   timbral, 117
   vocal, 169
affect, 13, 169, 191n.19
African American(s), 98–99, 149–50, 163–
   64, 194n.21
   See also Harlem; tuberculosis
agenda-setting theories, 16
aid, 12–13, 14–15, 16, 18, 33–35, 36–42,
   43, 44–45, 46–49, 50, 52, 57–58,
   83, 85, 88, 94, 98, 128, 145–46,
   179n.1, 179n.2

alcohol, 183n.12
Amala, 26–27
anticipation, 109, 112–13, 119–20, 121, 157
anxiety, 13–14, 30, 112–13, 123–24, 155–
   56, 171–74, 187n.10
arthritis, arthritic, 18, 161–62
asylum, 175nn.2–3
   political, 22–23
   seekers of, 5–6
Auschwitz, 2–3, 69–70, 75–76
   Auschwitz-Birkenau Museum, 2–
   3, 175n.1
Austro-Hungarian Empire, 59–60, 76,
   79–80, 93, 119
   Austrian Empire, Habsburg, 64, 76–77
avtentyka, 126–27

Babi Yar, 131
   See also Holocaust; Jews
balalaika, 118–19
   See also domra
Balkan, Balkans, 7–8, 25, 42, 57–58, 59, 60,
   61, 64, 97–98, 127, 164–65, 178n.17,
   181n.1, 183n.15
bandura, 118–19
baron, barony, 37–38, 49–50, 91–92
   robber, 59–60
Barranikov, Aleksei, 24
Bartok, Bela, 11–12, 80–81
bazaar, 62–63, 75–76, 92, 110, 111, 157–
   58, 183n.12, 189n.3
begging, 18, 100, 101, 102–3
Bessarabia, 23–24, 178n.12
birov, 37–38, 49–50, 165–66, 180n.17
   See also baron, barony; *bulibașă*;
   elders: Romani

214   INDEX

Bizet, Georges, 140–41, 143–44
  Carmen, 140–43, 193n.16
body, 15, 17, 18, 62, 78, 79, 91, 107, 109,
    111, 129–30, 132, 144, 145, 147, 148–
    49, 154, 155–56, 160–61, 180n.12,
    191–92n.1, 191n.19, 193n.11
borderland, 19
borders, 5–6, 7, 16, 19, 32, 44, 55, 64, 66,
    73, 93, 101, 131, 140, 176–77n.9,
    181–82n.4
Budapest, 9–11, 45, 46, 48–49, 66, 85–
    87, 119
bulibaşă, 179n.6
  See also *birov*; *baron;* elder
busking, 101
  See also music-begging

camp, camps, 2–3, 23, 24, 28–29, 40, 46–
    47, 69–70, 87, 90–92, 95–96, 125–26,
    130–32, 179n.5, 182n.9, 183n.18,
    185–86n.22, 188n.1
  See also *tabir, tabor*
Carmen. See Bizet, Georges
Carpathian Mountains, 59–60, 61, 64,
    74–75, 76
Carpathians, 74, 110
  Carpathian Ensemble, 64–66 (*see also*
    education; University of Pittsburgh;
    world music ensembles)
  Carpathian forests, 94
  Carpathian region, 78–79, 80–81, 184n.9
  Carpathian territories, 77
caste, 178n.13, 179n.7
censorship, 59, 88–90, 117, 130–31
  See also academic freedom
Chernobyl, 19, 125–26, 193n.11
children, Romani, 13, 18, 21–22, 39, 66–
    69, 75–76, 78–79, 88, 98, 100, 102–3,
    104–5, 107–8, 118, 124–25, 131,
    132–33, 134, 139, 145, 154, 162–64,
    166–67, 182–83n.10, 185–86n.22,
    188n.12
choirs, 24, 116–17, 118
  Roma, 32
  Romani, 24, 32, 116–17, 118
  Chornyĭ Tsyhan (Black Gypsy), 90, 91–
    92, 185n.17, 186n.26
  See also Kalo Rom

Chovka, Viktor, 105, 185n.19
cigarettes, 107–8, 135, 136, 138–40
cimbalom, 64, 84–85, 92, 119, 168–69
Ciocărlia, Fanfare, 9
citizenship
  rights of, 17, 35, 74, 87
civil society, 14–15, 35, 43–44
class, 33–34, 35, 36–37, 42–44, 82, 84, 88–
    90, 103, 115–16, 136–38, 144, 179n.3,
    190n.15, 194n.21
  lower, 143
  middle, 1–2, 6–7, 55–56, 85, 141–42, 150
  noble, 32
  postsocialist, 11–12
  tensions, 15
  upper, 116–17
Cold War, 116, 189–90n.10
collectivization, 7
  collective farms, 7, 101–2
communism, 2–3, 15, 25, 27–28, 44–45,
    64, 186–87n.5, 189n.5
concentration camp, 2–3, 69–70
  See also Auschwitz
concert(s), 65f, 75–76
  and coughing, 146–47
  and politics, 116
  of Romani music/musicians, 85–86, 87,
    88, 126–27, 183n.15
  tours, 9–11
  for Western audiences, 42
corruption, 180n.9
  and fieldwork, 112–13
  postsocialist, 64
  and Romani, 6–7, 9–11, 16, 96–97, 144
  and Ukraine, 19, 34, 35, 47–48, 95–96,
    145–46, 179n.1
cough, coughing, 13–14, 17, 129–30,
    145, 146–48, 150–51, 180n.18, 180–
    81n.19, 194n.20
  and health, 134, 136
  and infection, 193n.19
  and music, 18, 145–48, 193n.18,
    194n.20
  and sound, 191–92n.1
  See also death rattle; phlegm;
    tuberculosis; vocal cords
Crimean Peninsula, 19
  Crimean Tartars, 36–37, 116, 131

INDEX 215

Czechoslovakia, 73, 76, 90–91, 132–33, 174, 177n.8, 193n.9

death, 19, 62–63, 78–79, 111–12, 129, 133, 144, 147, 148, 154, 157, 183n.11, 192n.6, 193n.11, 194n.21
    See also funerals
Death by Hunger, 8, 192n.6
    See also *Holodomor*
democracy, 43–44, 181n.2
depression, 96–97, 103, 143–44
    era of, 63
    Great Depression, the, 13–14, 98–99, 103
    mental health, 13–14, 143–44, 154, 157, 168
diaspora, 61–62, 64–65, 127, 131–32
discrimination, 9–11, 22–23, 40, 46, 47– 49, 63, 78–79, 95, 97–98, 103, 184n.4, 185n.12, 195n.6
    systemic, 13–14, 105
disease, 13, 37–38, 98, 99–100, 129–30, 133, 134–35, 136, 148–49, 155–56, 186n.25, 193n.11, 194nn.20–21, 194n.22
    and coughing, 147–48
    heart, 136
    lung, 136
    tuberculosis, 17, 148–51
dissonance, 90, 117–18
Donbas, 19
donors, 33–34, 38–39, 43, 48–49, 52, 97– 98, 179n.7
    Western, 35, 40, 44
duress, 17

economic deprivation, 6–7
education, 6–7, 25–26, 36–37, 38, 39, 46, 47–48, 56–57, 59, 84, 92, 95, 97–98, 101, 102–3, 115, 124–25, 129, 167, 182n.5
    See also kindergarten; Košice, Slovakia
elders, 91–92, 159–60
    Romani, 37–38, 49–50, 62–63, 165–66, 179n.6, 185n.18
    See also *baron, barony*; *birov*
emotion(s), 101–2, 110, 138, 149, 154, 155– 56, 159–60, 164–65, 167, 168–69, 173
    music as emotional trigger, 17–18, 154– 55, 169

state of, 17–18, 29, 31–32, 101–2, 110, 149, 154, 155–56
    of tuning, 122–24
emotional labor
    fieldwork as, 156–60
ensembles
    folklór, 25, 60, 126–27
    world music, 7, 64–65, 118, 183n.14
    university-based, 55–56, 65
entertainers, 6–7, 28, 29–30, 32, 63, 178n.16
entrapment, 29–30, 45–46, 93
    ethnographic, 45–46
estrada, 85–86, 87
ethnicity, 14–15, 33–34, 36–37, 40, 43–44, 60–61, 112–13, 183n.18, 189n.5
ethnography, 154–55, 160, 186n.4
    salvage, 129
ethnomusicology
    applied, 2–3, 13, 57–58, 59, 70–71, 129–30, 143–44, 154, 157, 164–65, 182n.5, 195n.4
Euromaidan, 188n.1, 190–91n.18
European Roma Rights Center (ERRC), 23, 44–45, 49–50, 186n.1

failure, 95–96, 109, 119–20
    fieldwork as, 112–16
Fanfare Ciocărlia, 9
fieldwork, 2–3, 8, 12, 55–56, 74–75, 81–82, 84–85, 96, 99–100, 104, 135, 154– 55, 156–57, 159, 161–62, 163–64, 178n.12, 181–82n.4, 187–88n.11, 188n.13, 191–92n.1
    ethnographic, 94
    grief fieldwork, 2
    and healthcare, 144, 145, 150–51
    methods, 173–74
    recordings, 17
    and smoking, 138–39
    See also emotional labor; failure
financial
    aid, 33–34, 36, 37–39, 46–47
    assistance, 43
    backing, 44
    capital, 85–86
    compensation, 30–31
    crises, 12

216 INDEX

financial (*cont.*)
  exchanges, 140
  gains, 59–60
  growth, 95
  help, 94
  instability, 17–18
  means, 21–22, 149–50
  networks, 71
  poverty, 6–7
  resources, 40, 49–50
  rewards, 32
  standing, 115–16
  success, 9
  support, 12–13, 36–37
folklore, 7, 65, 80–81
  studies of, 81–82
  Tsygan, 78
  See also *folklór (Hungary)*; Folklore
    Division; Ukrainian Academy of
    Sciences
folklór (Hungary), 25
foreign, foreigners, 7, 14, 33, 35, 36–37,
    40–41, 46–48, 52, 53, 57–58, 73, 75,
    135–36, 190n.15
  See also *innozemni*
forgiveness, 162
Franko, Ivan, 77, 79, 81–82, 115, 184n.3
  See also Tsyhany
free speech, 33, 34
funding, 5, 38, 41, 43, 48, 80–81, 92, 97–98,
    134, 143, 182n.5, 182–83n.10, 184n.4
  ethnically-based, 35
funeral(s), 175n.3
  Romani, 61–63, 183nn.11–12

Gadjo, gadji, gadje, 9–11, 21–22, 25, 142, 176n.8
Gadjology, 9–11
gendarme, 77, 78–79
gender, 14, 33–34, 36–37, 94–95, 135–36,
    140, 148–49, 159, 188n.12, 195n.6
  male musicians, 11–12, 42–43, 61–63,
    82–84, 85, 90–91, 92, 107, 159, 168
Gogol Bordello, 7–8, 19, 125–27, 175n.4,
    183n.15
grants, 5–6, 11–12, 33–34, 37–38, 39–40,
    41–42, 43, 44–45, 46, 47–49, 50, 53,
    90, 97–98, 115, 131, 133, 145–46,
    179n.1, 185n.17, 188n.13
  ethnically-based, 35

Great Depression. *See* Depression, Great
grief, 153, 157, 159–60, 167–68, 176n.8
  fieldwork, 2
  tourism, 2
guitar, 18, 64, 66, 107, 108–9, 110, 111–12,
    117, 176–77n.9, 189n.9, 190n.11
  seven-stringed, 28–29, 124, 126, 136–38
gulag, 131–32
Gypsies, 9–11, 24, 27, 38, 65, 77, 78, 99–
    100, 176n.7, 184n.4
  Time of the Gypsies, 127
  Ukrainian, 29–30
  See also *Tsyhany*

Habermas, Jürgen, 38–39, 44
  See also ideal speech situation
Habsburg, 64, 76–77
happiness, 13–14, 30, 31–32
hardship(s), 2, 27, 59–60, 112–13, 133, 165
Harlem, 98–99, 149–50
  Spanish, 149
  See also African Americans
health, 2, 13, 15, 17–18, 25–26, 35, 50, 88–
    90, 97–98, 109, 112–13, 129–30, 132–
    33, 134, 135–36, 139, 145–46, 149–50,
    154, 180–81n.19, 192n.2, 193n.11
  health-conscious, 143
  mental health, 153–54
  and music, 143–44, 145
  women's health, 169
healthcare, 13–14, 25–26, 47–48, 115,
    132–33, 134–35, 136, 144, 149–50
Holodomor, 8, 192n.6
  See also Death by Hunger
Holocaust, xii, 2–3, 8, 64, 94, 123–24,
    129, 130–31, 184n.1, 191–92n.1,
    192n.6, 195n.2
  See also Auschwitz; Babi Yar; Jews;
    Porajmos
horse, 28–29, 73, 76–77, 78, 99–100, 104–
    5, 178n.16, 191n.21
Horvat, Bela, 85, 86–87
Horvat, Myroslav, 1, 105
Horvat, Kandra Josyp, 185n.19, 185n.20
hryvnia, 96–97
humanitarianism, humanitarian, 5, 41,
    46–47, 50
  and celebrity, 41
  and charitable organizations, 57–58

human rights, 5, 16, 22–23, 33–34, 35, 41–
42, 46, 47–49, 55–57, 59–60, 65–66,
69–71, 77, 166–67, 177n.7, 180n.12,
181n.2, 181–82n.4, 182n.7, 186n.1
Hungary, 9–11, 16, 22–23, 25, 48–49,
56–57, 61, 62, 65–66, 73, 74–75,
76, 80–81, 85–86, 87–88, 93, 102,
119, 125–26, 140, 183n.17, 184n.9,
188n.12, 191n.21
hunger, 1–2, 78, 98, 171, 186n.1
See also hunger strike
hunger strike, 171, 174
Husserl, Edmund, 120
See also anticipation
Hutsul, 119
Hutz, Eugene, 125–27

ideal speech situation, 38–39, 44
See also Habermas, Jürgen
illegal, 46, 94, 99–100, 118, 124–25, 132,
133, 134
immigrant, 59–60, 61, 64, 125–26
See also diaspora
impoverished, 66–67, 94–95, 103, 134, 149–
50, 168, 169, 179n.1, 179n.3, 183n.11
See also economic disparity; poverty
improvisation, 90
India, 6–7, 24, 27, 120–21, 178n.13,
178n.15
inflation (hyper), 48, 96, 111–12
innozemni, 75
See also foreign
instability, 96–97
political, 16, 17–18, 19
institution(s), 149–50, 182n.5
instrument(s), 111–13, 115–16, 126,
154, 158–59, 168–69, 188n.2,
189–90n.10, 190n.15, 190–91n.18,
191n.19, 195n.3
and health, 150–51
and identities, 108–9
musical, 7, 12, 17, 42, 60, 61–62, 64, 67–
68, 90–91, 96, 107
of peace, 57–58
and quality of, 110–11
and tuning, 116–25, 128
See also accordion; guitar; piano; violin
integration, 14–15, 21–22, 24, 25, 27, 35,
36–37, 97–98, 186–87nn.5–6

International Renaissance Foundation, 39,
46, 48–49, 168, 185n.17
intervention, 5–6, 12, 14, 16, 17, 35, 37–39,
43–44, 47–48, 97–98, 128, 130, 131–
34, 135–36, 149–50
interview(s), 45, 50, 125–26, 135, 138–39,
145, 153–54, 156–60, 162–64, 165–
66, 167, 168, 169, 182n.5, 192n.2
as ethnographic method, 3, 111–12,
154–55, 161
See also lament
Interwar Period, 73, 90–91
intonation, 160
Ivano-Frankivsk (Ukraine), 83, 186n.3

jazz, 90, 92, 105, 136–38
Pap Jazz Fest, Pap Jazz Kwartet, 88–90
See also *manouche*
Jews, 69–70, 75–76, 131
See also Auschwitz; Babi Yar; Holocaust
Josef II, 76–77
Jurkova, Zuzana, 56–57, 65–66, 183n.16

Kalderari (Kalderash), 131, 193n.9
Kalo Rom, 90, 185n.17
See also Chornyĭ Tsyhan (Black Gypsy)
Kalyi Yag, 25, 66
See also Gustav Varga
Khamoro Music Festival, 65–66, 183n.16
kindergarten
Romani, 48–49, 66–69
Kolessa, Filarett, 80–82
Košice (Slovakia), 66–68, 70*f*
Kostenko, Lina, 7–8
"Tsyhanska Muza," 7–8, 45, 79–80,
178n.14
Krykunov, Ihor, 26–27, 168
kupon, kupony, 96–98
See also *hryvnia*; ruble
Kvitka, Klement, 81–82
Kyiv, 19–22, 23, 26–29, 39, 46–47, 73,
74, 93, 96–97, 100–2, 116, 125–27,
131, 168, 169, 171–73, 189n.4, 190–
91n.18, 195n.5

labor, 6–7, 12–13, 35, 59–61, 63, 93, 94–96,
100–2, 104–5, 132, 133, 134, 140,
142–44, 156–57, 167–68, 173, 182n.8,
188n.12

218 INDEX

lament, 156–57, 162, 167, 173–74, 195n.3
  interview as, 156–60
  See also interview
language, 3, 23, 33–34, 36, 41–42, 47–48,
    64, 73–74, 76, 80–81, 94, 138–39, 153,
    154–55, 160, 169, 171, 185n.12
  English, 103, 164–65, 166–67, 174,
    183n.15, 190n.11
  of in-tuneness, 115–16
  and music, 122, 124
  Romani, 1, 9–11, 23, 39, 48–49, 69, 74–
    75, 76–77, 177n.9, 178n.13
  Russian, 28–29, 107
  tonal, 118–19
Latsko, Sasha, 1–2
Lăutar, 88, 92, 180n.11
leader(s)
  Communist, 88–90
  community, 1, 64
  foreign, 7, 33, 76, 186n.2
  political, 11–12
  Romani, 5, 23, 24, 26, 37–38, 40, 46–47,
    48–49, 90–91, 97–98, 104, 105, 159–
    60, 174, 184n.4, 185–86n.22
  Soviet, 118
  See also *romskií lider*
Lenin, Vladimir, 96
Liszt, Franz, 9–11, 62, 81, 90
Lovara, 23, 177–78nn.10–11
Lunik IX, 66–67, 69–70
Lviv, 22, 23, 27–29, 39, 80–82, 83,
    100–1, 104, 127, 178nn.15–16,
    178n.18, 192n.5

magnitizdat, 117
manele, 9–11, 179n.4
manouche, 136–38, 193n.13
Maria Theresa, 76–77
Maty- Heroinia, 133
media, 171, 173–74, 175n.3, 179n.5
  visits to Romani settlements, 165–68
mental health, 13–14
Merimee, Prosper, 140–42
migrant labor, 104–5, 188n.12
"Migrant Mother," 98–99, 100, 102
minorities, minorization, 14–15, 141–42, 149–50
mobility, 25
  economic, 127–28

social, 66
Moscow (Russia), 7–8, 29, 32, 48, 64–65,
    84–85, 93, 116, 139, 140–42
Mukachevo, 82–83, 87
museum(s), 187–88n.11
music-begging, 100, 101, 102–3
  See also busking

(ultra)nationalists, 9–11, 17, 21–23,
    36–38, 39, 43, 45–47, 61, 81–82, 88,
    90–91, 130, 165–66, 167, 174, 175n.3,
    177n.1, 180n.8, 180–81n.19, 182n.5,
    183n.17, 187n.6, 195n.6
nationality policies, 44–45
  See also Soviet
Nazi, 3, 8, 64, 88–90, 123–24
neoliberal, neoliberalism, 6–7, 12, 14–15,
    18, 35, 45–46, 55–56, 186–87n.5
nobles, 24, 28–29, 32
"noble savage," 91–92
nomad, nomadic, nomadism, 7–8, 24, 28–
    29, 30–31, 32, 42, 53, 66, 77, 95–96,
    124–25, 130–31, 133, 134, 154–55,
    178nn.15–16, 184n.5, 191n.21
  See also Roma, Romani
non-governmental organizations (NGOs),
    5, 6–7, 12, 13, 14, 16, 25–26, 33–35,
    36–38, 39–40, 43–44, 45, 46–48,
    49–50, 55–58, 65–66, 71, 83, 88–90,
    91–92, 94, 95, 97–98, 99–101, 103–4,
    105, 113–14, 129, 134–36, 139, 159,
    165–66, 179n.3, 179n.6, 180n.9,
    180n.16, 181n.3, 184n.4
nonprofit organizations, 5, 192n.7
nonprofit sector, 12–13, 33, 179n.1
  See also nonprofit organizations

oblast, 32, 47–48
observer effect, 16
oligarch(s), 73, 96–97, 112–13, 179n.4, 189n.3
Open Society Institute, 46
Orange Revolution, 18, 19, 33, 34, 81–82,
    96–97, 114, 126–27, 163–64, 171–73,
    180n.9, 189n.4
Orban, Viktor, 22–23
orientalism, 9–11
Ottoman Empire, 19
  Ottoman contexts, 9–11

Pap Jazz Fest. *See* jazz
Pap Jazz Kwartet. *See* jazz
passport(s), 22–23, 74, 114, 159, 188n.12
perestroika, 93
performance, 7–8, 12–13, 24, 25–26, 28,
    32, 36, 48, 55–56, 58, 64–65, 85–86,
    91–92, 101, 117, 118–19, 120–21,
    122–23, 126–27, 136, 147, 148, 150–
    51, 165–66, 175n.4, 189n.4, 190n.15,
    190–91n.18
  aesthetics, 2, 9, 15, 17, 109, 127,
    135, 168–69
  arts, 13, 176n.7
  groups, 27, 183n.15
  musical, 3, 190n.12
  opportunities, 17, 127–28
  practices, 17, 91, 143–44
  public, 27–28
  Romani, 83
  space, 146–47
  stage, 124–25, 167–68
  vocal, 167–68
Pettan, Svanibor, 9–11, 13, 58, 186n.4
philanthropic, 36–39, 41, 71, 99–100, 104
photography, 66–67, 103
  as ethnographic method, 105
piano, 116–17, 119, 122, 123–24, 190n.15,
    190–91n.18
  Romani player, 104
  See also *The Pianist*
pitch, 107, 111–12, 115–17, 118–20, 121,
    122–24, 147, 154, 160–61, 167, 189–
    90n.10, 190–91n.18
Pittsburgh (Pennsylvania), 60, 61, 67–68
  diaspora in, 2, 27, 61–62, 64–65,
    127, 131–32
  Roms, 59–60, 61–62, 63, 86–87, 175n.3
  university, 3, 9, 56–57, 59–60, 64, 65–66,
    146–47, 171, 182–83n.10
  labor, 73, 182n.9
  See also immigrants
pleasure, 87, 116–17, 119–20, 122, 141,
    185n.12
pluralism, 43–44
  cultural, 44
pogroms, 22
Poland, 2–3, 14, 16, 56–57, 61, 69–70, 93,
    102, 123–24, 125–26, 184n.2

police, 40, 46, 47–48, 50, 69–70, 77, 94,
    101–2, 129, 154–55, 166–67, 186n.1
  See also *Polizai, polizai*
politics, politicians, 6–7, 11–12, 14, 56–57,
    58–59, 95–96, 115–16, 119, 168,
    171, 179n.1, 180n.9, 186–87nn.5–
    6, 195n.6
  identity, 12–13, 92
  minority, 14–15, 22–23
  Romani, 15, 18, 27, 40, 42
Polizai, polizai, 69
Porajmos, 8
postsocialism, 115
post-traumatic stress (PTS), 156, 195n.1
prison, 21–22, 131–32, 163–64
  See also *gulag*
prisoners, 3
  of war, 69–70
project speak, 40
propyska, 154–55, 191n.21
pysanka, 178nn.14–15
  See also *Tsyhanska doroha*

Rada, 28–29, 91–92
  See also *tabir, tabor*: *Tabor
    ukhodit v Nebo*
Radulescu, Speranta, 9–11, 176n.8
Radvanka, Radvankakere, 75, 79–81,
    82–83, 86–87, 90–91, 185n.12,
    185–86n.22
Redžepova, Esma, 126–27, 178n.17
"reflexive turn," 59
Reinhardt, Django, 88–90, 136–38,
    193n.12, 193n.13
  "Memory of Django," 88–90
Revolution of Dignity, 18, 19–22, 23,
    33, 96–97, 114, 126–27, 171, 173–
    74, 180n.9
Romania, Romanian, 9–11, 16, 23, 25–26,
    32, 38, 76–77, 88, 93, 102
Romani Yağ (Romani Fire, Roma Fire), 16,
    26–27, 33–34, 37–38, 39, 48–50, 66,
    82–83, 84, 92
Romani rights, 5, 6–7, 13, 14–15, 16, 17,
    23, 24–26, 27, 39, 49–50, 56–57, 87,
    104, 175–76n.6
romskiĭ lider, 40
ruble, 96–97

220 INDEX

Rumungri, 23, 177–78n.11
Russia, 7–8, 14, 15–16, 19, 23–24, 25–26,
    27, 32, 33, 49–50, 73, 75–76, 116–
    17, 161–62
    See also Putin, Vladimir
Russian Empire, 15–16, 24, 88–90, 96,
    116–17, 118, 124, 156
Russian Federation, 22–23
Rusyn, 74–75

saman, 13, 18, 79, 94, 110, 134, 165–66
Serbia, 9–11
serfs, 24
Servy, 23, 125–26
settlement(s), 36, 180n.17
    Romani, 37–38, 40, 45, 46–47, 48–
    52, 53, 62–63, 69–48, 74–75, 85,
    90–91, 125–26, 129, 134, 139, 154–
    55, 165–66
    See also Tabir, tabor
sexuality, 14, 29, 140, 141, 143, 148
Shevchenko, Taras, 30–31, 80–81
    Shevchenko Scientific Society, 184n.6
silence, silenced, 5–6, 8, 13, 17–18, 59, 109,
    121, 123–24, 146–47, 150–51, 153–
    54, 155–56, 160–61, 163–64, 165, 169
Silverman, Carol, 9–11, 42, 59
Slovakia, 16, 27, 52, 56–57, 61, 66–67,
    69–70, 74, 76, 93, 101, 132–33,
    140, 149–50
Slovākika, 23, 75
    See also Romani groups
smoking, 13–14, 17, 107, 129–30, 135–39,
    140, 143, 183n.12
sonic, 15, 17, 110, 119–21, 122, 124, 125–
    26, 157
Soros, George, 27, 36, 38–39, 48–49
Soros Foundation, 36, 60
Soviet nationality policies, 44–45
Soviet Union, 6, 7–8, 11–13, 24, 25–26,
    28–29, 32, 38, 48, 55, 73, 74, 76, 81–
    82, 83, 84–86, 88–90, 93, 96, 99–100,
    107–8, 112–13, 114, 116, 117, 124–
    25, 133, 134–35, 136, 139, 141–42,
    154–55, 163–65
    See also USSR
spektakli, 28
Stalin, Josef, 88–90, 131–32

Starytskyĭ, Mykhaĭlo, 26
steel. *See* Pittsburgh; Kosice; labor
stereotypes
    Romani, 63, 84, 95, 100, 101, 124–25,
    127–28, 130
    East European, 56–57, 91–92, 140–41
study-abroad, 56–57, 65–67, 69–
    71, 138–39
suffering, 13–14, 17–18, 101, 109, 148–
    49, 166–68
    Romani, 32, 78–79
suicide, 96–97
synthesizers, 85–86, 117

tabir, tabor, 24, 28–29, 40, 46–47, 87, 91–
    92, 95–96
Tabor ukhodit v nebo, 28–29, 91–92
Taraf de Haïdouks, 9, 42, 88
Teater Romance, 153–54, 168
Teater Romen, 7–8, 24, 26, 28–29,
    140, 141–42
Ternopil, 83
testimonies, 5–6
The Pianist, 123–24
thievery, 21–22
timbre, 107, 120–21, 122, 147–48, 167
time, local, concepts of, time poverty,
        timeless time, real time
    ethnomusicology in, 2–3
    as guiding factor, 5–6
    and illness, 144, 148–49
    keeping time, 93, 94–95
    loss of time, 174
    and place, 157
    and poverty, 97–98
    progression of, 18
    stuck-in-time, 64
    "timeless time," 173
    and trauma, 153
tobacco, 136, 138, 140, 142–43
    See also smoking
tourism, 51–53, 55–56, 76
    dark tourism, 2–3
    ethical, 51
    ghetto, 51
    green (zelenyi) tourism, 76
    "grief tourism," 2, 76
    musical tourism, 51, 52

INDEX   221

"niche tourism," 50–51, 52
poverty, 51–52
slum tourism, 51
voluntourism, 51
Transcarpathia, 16, 18, 22–23, 24, 27–29,
   32, 33–34, 37–38, 39, 40, 46–47,
   48–50, 61–62, 73–75, 76, 79–81, 82,
   84–86, 87–88, 90–91, 92–76, 93, 94,
   95–96, 100–2, 105, 107, 110, 111–12,
   125–26, 129–30, 134, 138–39, 159–
   60, 163–64, 165–66, 168–69, 174
transportation
   networks, 115
   trains, 101–2, 111–12, 123–24, 144, 165
trauma, 2, 15, 17–18, 25–26, 69–70, 75–76,
   96–97, 123–24, 153–54, 155–57, 160,
   164–65, 167–68, 174
   inter-generational, 13–14
travel, 2, 3, 7, 9, 22–23, 24, 26, 42, 47–49,
   50–51, 52, 59, 61, 65–66, 94, 95–96,
   99–101, 102, 110–12, 114, 133, 136–38,
   139, 144, 145–46, 157–58, 162, 163–65
Tsyhan, Tsyhany, 24, 91–92
Tsyhanka Aza, 26
   See also Starytskyĭ, Mykhaĭlo
Tsyhanska doroha, 178n.14
   See also *pysanka*
Tsyhanska krov, 45
Tsyhanka-Vorozhka, 30–31
   See also Shevchenko, Taras
Tsyhanshchyna, 32
Tsyhanske schastia, 13–14
   See also happiness
tuberculosis, 13–14, 17, 18, 39, 130, 134–
   35, 136, 147–51
tuning, 2, 17, 107, 108–9, 115–16, 117,
   118–19, 122–23, 124, 128
   instrumental, 120–21
   tempered, 116–17
   "tuning in," 109

Ukrainian SSR, 7, 28–29, 83
ultranationalists, 22, 167
UNESCO, 43–44
Ungrika, 23, 75

Ungvar, 76, 79–80
USSR, 19, 24, 29, 75, 90, 93, 131–32, 134
   See also Soviet Union
Uzhhorod, 1, 16, 24, 26, 27–29, 38, 39, 48–
   50, 61, 62–63, 74–76, 79–80, 82–83,
   84–87, 88, 90–91, 92, 99–100
Uzh River, 75–76, 79–80
Uzh Romani, 74
   See also language: Romani

Varga, Gustav, 66
   See also Kalyi Yag
Via Romen, 7–8
victim-blaming, 46–47, 103
video, 3, 66–67, 104–5, 107, 111–12,
   162, 167
   as ethnographic method, 105
   See also photography
Vienna, 1, 138–39
villages, 1–2, 11–12, 17, 23–24, 37–38, 39,
   48, 53, 73, 78, 79–80, 94, 96, 97–98,
   102–3, 112–13, 115, 131–32, 134,
   145–46, 165–66
violence, 1, 5–7, 19, 22–23, 46, 58, 156–57,
   165–66, 171, 173–74
violin, violinist, 24, 61–62, 80–81, 84–87,
   92, 101, 107, 108, 110, 111, 121, 168–
   69, 176–77n.9, 185n.12
Vlax, 23, 66, 80–81
Vysotsky, Vladimir, 117

Wallachia, 23
weather, 78
witness, 111–12
Works Progress Administration (WPA),
   63, 149

Zajdel, Evan, 69–70
   *Narrative Threads Ethnographic Tourism,
      Romani Tourist Tales, and Fiber Art*, 3
Zobar, Loiko, 28–29, 91–92
   See also Rada; *tabir, tabor: Tabor
      ukhodit v Nebo*
zoo
   animals, 45

The manufacturer's authorised representative in the EU for product safety is Oxford
University Press España S.A. of El Parque Empresarial San Fernando de Henares,
Avenida de Castilla, 2 – 28830 Madrid (www.oup.es/en or product.safety@oup.com).
OUP España S.A. also acts as importer into Spain of products made by the manufacturer.

Printed in the USA/Agawam, MA
March 21, 2025

884675.005